SCOTTISH PAGEANT

SCOTTISH PAGEANT

1513-1625

EDITED BY

AGNES MURE MACKENZIE
C.B.E., M.A., D.LITT.

OLIVER AND BOYD
EDINBURGH AND LONDON

1948

FIRST EDITION 1948

The portrait of Mary, reflected in the
mirror of the vignette on the title-page,
is after Clouet's drawing of the Queen
in her girlhood.

Title-page and Jacket designed and embellished by
Joan Hassall

PRINTED AND PUBLISHED IN GREAT BRITAIN BY
OLIVER AND BOYD, LTD., EDINBURGH

I hafe in this vacant time compiled and gathered (and nocht maid) out of divers, alsweill foreine as Scottis wreittaris, this sempill treatise for the commodite of my countrey.

From the Scots version of *De origine moribus et rebus gestis Scotorum* of John Lesley, Bishop of Ross, 1578

PREFACE

THE business of this book is not to give what is commonly known as the history of its time—the great shaping events, their cause and their consequence. What is here is the texture and atmosphere of life as the folk of the time unconsciously reproduced them. Here speaks for itself the age of Knox and of Mary, of silken songs and bitter pamphleteering, of three-hour sermons and the Riding Ballads, of courtly masques in Italian or Latin and the clash of swords in the street on a winter night, of brocaded dancers and of total war, and through them all danger and a high-headed courage, and a certain fierce sureness, a style, in the process of life. It is grimly like our own time in many ways—the less pleasing ways of its politics and its war, and of the transitional conflict of ideas that ran across and complicated its war; and unlike our own time in certain of its virtues, the dignity it combined with such vivid life and the arrogant individuality that resembles so little our mass-produced civilisation, whose conscientious breaches of convention all run so wearily to a stock pattern.

I have, as before, let its people speak for themselves, choosing at random from the great mass of material whatever happened to hit my own personal fancy, stringing together in groups those passages which chanced to have some connection in their subject, and presenting them with just enough explanation to let the reader know who is talking, and when, and so much of the background as may be necessary to let him get the point of what is said. If I have had any other principle, it has been to choose the less-known passages rather than those which are well known and easy to come by.

The result, now I have put it in a rough order, is a fairly complete cross-section of the time, save for one element which in fact was conspicuous. There is a glimpse here of the time's religion, but none of the theological disputation that was as much the background of its thought as theories of the state are the background of ours. It is unhistorical to leave it out: but the present age is so terrified of the subject, so convinced that who says theology says dullness (which is, in fact, conspicuously absurd) that I have let it be. In any case, it is not a thing one fairly can give in snippets.

A word on the language. Texts written in French, Latin, and one or two Continental languages are given here in modern standard English, and the English in its own racy idiom, but with modernised spelling. The Scots provided a problem. The courtly and literary Scots of the time has become for practical purposes a dead language, and frightens readers: which is a very great pity. Yet it seems to me that their path is made harder than need be, by presenting them with too literal a text. The twentieth-century reader of Shakespeare, for instance, is not expected to take his *Lear* or *Hamlet* from a literal version of the First Folio: and he would not get far with them if he were. I do not see why he should be expected to cope with the Bannatyne songs in George Bannatyne's spelling, which is not even that of the actual writers.

Modern Scots strikes as wrong a note as modern English: so it seems that a compromise is indicated, and I have endeavoured to find one which may serve. A good deal of the reader's difficulty comes from the wild variations in the spelling, with three or four forms of the same word on a page, that are common in most vernaculars of the time, even in the writing of very learned men. So, as an experiment, I have tried to achieve a standardised form of the curial speech of the time, and have used it throughout, basing it on the most characteristic forms, but avoiding one or two really difficult ones, like the vowel ȝ and the change of *u* and *v*, though I have kept, as too characteristic to change, the use of *quh-* for the sound that we spell *wh-*. After all, we are still well used to it in place-names.

If the reader is now and then slightly bothered at first, he will soon find himself getting the hang of it, especially if he will read aloud a little. Really obsolete words, or obsolete senses of words, have all been glossed, as in the previous volume, at the end of the extract, and the stranger will find an additional glossary (on page 325) of purely Scottish words which are for the most part still in living use. The punctuation, and sometimes the paragraphing, have been frankly modernised in all the languages.

This compromise will scandalise the pedant: but—at least till our schools take a little cognisance of the older literature of their own country—it seems that something of the sort is needed if the ordinary fairly intelligent reader is to have some first-hand contact with our rich past. And, until he has that contact, he is likely to remain in that unhealthy ignorance of it which so long has been characteristic of our country.

I do not wish in the least to seem to belittle the work of the Scottish Text Society, the older Bannatyne and Maitland Clubs, and other such bodies. Their work is truly priceless to the scholar. But it does not greatly help the general reader: and to leave a country's past literature wholly to scholars is neither usual nor advisable. This book is no more for the expert than for the fool.

I do not want to sound too solemn about it. I hope to combine some instruction with entertainment: but, to be frank, my fundamental motive was to share with like-minded folk what I like myself. And I hope they will enjoy it as I have done, and feel, when they have reached the end of it, that their forebears are not mere names in a page of print, but men and women as human as themselves . . . for history will serve them little till they know that.

Highgate, *March* 1948

CONTENTS

xi

I

LANDSCAPES

An auld fre realm, as it lang tym hes bein.
SIR RICHARD MAITLAND, *A New Yeiris Gift*

1. PERSPECTIVE

In 1544 Sebastian Munster, Professor of Hebrew and Theology in the University of Heidelberg, published his famous " Cosmographia," one of the standard reference books of its time. What follows is from the second, French, edition, published in Paris in 1575, with additions by its editor François de Belleforêt. The two British kingdoms are described together.

Scotland is not equal in fertility to England, except that it has more fish and more white beasts, because the harbours are very good and safe and the tide enters more easily : also the lakes, marshes, rivers, and springs are full of fish, so that the salmon there are so large they sell for a crown apiece.   In many places it is mountainous, and above the mountains is an even plain, which gives abundant pasture to cattle.   Near the city of Aberdeen there is much forest, and it is thought that this is the Caledonian Forest, of which Ptolemy makes mention : and it begins about two leagues from Edinburgh, where is the palace of the King of Scotland.   Beyond Scotland, towards the North, are the Orkney Isles, which in our time are all inhabited, and oats and barley grow there, but no wheat.   They have very good pasture, and many white beasts. . . .

Between England and Scotland is perpetual war, and there is no hope of composing it unless the two kingdoms should be united by royal marriage. . . .[1]   The Scots today do not differ in manners and customs from the Irish, from whom they

[1] When the original edition was published, the proposed marriage of the infant Queen Mary and the heir of England was very much in the news.

originated, as we have said above : for when the sky is clear, one can see Ireland from Scotland. Further, their language, their customs, and their dress are alike. They are very intelligent, as their learning shows, for whatever subject they apply them-selves to, they readily profit by. They are proud and quick to revenge, strong in war, and to endure hunger, thirst, and wake-fulness. Those who dwell in the southern part, which is the best, are very courteous, and as it were more highly civilised than the rest : they use the English language. Because there is hardly any forest, they make fire of black stones, which they extract from the ground. In the other part, which is moun-tainous, dwell a kind of people much tougher and fiercer, who are called the Wild Scots. These are dressed in such a manner and in such shirts dyed with saffron as the Irish, and go with legs bare to the knee. Their arms are a bow and arrow with a very large sword, and the dagger with a single cutting edge. The Scots differ in law and government from the English, for they use the Civil Law [1] like other folk, and the English have nothing but their statutes and customs.

There follows a quotation from John Major, on agriculture, a catalogue of towns and universities, a detailed description of Edin-burgh, quoted in § 3, and a long annotated list of Scottish Kings, filling four folio pages. This last shows the influence of the Auld Alliance, as Munster himself only gives the later ones. The English Kings are dismissed in a third of a page.

2. FOREGROUND

It is to the credit of Sir David Lindsay that when, in 1524, the Queen-mother and the quisling Douglases defeated at last the Regent Duke of Albany, Lindsay lost his place about the harried bairn who was the King. For the next four years the boy, growing into his teens, was held captive and deliberately debauched : but in

[1] The Roman Code, still the foundation of what remains to us of our native system.

1528, *being then sixteen, he escaped, disguised as a groom, from the hands of his gaolers, and put himself at the head of the Government.*

Lindsay celebrated his master's liberation by a poem of good advice, " The Dreme."   In the manner traditional for some three centuries, he falls asleep (in a cave by the winter shore) and Dame Remembrance brings him a vision of the universe, which culminates in one of his own country, that could be, and is not, a paradise . . . but will be yet if the King shows courage and wisdom.

> . . . Of Scotland I persave the properteis,
> And als considder, be experience,
> Of this countrey the greit commoditeis :
> First the aboundance of fischeis in our seis,
> And fructuall mountainis for our bestiall,
> And for our cornis, monie lustie vaill.
>
> The rich riveris, pleasand and profitabill,
> The lustie lochis, with fische of sindrie kindis,
> Hunting, hawking, for nobillis convenabill,
> Forestis full of da, ra, hartis, and hindis,
> The fresche fountainis, quhais halesum cristal strandis
> Refreschis sa the flourischit grein medis :
> So lak we nathing that to nature neidis.
>
> Of everie metal we haif the rich mynis,
> Baith gold, silver, and stanis precius.
> Howbeit we want the spycis and the wynis
> Or uthir strange fruitis delicius,
> We haif als guid, and mair neidfull for us—
> Meit, drink, fyre, claithis, that micht be gart abound,
> Quhilkis als is nocht in al the Mapamound :
>
> Mair fairar pepill, nor of greiter ingyne,
> Nor of mair strenth greit deidis til indure . . .

B

I marvel greitlie, I yow assure,
Considderand the pepill and the ground,
That richis sould nocht in this realm redound.

da, *ra*, doe and roe.   *flourischit*, blossoming.   *Quhilkis als*, which also.
    Mapamound, mappemonde, map of the world.   *ingyne*, intelligence.

3. THE EDINBURGH OF JAMES V

This description of Edinburgh was written, in Latin, for Munster's " Cosmographia." The writer was an Edinburgh man of a burgess family, Alexander Hailes, called Alesius, Sacrae Theologiae Doctor. Born about 1500, he took his degree at St Andrews, and was one of the first Scots to follow Luther's doctrines, being a convert of Patrick Hamilton. Imprisoned, he was set free on the order of James V, and went abroad. First he sought Luther at Wittenburg, but, disappointed by his lack of " moderation and fairness," went to England, where he succeeded Erasmus at Cambridge and made the official Latin translation of the first English Book of Common Prayer. Later, after filling the Chair of Theology at Frankfurt, he became Rector of the University of Leipzig, where he was one of the leaders of the group who sought a concordat between the Lutherans and the Catholics. He died at Leipzig in 1565, towards the end of Mary's brief personal reign.

Alesius's Edinburgh was still unburnt by Hertford, and was substantially the city of James IV, though by this time, probably, somewhat the worse for wear.

Edinburgh is situated in the province of Lothian, an Italian mile to the south of an arm of the sea into which flows the river Forth, coming from the west. The city has also two hills to the east : the southern is called Arthur's Seat, and that which looks to the north Boar's Hill. The land about is most fertile, with pleasant fields, groves, lakes, burns, and more than a hundred castles round the city, within a German mile.[1] To the

[1] Fynes Morison gives a German mile as three English ones and five Italian. The Italian mile is the old Roman *mille passuum*.

north, at the distance of an Italian mile, as we have said, is an arm of the sea, close to which is situated the town of Leith, in the midst of which has been made a harbour, in which at the one time may be seen a hundred great merchant ships. On the other side, one can see a town, the New Haven.

To continue, Edinburgh is situated on a hill, like Prague, in length an Italian mile, in breadth half that. From the west of the town rises a high rocky hill, and a citadel on the rock, below which is a deep valley, except on that side which looks towards the town, so that the castle is impregnable save from the town, nor can it be scaled by ladders, so steep and difficult is the rock, in which hawks nest.[1] These nests are robbed by over-daring young fellows who are sent out from the Castle to take their play. This citadel is called the Castle of Maidens, and it closes in the city on the west.

For the rest, on the east of the town is the Augustinian monastery of Holyrood, having joined to it the palace of the King and most pleasant gardens, shut in by the lake at the foot of the hill Arthur's Seat. In this hill are found precious stones, crystals which shine nobly with a clear light. In the town are two great streets, from the Castle of Maidens to the monastery and the King's palace, paved with squared stones : the chief is the Royal Way. There is a suburb to the west, a half mile long, called St Cuthbert Street.[2] There are in the town many monasteries and churches, in special the Greyfriars, the Blackfriars, and the Church of St Mary in the Fields, a college of priests : and elsewhere are the College of the Trinity and the Hospital of St Thomas.

The town itself is built not of brick, but of stone both hewn and unhewn, so that single houses may be compared to great official buildings (*palatia*). In the midst of the town is the Tolbooth (*capitol*) and the collegiate church of St Giles. The

[1] There is probably a personal reminiscence here : Alesius as a boy had a near escape from breaking his neck on the Rock.
[2] Portsburgh.

bishops, dukes, earls, barons, and nobles of all the kingdom have their palaces in this same town, when they are called to the Estates. The King's Palace, very large and proud, is placed above a monastery, and from it to the Castle of Maidens extends an unbroken street called the Royal Street, which is broader towards the castle and narrower towards the monastery. And this Royal Street has on either side notable houses, built for the most part of dressed stone. Further, another long street which is called the Canongate is narrower, and divided from the Royal Street by a wall, gates, and towers, and ranks as a suburb. From the Royal Street, between south and north, stretch an infinity of small streets, all adorned with tall houses, such as the Cowgate, in which dwell the gentry and the high municipal dignitaries, and in which are the palaces of the princes of the kingdom, where is nothing humble or rustic, but all is magnificent.

Among the greater churches of Edinburgh, after the noble basilica of the monastery, the first place is held by the collegiate church of St Giles, built in the middle of the Royal Street. After it, in the street which divides Edinburgh from the Canongate and the suburbs, is a splendid church called Queen's College within the Walls. Also between the Greyfriars and the Blackfriars is the Church of Mary in the Fields, where also there is a college of priests. And under the rock of the Castle of Maidens is placed the new parish church of St Cuthbert.[1]

In the Paris edition of the " Cosmographia," this description is illustrated by a careful but highly imaginative woodcut. The city, in a circle of craggy mountains, so bristles with towers that it looks like a small New York. The main " sights " are carefully indicated by letters, from Holyrood—down on the shore, close to the walls of Leith—to La Tour des Filles and St Giles, which has lost its crown.

[1] Alesius says *parochia* merely, but the parish itself had existed since at least the early twelfth century.

4. Spring Morning

This is spring morning outside a royal palace, perhaps Lin-lithgow above its lake with the swans. The author, Alexander Montgomerie, an impecunious cadet of Eglinton, is almost the last of the courtly poets to use Scots. The light of the Makaris by his day was burning low, for his verse in the main is thin, though accomplished in form. Here there is more than conventional delight.

Hey, now the day dawis,
The jolly cok crawis,
Now schroudis the schawis
　　Throw Nature anone.
The throssil-cok cryis
On luvaris quha lyis :
Now skaillis the skyis :
　　The nicht is neir gone.

The fieldis ourflowis
With gowans that growis,
Quhair lileis lyk lowe is,
　　Als reid as the rone.
The turtill that trew is
With notis that renewis
Hir pairtie pursewis :
　　The nicht is neir gone.

Now hartis with hindis,
Conform to thair kindis,
Hie tursis thair tyndis
　　On grund quhair thay grone.
Now hurcheonis with haris
Ay passis in paris,
Quhilk dewlie declairis
　　The nicht is neir gone.

The sesoun excellis
Throw sweitnes that smellis.

Now Cupid compellis
  Our hartis eche one
On Venus quha waikis,
To muse on our maikis,
Syne sing for thair saikis,
  " The nicht is neir gone."

All corageous knichtis
Aganis the day dichtis
The breist-plate that bricht is,
  To fecht with thair fone.
The stonit steid stampis
Throw corage, and crampis,
Syne on the land lampis :
  The nicht is neir gone.

The freikis on fieldis
That wicht waponis wieldis
With schining bricht schieldis,
  As Titan in trone—
Stiff speiris in restis,
Our coursaris crestis,
Ar broik on thair brestis :
  The nicht is neir gone.

Sa hard ar thair hittis,
Sum swayis, sum sittis,
And sum perforce flittis
  On grund quhair thay grone.
Syne grumis that gay is,
On blonkis that brayis,
With swerdis assayis :
  The nicht is neir gone.

Schroudis the schawis, probably, mist hangs on the patches of woodland. *skaillis*, clear. *rone*, rowan. *pairtie*, parti, mate. *tursis*, tosses. *tyndis*, tines. *hurcheonis*, hedgehogs. *stonit steid*, stallion. *crampis*,

? capers.   *lampis*, leaps.   *freikis*, bonny fechters.   *grumis*, young fellows.
blonkis that brayis, white horses that nicker.

5. PASTORAL SYMPHONY

*In the " Compleynt of Scotland" of 1549 the writer looks back
from the gloom and misery of his own time to the old kindly world
" before the war." Here is a midsummer morning, done almost
all in terms of sound and movement.*

First furth on the fresche feildis the nolt maid nois with
monie loud low.   Baith hors and meiris did fast neigh, and the
foalis nikir.   The bullis began to bullir quhen the scheip began
to bleit, becaus the calfis began to moo, quhen the doggis
berkit.   Then the swyn began to quhryne quhen thay herd the
ass rair, quhilk gart the hennis kekkil quhen the cokkis creu.
The chikkinis began to peu quhen the gled quhissilit.   The fox
followit the fed geis, and gart them cry claik.   The gaislingis
cryit quhilk quhilk, and the deukis cryit quaik.   The rouping
of the ravinnis gart the cranis croip.   The huddit crawis cryit
varrok, varrok quhen the swannis murnit, becaus the gray
goulmaw prognositicat ane storm.   The turtil began for to greit
quhen the cuschat youlit.   The titlin followit the gouk, and
gart hir sing guk guk.   The dou croutit hir sad sang, that
soundit lyk sorou.   Robene and the litil wran war hamelie in
wintir.   The jargoling of the swallou gart the jay jangil.   Then
the mavis maid mirth, for to mok the merl.   The laverok maid
melodie up hie in the skyis.   The nichtingal al the nicht sang
sweit notis.   The teuchatis cryit thevis nek, thevis nek, quhen
the pyotis clatterit.   The garruling of the stirlen gart the
sparou cheip.   The lintquhyte sang counterpoint quhen the
ousil yelpit.   The grein serein sang sweit quhen the goldspink
chantit.   The reidschank cryit my fut, my fut, and the oxee
tweit.   The heronis gaif ane wyld skreich, as the kiln had bein
on fyir, quhilk gart the quhaupis for fleitnes flie far fra hame.

Quhryne, grunt.   *rouping*, hoarse note.   *croip*, *?* croak.   *goulmaw*,
guillemot.   *titlin*, hedge-sparrow.   *teuchatis*, whaups, lapwings.   *lintquhyte*, linnet.   *serein*, greenfinch.   *oxee*, tomtit.

6. SUMMER DAY

This is a slightly shortened version of the " Day Estivall " of Alexander Hume.   He was of the Polwarth family—a collateral forebear of the delightful Lady Griʒel.   His " Hymnes or Sacred Songs wherein the Right Use of Poetry may be espied " was printed in Edinburgh in 1599, and the title places his religion, and therefore his politics.   He was not much of a poet, but once his sheer content in landscape and light and sunwarmth made him one. His party were strong anglicisers in letters, and his language already is rather Scoto-English than classical Scots.

O perfite Light, whilk shed away
   The darkenes from the light,
And set a ruler our the day,
   Ane other our the night—

Thy glorie when the day foorth flies
   Mair vively does appear,
Nor at midday unto our eyes
   The shining sun is cleare.

The shadow of the earth anon
   Removes and drawes by ;
Syne in the east, when it is gone,
   Appeares a clearer sky :

Whilk sune perceives the little larks,
   The lapwing and the snyp,
And tunes thair sangs like Nature's clarks
   Our medow, muir, and stryp.

They dread the day, fra it they see,
   And from the sight of men,
To seats and covers fast they flee,
   As lyons to their den.

Our hemisphere is poleist clean
　　And lightened more and more,
While every thing be clearly seen,
　　Whilk seemed dim before. . . .

The golden globe incontinent
　　Sets up his shining head,
And our the earth and firmament
　　Displayes his beams abraid.

For joy the birds with boulden throtes
　　Aganis his visage sheen
Takes up their kindlie musicke notes
　　In woods and gardens green.

Upbraids the carefull husbandman,
　　His corn and vines to see :
And every tymous artisan
　　In buith works busilie.

The pastor quits the slothfull sleep,
　　And passis forth with speede
His little camow-nosed sheep
　　And rowting kye to feede.

The passenger, from perils sure,
　　Gangs gladly forth the way :
Brief, everie living creature
　　Takes comfort of the day.

The dew upon the tender crops,
　　Like pearles white and round,
Or like to melted silver drops,
　　Refreshes all the ground.

The misty rouke, the clouds of rain
　　From tops of mountaines skails.
Cleare are the highest hills and plaine,
　　The vapour takes the vales.

Begaried is the saphire pend
　　With spraings of scarlet hue,
And preciously from end to end
　　Damasked white and blue.

The ample heaven of fabric sure
　　In cleannes does surpas
The crystall and the silver pure
　　Or clearest poleist glass.

The time sa tranquil is and still
　　That na where sall ye find,
Saif on ane high and barren hill,
　　Ane aire of piping wind.

All trees and simples great and small
　　That balmie leaf do bear,
Nor they were painted on a wall,
　　Na mair they move or steir.

Calm is the deep and purpour sea,
　　Yea, smoother nor the sand :
The wavis that woltering wont to be
　　Are stable like the land.

Sa silent is the cessile air
　　That every cry and call,
The hills and dales and forest fair
　　Againe repeats them all.

The rivers fresh, the caller streams
   Our rockes can softelie rin,
The water clear like crystall seems,
   And makes a pleasant din.

The flourishes and flagrant flowers
   Throw Phoebus fostring heit,
Refresh'd with dew and silver showres,
   Casts up ane odour sweet. . . .

The sunne maist like a speedie post
   With ardent course ascends,
The beautie of the heavenlie host
   Up to our zenith tends.

The burning beams down from his face
   Sa fervently can beat
That man and beast now seeks a place
   To save them fra the heat. . . .

The herds beneath some leafie tree
   Amids the flowers they lie.
The stable ships upon the sea
   Tends up their sails to dry. . . .

Back from the blue paymented whin
   And from ilk plaister wall
The hot reflexing of the sunne
   Inflames the aire and all.

The labourers that timelie raise,
   All wearie, faint, and weake,
For heat, down to their houses gais,
   Noon-meate and sleepe to take.

The caller wine in cave is sought
   Men's brothing breists to cule :
The water cauld and cleare is brought,
   And sallets steipt in ule.

Some plucks the honie plum and peare,
   The cherrie and the peache ;
Some likes the reamand London beer
   The bodie to refresh. . . .

The corbies and the kekling kais
   May scarce the heate abide ;
Hawks prunyeis on the sunnie braes
   The wedder's back and side.

With gilded eyes and open wings
   The cock his courage shaws ;
With claps of joy his breast he dings
   And twentie times he craws.

The dow with whistling wings sa blue
   The winds can fast collect ;
His purpour pennis turnes mony hue
   Against the sunne direct.

Now noone is went, gane is midday
   The heat does slake at last.
The sunne descends downe west away,
   Fra three of clock be past.

The rayons of the sun we see
   Diminish in their strength :
The shade of everie tower and tree
   Extended is in length.

Great is the calme, for everie where
  The wind is sitten downe :
The reek thrawes right up in the air
  From everie tower and towne.

The mavis and the philomene,
  The stirling whistles loud,
The cushats on the branches green
  Full quietly they crowd.

The gloaming comes, the day is spent,
  The sun goes out of sight,
And painted is the occident
  With purpour sanguine bright.

Our west horizon circuler,
  Fra time the sunne be set,
Is all with rubies, as it were,
  Or rosis reid ourfret.

What pleasure were to walke and see
  Endlang a river cleare,
The perfite form of everie tree
  Within the deepe appeare.

O then it were a seemlie thing,
  While all is still and calme,
The praise of God to play and sing,
  With cornet and with shalme.

Vively, livingly.   *stryp*, burn.   *boulden*, ? emboldened.   *kindlie*,
according to their kinds.   *buith*, booth, shop.   *camow-nosed*, flat-nosed.
begaried, vari-coloured.   *pend*, hanging curtain.   *simples*, herbes.   *cessile*,
yielding.   *flourish*, tree-blossom.   *ends*, stretch.   *whin*, here whinstone.
ule, oil.   *kais*, daws.   *pennis*, eat s.   *philomene*, nightingale.

7. THE EDINBURGH OF JAMES VI

This is the city as seen by an English visitor. Fynes Morison was born in 1566 : after leaving Cambridge he travelled all over Europe, describing his impressions in his famous " Itinerary," which appeared in 1617. He had ridden to Edinburgh from Berwick, in the April weather of 1598. Since the days when Alesius had written of it the city had been comprehensively sacked and burnt, and had witnessed years of war, foreign and civil.

This city is high seated, in a fruitful soil and wholesome air, and is adorned with many noblemen's towers lying about it, and aboundeth with many springs of sweet waters. At the end towards the east is the King's palace, joining to the monastery of the Holy Cross, which King David the First built, over which in a park of hares, conies, and deer a high mountain hangs, called the Chair of Arthur (of Arthur the Prince of the Britons, whose monuments famous among all ballad-makers are for the most part to be found in these borders of England and Scotland.) From the King's palace at the east, the city still riseth higher and higher towards the west, and consists especially of one broad and very fair street (which is the greatest part and sole ornament thereof) the rest of the side streets and alleys being of poor building, and inhabited with very poor people ; and this length from the east to the west is about a mile, whereas the breadth of the city from the north to the south is narrow and cannot be half a mile. At the furthest end towards the west is a very strong castle, which the Scots hold inexpugnable. Camden saith this castle was of old called by the Britons Castle Myned Agned ; by the Scots, the Castle of the Maids or Virgins (of certain virgins kept there for the Kings of the Picts) and by Ptolemy the Winged Castle. And from this castle towards the west is a most steep rock, pointed on the highest top, out of which this castle is cut. But on the north and south sides without the wall lie plain and fruitful fields of corn. In the midst of the foresaid street, the Cathedral Church is built,[1] which is large and lightsome, but little stately for the building and nothing at all for the beauty and the ornament.[2]   In this church the King's seat is built some few stairs high of wood, and leaning upon the pillar next to the pulpit, and opposite to the same, is another seat very like it, in which the incontinent use to stand to do penance ; and some few weeks past a gentleman, being a stranger, and taking it for a place where men of better quality use to sit, boldly entered the same in sermontime, till he was driven away with the profuse laughter of the common sort, to the disturbance of the whole congregation.

The houses are built of unpolished stone, and in the fair street good part of them is of freestone, which in that broad street would make a fair show, but that the outside of them are faced with wooden galleries built upon the second storey of the houses ; yet these galleries give the owners a fair and pleasant prospect into the said fair and broad street, when they sit or stand in the same.   The walls of the city are built of little and unpolished stones, and seem ancient, but are very narrow, and in some places exceedingly low, in other ruined.

Morison, unluckily, had to turn home when he had only just crossed into Fife, so that he had little more to say of the country.

8. THE SCOTTISH RIVERS

James VI, on his visit in 1617, *was greeted with a number of learned diversions.   Certain members of the University of Edinburgh entertained him with Latin debates on various subjects, from the origin of fountains to the question of heritable sheriffdoms. James was delighted, and took a hand himself, winding up with a lively speech in Scots, punning upon the name of each debater.   A*

---

[1] Morison was misinformed.   Until a diocese of Edinburgh was established in 1633, St Giles was only a collegiate church, and Edinburgh and Lothian formed part of the diocese of St Andrews.

[2] Edinburgh was a stronghold of the Saints, who by this time had worked their will upon its churches.

*collection of fifty-five " copies of verses " in Latin and Greek,
magnificently bound, was presented to him, and there were other
literary celebrations, among them William Drummond of Hawthornden's " River of Forth Feasting."   Here is Forth's invocation
of the waters of Scotland.*

> Whate'er beneath Albania's hills do run,
> Which see the rising or the setting sun,
> Which drink stern Grampius' mists or Ochil's snows,
> Stone-rolling Tay, Tyne tortoise-like that flows,
> The pearly Don, the Dee, the fertile Spey,
> Wild Naver which doth see our longest day,
> Ness, smoking sulphur, Leave with mountains crowned,
> Strange Lomond for his floating isles renowned,
> The Irish Ryan, Ken, the silver Ayr,
> The snaky Dun, the Ore with rushy hair,
> The crystal-streaming Nid, loud bellowing Clyde,
> Tweed which no more our kingdoms shall divide,
> Rank-swelling Annan, Lid with curled streams,
> The Esks, the Solway where they lose their names :
> To every one proclaim our joys and feasts,
> Our triumphs : let all come to be our guests.

*The verse is interesting : Drummond was a pioneer of the
" closed " couplet which was to become the major form of English
verse, and hold that place for a good century.*

9. SCOTLAND AT PEACE

*This passage, from the travels of William Lithgow, was actu-
ally published a few years after King James's death, but it has
been included here, as there are several other extracts from this
writer's work.   It describes the peaceful Scotland of the last dozen
years of the reign and the first eight, at any rate, of the next, that
was to conclude in such a mortal storm.*

As for the nobility and gentry of the kingdom [of Scotland], certainly as they are generous, manly, and full of courage, so are they courteous, discreet, learned scholars, well read in best histories, delicately linguished the most part of them, being brought up in France or Italy : that for a general complete worthiness, I never found their match among the best people of foreign nations, being also good housekeepers, affable to strangers and full of hospitality.

Later, he calls them " the best and most bountiful Christmas-keepers, the Greeks excepted, that ever I saw in the Christian world." It must be recalled, of course, that at this time the Episcopal party in the church had been dominant for over thirty years : and the Bishops believed in observing the Church's Year.

. . . In a word the seas of Scotland and the Isles abound plentifully in all kinds of fishes, the rivers are engorged with salmon, the Highlandish mountains overclad with fir-trees, infinite deer, and all sorts of other bestial, the valleys full of pasture and wild fowl, the low laid plains enriched with beds of grain, justice all-where administered, laws obeyed, male-factors punished, oppressors curbed, the clergy religious, the people sincere professors, and the country peaceable to all men.

The chiefest commodities whereof transported by sea are these : wheat, corns, hides, skins, tallow, yarn, linen, salt, coal, herrings, salmon, wool, keilling, ling, turbot, and saithes. And last and worst, all the gold in the kingdom is daily transported away with superfluous posting for court. Whence they never return anything save spend all, end all, then farewell fortune : so that numbers of our nobility and gentry now become with idle profits, down-drawers of destruction upon their own necks, their children, and estates : and posting postillion by dissolute courses, to enrich strangers, leave themselves deservingly desolate of lands, means, and honesty forever. Doing even with their virtue, long continuance, and memory of their noble ancestors as M. Knox did with our glorious churches of abbacies and monasteries (which were the greatest beauty of the kingdom) knocking down all to desolation, leaving naught to be seen of admirable edifices, but like to the ruins of Troy, Tyrus, and Thebes, lumps of walls and heaps of stones.

II

FIGURES

Adorned with cuffs and flounces in a style of such affluent magnificence that we question if any grander has since been seen in Glasgow.

JOHN GALT, *The Entail*

10. THE FINE LADY

This day in the life of an expensive lovely comes from the only surviving specimen of Scots Renaissance drama, the romantic comedy " Philotus." The play is extant in a fine black-letter edition of 1603, *but internal evidence suggests that it was actually written in the reign of James V—that is, before* 1542. *It is primitive enough, but it shows Scots drama working clear of the allegorical chrysalis that is barely cracking in Lindsay's contemporary " Thrie Estaitis." It may be the work of one of the lost dramatists whom Lindsay himself mentions in " The Testament of the Papyngo."*

The Macrell or Go-between is trying to induce the young and pretty Emily to marry the rich and elderly Philotus.

> . . . Heir quhat honour, welth, and eis
> Ye may get with him, an ye pleis
>   To do as I devise.
> Your fyr sall first be birnand cleir :
> Your maidinnis then sall haif your geir
> Put in guid ordour and effeir
>   Ilk morning or yow ryse,
>
> And say, " Lo, maistres, heir your muillis.
> ' Put on your wylicoat, for it cuillis :
> ' Lo, heir ane of your velvot stuillis,
>   ' Quhairon ye sall sit doun."

Then twasum cumis to kaim your hair,
Put on your heidgeir soft and fair.
Taik then your glas, sie all be clair,
    And sa gais on your goun.

Then taik to stanch the morning drouth
Ane cup of Mavesie for your mouth—
[And] sum cast sukre in at fouth,
    Togidder with ane toist.
Thrie garden goups taik of the air,
And bid your page in hast prepair
For your disjune sum daintie fair,
    And cair nat for no cost.

Ane pair of pluvaris pyping het,
Ane pairtrick and ane quailzie get,
Ane cup of sack, sweit and weil set,
    May for ane braikfast gane.
Your cater he may cair for, syne,
Sum delicat aganis ye dyne.
Your cuik to sesoun all sa fyne
    Then dois employ his pain.

To sie your servandis may ye gang,
And luik your maidinnis all amang :
And gif thair onie wark be wrang,
    Then bitterlie thaim blaim.
Than may ye haif baith coiffis and kellis,
Heich candie ruffis and barlet bellis,
All for your weiring, and nocht ellis,
    Maid in your hous at haim.

And now quhen all thir warkis is dune,
For your refresching eftirnone

Gar bring intil your chalmer sune
   Sum daintie dische of meit,
Ane cup or two with muscadall,
Sum uthir licht thing thairwithall :
For rasinnis or for caperis call,
   Gif that ye pleis to eit.

Til supper tyme than may ye chois
Unto your garden to repois,
Or merelie to taik ane glois,
   Or taik ane buik and reid on.
Syne to your supper ar ye brocht,
Til fair ful far that hes bein socht
And daintie dischis deirlie bocht,
   That ladeis luve to feid on.

The organis then into your hall
With schalm and timbrell sound thay sall,
The viol and the luit withal,
   To gar your meit digest.
The supper dune, then up ye ryse,
To gang ane quhyle, as is the gyse.
Be ye haif romit ane alley thryse
   It is ane myle almaist.

Then may ye to your chalmer gang :
Begyle the nicht, if it be lang,
With talk and merie mowis amang
   To elevat the splein.
For your collatioun taik and taist
Sum litel licht thing to digest.
At nicht use Rense wyn ay, almaist,
   For it is cauld and clein.

And for your bak I dair be bold
That ye sall weir evin as ye wold,

With doubil garnishingis of gold
   And craip abuve your hair,
Your velvot hat, your hude of stait,
Your missell quhen ye gang to gait,
Fra sun and wind, baith air and lait,
   To keip that face sa fair.

Of Paris wark wrocht, by the laif,
Your fyne half-cheinzie ye sall haif;
For to decoir, ane carkat craif,
   That cumlie collar bane. . . .

And for your gounis ay the new guise
Ye with your tailzeour may devise,
To haif thaim louse with pleitis and plyis,
   Or claspit close behind.
The stuff, my hart, ye neid nocht hain—
Pan velvot, raisit, figurit, or plain,
Silk, satin, damas, or grograin,
   The fynest ye can find.

Your claithis on cullouris cuttit out,
And all pasmentit round about. . . .
My blessing on that semelie snout,
   Sa weill I trow sall set thaim !
Your schankis of silk, your velvot schune,
Your borderit wylicoat abune.
As ye devise, all sall be dune,
   Uncraisit quhen ye get thaim.

Your tablet be your hals that hingis,
Gold bracelettis and all uthir thingis,
And all your fingaris full of ringis,
   With perl and precius stanis.

Ye sall haif ay, quhill ye cry ho,
Rickillis of gold and jewellis, jo.
Quhat reck to taik the bogill-bo,
My bonie burd, for anis ?

Emily, however, declines the bait.

effeir, readiness.　　*muillis,* mules, slippers.　　*wylicoat,* here probably petticoat.　　*Mavesie,* Malvoisie, malmsey, a strong sweet wine of Greece or Spain. *at fouth,* in plenty.　　*sack,* sherry.　　*cater,* caterer.　　*kellis,* headgear. *candie ruffis,* ? open ruff—or perhaps held up in cane framework ?　　*barlet bellis,* ? may be a bell-shaped unpleated ruff as in some contemporary portraits, with a roll edging—Fr. bourrelet.　　*muscadel,* strong sweet wine from Muscat grapes.　　*glois,* chat.　　*as is the gyse,* as is the fashion.　　*mowis,* strictly pouts : suggests lively conversation with a good deal of facial expression.　　*collatioun,* a light meal, a snack.　　*Rense,* Rhenish.　　*missell,* mask.　　*half-cheinzie,* broad chain looped from shoulder to shoulder.　　*carkat,* carcanet, necklace. *plyis,* folds.　　*pan velvot,* panne, thin supple velvet.　　*grograin,* grosgrain, heavy silk.　　*on cullouris,* etc., slashed over a contrasting lining.　　*pasmentit,* trimmed with strips of embroidery.　　*schankis,* stockings.　　*uncraisit,* uncrushed.　　*tablet,* little note-book, often jewelled, a fashionable toy.　　*cry ho,* ask for mercy.　　*rickles,* confused heaps.　　*bogill-bo,* craw-bogle, scarecrow.

11. The Dandy

This picture of the gallant of Mary's court comes from a MS. collection of poems, apparently made by Mary Maitland, sister of the famous Lethington, and herself something of a poet. The author is unknown.

Thair meit doublet dois thaim rejois :
Thay spred abroad thair buffit hois,
Thay taik delyt in nedill wark,
Thay gloir into thair ruffit sark.
Thair litill bonet or braid hat,
Sumtym heich and sumtyme plat,
Wattis nocht how on thair heid to stand.
Thair gluvis perfumit in thair hand
Helpis meikil thair contenance,
Et tout est à la mode de France.
Thair dry scarpenis baith trim and neit,
Thair mulis glitterand on thair feit,

Thair gartenis knottit with ane rois
Puttis al the lassis in thair chois.
Thay snyte though ther na mister be,
That ye may thair trim napkin see,
And gif ye richtlie it considder,
The goldin knoppis sall hing togidder.

meit, seemly, well-fitting. *buffit*, puffed. *plat*, flat. *wattis*, knows.
scarpenis, pattens, overshoes. *mulis*, low shoes. *gartenis*, garters. *snyte*,
blow their noses. *mister*, need. *knoppis*, here the gold tassels on the
corners, which made it drape gracefully when it was flourished.

12. She Would Be

*Here, from the same collection, is the would-be fine lady of
Mary's time—the equivalent of the modern patroness of the expensive road-house. She shows the same addiction to the catch-
phrase.*

(Thay) maun be buskit up lyk brydis,
Thair heidis heisit with silken sailis,
With clartie silk about thair tailis.
Thair hois maid of sum vantour hew,
And quhen thay gang, as thay nocht knew,
Thay lift thair goun abune thair schank,
Syne lyk a bridlit cat thay brank.
Sum taunting wordis thay haif parquier,
That servis thaim in al mateir. . . .

heisit, hoisted, " spreading canvas "—a good word for the veil spread on
high arches. *clartie*, muddy. *vantour*, boastful. *brank*, cognate with
prance, but with some untranslatable Scots overtones. *parquier*, par coeur,
by rote.

13. Lowland Dress

*In his " Itinerary," the Englishman Fynes Morison has a
chapter " Of the Turks, French, English, Scottish, and Irish
apparel." He was in Scotland in 1598.*

The husbandmen in Scotland, the servants, and almost all in
the country did wear coarse cloth made at home, of grey or sky-

colour, and flat blue caps, very broad. The merchants in cities were attired in English or French cloth, of pale colour or mingled black and blue. The gentlemen did wear English cloth, or silk, or light stuffs, little or nothing adorned with silk lace, much less with lace of silver or gold, and all followed at this time the French fashion, especially at court. Gentlewomen married did wear close upper bodies, after the German manner, with large whalebone sleeves, after the French manner, short cloaks like the Germans, French hoods, and large falling bands about their necks. The unmarried of all sorts did go bareheaded, and wear short cloaks with most close linen sleeves upon their arms, like the virgins of Germany. The inferior sort of citizens' wives and the women of the country did wear cloaks made of a coarse stuff, of two or three colours of checkerwork, vulgarly called ploddan. To conclude, in general they would not at this time be attired after the English fashion in any sort, but the men, especially at court, followed the French fashion, and the women, both in court and city, as well in cloaks as naked heads and close sleeves on the arms and all other garments, follow the fashion of the women of Germany.

whalebone sleeves, sleeves stretched on whale-bone hoops.   *vulgarly*, commonly.   *falling bands*, a deep linen collar, turned down.

14. MINISTERS MUSTN'T

This act of the General Assembly of 1575 throws a gay-coloured light on the general dress of the time.

Forsamekil as ane comelie and decent apparell is requisite in all, namelie in the ministerie and sic as beiris functioun in the Kirk ; First, we think all kindis of broidering unseemlie, all bagarris of velvot on gounis, hosis, or coatis, and all superfluous and vain cutting out, steiking with silkis, all kindis of costlie sewing of passementis, or sumptuous and large steiking with silkis, all kind of costlie sewing or variant hewis in sarkis, and kindis of licht and variant hewis in clothing, as red, blew, yellow,

and siclyke, quhilk declairis the lichtnes of the mind ; all weiring
of ringis, bracelettis, buttonis of silver, gold, or uthir metal, all
kindis of superfluitie of claith in making of hois ; all weiring of
plaidis in the kirk be reidaris or ministeris, namelie in tyme of
their ministerie and using thair office ; all kinds of gowning,
coating, doubletting or breitchis of velvot, satin, taffetie and
siclyke ; all costlie gilting of whingeris and siclike ; all silken
hattis and hattis of divers and licht colouris : Bot that thair
haill habitis sall be of grave colour, as black, russet, sad gray,
sad broun, or of sergis, winsett, camlet, growgram, lytes,
worsett, or siclyke, and to be schort, that the guid Word of God
be thaim and thair immoderatenes be nocht sclaunderit.   And
thair wivis to be subject to the same order.

bagarris, facings of different colour.   *steiking*, stitching.   *winsett*, wool
and cotton or flax.   *camlet*, camel-hair or fine wool.   *growgram*, silk and
wool.   *lytes*, ?.

15. HIGHLAND DRESS

*In the fifteen-forties Jean de Beaugué (whom we shall meet
again) described the Highlanders as wearing " dyed shirts " and a
" light wrap of wool of different colours."   In the fifteen-seventies
Bishop Lesley describes this, the old dress that preceded the kilt, in
rather more detail.   The original is Latin.*

They also made of linen very full tunics with many folds
and wide sleeves, flowing loose to their knees.   The wealthy
dyed these with saffron, and others oiled them, to keep them
longer clean among the exertion and exercise of a camp. . . .
In making these, grace and ornament were not lacking, and the
different pieces of the garments were seamed together with silk,
commonly green or red.

*Nicholas d'Afreville, Cosmographer to the King of France,
described a similar costume a few years later, but in George
Buchanan, writing in the same generation, we already find that*

The Highlanders take pleasure in clothing of various colours, especially striped, and their favourite colours are purple and blue. Their forebears wore plaids of many colours, and numbers still keep to this custom, but most now prefer to wear a dark brown, matching the leaves of the heather, so that, while lying among it in the day-time, they may not be revealed by a sight of their clothing. In these, wrapped rather than covered, they face the worst storms of the open, and at times will lie down and sleep, even in snow.

By the fifteen-nineties, however, O'Clery described the Islesmen who fought against the English in Ulster as wearing what sounds more like the belted plaid.

A speckled garment of many colours, hanging in folds to the calf, with a girdle round the loins over the garment.

Certainly by the time of Charles I the old leine chroich, the saffron-dyed linen shirt, centuries old, had disappeared, and its place had been taken by the breacan feile—the belted plaid—or the triubhas. Curiously enough, neither kilt nor any sort of nether garment at all is mentioned by John Taylor in 1618. Taylor was a well-known London character, the water-man—as we might say the taxi-man—poet. He was not much of a poet, but his ready tongue and cheerful cheek made him something of a pet wherever he went. In 1618 he tramped to Scotland, where he was received with an amused friendliness. The Earl of Mar took him on a hunting party, where he was surprised to find that " lords, knights, esquires, and their followers, all and every man in general, were in one habit, as if Lycurgus had been there."

Their habit is shoes with but one sole apiece ; stockings (which they call short hose) made of a worsted stuff of divers colours, which they call Tartane ; as for breeches, many of them, nor their forefathers never wore any, but a jerkin of the same stuff that their hose is of, their garters being bands or wreaths of hay or straw, with a plead about their shoulders,

which is a mantle of divers colours, much finer and lighter stuff
than their hose, with blue flat caps on their heads, a handkerchief
with two knots about their neck; and thus they were attired.
Now, their weapons are long bows and forked arrows, swords
and targets, harquebuses, muskets, durks, and Loquhabor axes.
With these arms I found many of them armed for the hunting.
As for their attire, any man of what degree soever that comes
amongst them must not disdain to wear it; for if they do, then
they will disdain to hunt, or willingly to bring in their dogs;
but if men be kind unto them and be in their habit, then are they
conquered with kindness, and the sport will be plentiful. This
was the reason that I found so many noblemen and gentlemen
in these shapes.

*Bishop Lesley describes the dress of the Highland lady. It
sounds rather like that described by Martin Martin a long life-
time later. We know that Queen Mary occasionally wore it, and
even had a lost portrait painted in it : and Brantôme declares that
it suited her very well.*

The dress of the women among them is most becoming, for
over a gown reaching the feet, and very richly adorned by the
Phrygian art, they wear very full cloaks, of several colours,
such as I have described—loose and flowing, yet gracefully
drawn into folds, as they will. With their arms tastefully
(*elegantius*) adorned with bracelets, and their throats with neck-
laces, they have great grace and beauty.

*The Phrygian art is embroidery. The Bishop's word for the
gown is tunica, which suggests a straight-hanging fullness like the
mediaeval gown, and in very marked contrast to the stiff spread of
the fashionable farthigale . . . though considerably more convenient, one imagines, riding across the Long Fords of the Uists.*

16. IMPORTED LUXURIES

The customs tariff for the year 1612 *throws a good deal of glittering and coloured light on the gear that filled the shops of the wealthy merchants, like the builder of the Saltire Society's Edinburgh home, Gladstone's Land in the Lawnmarket. David Masson, who edited it as long ago as* 1889, *remarks:* " *The list is a most valuable corrective of the common conception of the extreme rudeness of the domestic habits of Scotland in the early part of that century, and indeed a most valuable snub generally to that crude* ' *barbarism of our ancestors* ' *notion, which more than anything else blocks historical research.*" *But a notion driven home by a century of constant propaganda needs more than a mere fifty years to overthrow.*

The full list, in its tabular form, is too long to give, but it includes:

Alabaster, amber, coral, jet, and pearls; dolls and rattles; Brunswick, China, Turkish, and Venice carpets; Polish and Irish rugs; carvies; caviare; a wide variety of fine furniture, including mirrors of both steel and crystal; fitted dressing-cases of velvet; an enormous list of drugs; ivory and ostrich feather fans; fine furs, both real and imitation; musical instruments; globes; groceries, including almonds, apricots, spices of many kinds, pomegranates, oranges, jam, and marmalade; olives and salad oil; fine leather, both Russian and Spanish; Chinese, Levantine, and Italian silks; Milanese and French silk stockings; fine linen; Venice and Castile soap; surgical instruments; tapestry, some of it woven with gold and silver; tobacco; and of course wines, from the Levant, Italy, Spain, and the Rhineland, as well as the old staple import of wines of Gascony.

III

FOOD, DRINK, AND TOBACCO

> Good claret best keeps out the cauld,
> And drives away the winter sorn ;
> It makes a man baith gash and bauld,
> And heaves his saul beyond the morn.
>
> ALLAN RAMSAY, *To the Ph—*

17. CHRISTMAS DINNER AT HOLYROOD

No doubt some of these imported luxuries graced the Christmas tables of Holyrood in 1528—the first of the actual reign of the young James V. We have no account for them, or for the wines, but this is the butcher's bill, in Latin.

Expended 6 marts 2 quarters, and in liveries outbye, 1 mart 3 quarters, item bought 6 carcases of grass marts, £12-8 : item bought 100 sheep carcases, price £34 . . . item 3 large calves at 44/- : a boar, £3-5 : 42 hough fillets, 57/4 : 3 stone of suet, 24/- : 18 ox tongues, 12/- : 1 boar's head, 2/- : 1000 ox feet, price £10 : 1340 sheep's feet, price £3-6-8 : in milk and carriage, 14/4 . . . item, bought 98 tame geese, at 2/2 apiece : item, 11 kain geese from Fife : item bought 16 pigs, 21/4 : 12 cocks, 16/- : 10 chickens, 6/8 : 21 fowls, 17/6 : 42 capons, £3-3 : also entered five score and 2 capons of Fife, and 12 fowls, of the said kain . . . item, bought 7 fed capons, 21/- : 18 redshanks, 9/- : 27 sea-fowl, 31/6 : 29 partridges, £4-7 : 43 plovers, £3-4-6 : 30 woodcock, 45/- : 5 score and 4 muirfowl, £7 : 45 blackcock, £4-2-6 : 34 ducks, 45/- : 5 score and 9 rabbits, 2/8 apiece . . . 15 wild geese, £4.

The mart is the fatted ox, killed normally at Martinmas for salting down. Kain was rent paid in kind : the hens would be from the royal estates in Fife. 560 eggs were issued, but only 240 apples and pears : and 40 gallons of ale went into jellies.

18. Rationing

*Besides penalising profane swearing, the Parliament of 1551
took in hand a rationing scheme. As usual, its provisions are
graded : the more privilege the higher penalty. The privileges
here are not so unfair as they look, since the higher the rank, the
greater the tail, who considered the remains of their master's meal
to be their perquisite.*

*The scale may make the nineteen-forties girn : but we notice
that, then as now, the victims are informed that austerity is very
good for them.*

Item, it is statut and ordainit that . . . havand respect to
the greit and exhorbitant derth risin in this realm, of victualis
and uthir stuff for the sustentatioun of mankind, and dailie
increassand ; and understandand that the occasioun thairof is
becaus the superflous cheir usit commounlie in this realm,
alsweill amangis small as greit men, to the greit hurt of [the]
commoun weill of the samyn, and dampnage to bodie, quhilk
maikis ane man inhabill to exerce all liefull and guid warkis
necessair. And for remeid heirof and stanching of sic derth
and exhorbitant priceis foirsaidis, it is devisit and ordainit that
na archbischop, bischop, na erl haif at his meis bot viij dischis of
meit, nor na abbot, lord prior, nor dein haif at his meis bot vj
dischis of meit, nor na baroun nor frehalder haif bot iv dischis of
meit, nor na burges nor uthir substantious man, spirituall na
temporall, sall haif at his meis bot iij dischis, and bot ane kind
of meit in everie dische.

*The penalties were to be, for the first class, £100 : for the
second, 100 merks : for the third, £40 : and for the fourth, 20
merks, with this further,*

And quhatsumevir uthir persoun or persounis of quhatsumevir estait, degre, or conditioun that evir thay may be of,
that failzies and breikis this act and ordinance, thay sall be

haldin ane man gevin to his voluptuositie, and contempnar of
the auctoritie, and nocht to the comoun weill. . . .

*But none the less, they were Scots legislators, making laws for
men and not for a card-index—and for men, too, of a hospitable
country. So certain exceptions were formally recognised. When
a man of a lower rank entertained one of higher, he might feed him
only on the scale of his own table, unless the superior brought his
own provisions : but it was provided that*

this present act and ordinance stryke nocht upoun Yule and
Pasch, Patron Dayis, Mariageis, nor bankettis to be maid to
strangeris of uthir realmis : and the said bankettis to be maid
allanerlie be archbischoppis, bischoppis, erlis, lordis, abbottis,
prioris, deinis, baronis, provostis and baillies of burrowis. And
in lykewise providing that na Scottisman maik bankett to onie
uthir Scottisman bot in maneir foirsaid.

Pasch is Easter.   The *Patron Day* was the day of one's patron saint, kept
as still is the fête in France, rather than one's birthday.   *meis* is the word
mess, as it survives in the Services.

19. Dignity Dines

*This is from a Holyrood Table-list of Mary's time. The
original is in French.*

Table of the Master of the Household, where will eat : the
Chief Master of the Household, the Master on duty, an equerry,
the Marshal of the Household, two Secretaries, the Comptroller,
the Purveyor, the Keeper of the Plate, the Doctor, an Apothecary, the Billeting Officer, and the Captain of the Guard.

*The remains of the meal are to go to their servants—a man
apiece, except for the Doctor, who has two. A few hours after
leaving that sedate company, one of the Secretaries was to die,
hacked and screaming, at the Queen's feet, and the Captain of the
Guard was to gallop through Lothian in the March night wind,
with a Queen and her unborn heir riding pillion behind him.*

20. THE FEAST OF REASON

In the sixteenth-century statutes of the Faculty of Arts of Glasgow University, there is this agreeable provision :

Item, let those who are to be made bachelors or masters make seemly festival, inviting to a debate and a dinner, in honest assembly, at least the masters of the Faculty, with the Bedellus, calling on them in their chambers or lodgings, unless by chance they meet them in the way.

Their normal fare would seem to have been plain but ample. In 1602 that extremely versatile body the Privy Council had set a commission to work on the University of Glasgow. This is " The Allowance prescrivit be the Commissionaris to the Economus for halding of the Comoun Tabil within the College."

The first meis, consisting of the fyve maisteris, sall haif to thair disjune ane quhyte breid of ane pund wecht in a soupe, with the remainis of a peice beif or muttoun resting of the former day, with thair pint of aill amangis thaim.   To thair denner they sall haif ordinarilie quhyte breid eneuch, with fyve choppinis of sufficient guid aill, bettir nor the comoun sell aill in the toun, with ane dische of brewis and ane uthir of skink or kaill, a peice of sodden muttoun, ane uthir of beif salt or fresche according to the sesoun, ane roist ox veill or muttoun with a fowll or cunzie or a pair of dowis or chikkinis or uthir siclyke secund roist, as the sesoun gevis : and siclyke to thair supper.

The bursaris on the flesche dayis to haif for thair disjune, thrie and thrie, ane ait loif in ane soupe, quhairof thair sall be aucht scoir in the boll : at denner twa ait loifis amang four, ane dische of kaill or brewis, ane piece of beif, and siclyke to thair supper.

On fische dayis, the maisteris to haif for thair disjune ane dische of eggis with breid and drink sufficient, at denner a dische of kaill, a dische of eggis, with thrie dischis of weill graithit fische or uthir equivalent, with breid and drink as of befoir, and

to thair supper siclyke.   To the bursaris on sic dayis, breid and
drink to thair disjune, and to thair denner breid and drink as in
flesche dayis, and at supper siclyke.   And this to stand to the
saidis persounis for a constant and ordinar allowance till farder
order be tane.

*The pint is of course a Scots pint—about three times the
meagre English measure now in use.   The bursars probably drank
tippenny, as the absence of direct mention seems from the last
paragraph to be an oversight.   The " comoun sell aill " was the
minimum standard permitted by the burgh inspectors.   " Brewis,"
" skink," and " kaill " were soups.   " Sodden " (as in the A.V.)
is boiled.   A " cunzie " is a cony or rabbit.   " Graithit " is
dressed or prepared.   The Masters' Table represents the equivalent
of " la bonne cuisine bourgeoise."   One notices that there is no
sweet course.*

21. My Lords on Beer

*Until the end of the eighteenth century, ale and beer played
much the part that tea does today.   Now, in the years of peace that
followed the Union of Crowns, the Privy Council were much concerned with the improvement and protection of Scots manufactures.
In 1620 they were greatly annoyed because imported beer and ale,
English and Easterling (Baltic), were preferred to native.   After
a preamble declaring that it is not good that foreign commodities
should fetch higher prices, they complain of the large imports of
foreign ale,*

and the awneris thairof hes tane libertie without controlment to
alter and change, hight and raise the priceis thairof at thair
plesour, sa that the samyn ar alwayis sauld at ane heicher pryce
nor the propir drink of the countrey, outher aill or beir, althouch
thair be mair strenth and substance in the countrey drink nor in
the said foreigne beir, quhairthrow the countrey pepill ar heavilie
prejudgit, and monie of thaim, out of thair idill curiousitie,

without onie grund of resoun, dois maik chois of this foreigne drink for no uthir resoun bot this, becaus it is deirer nor the countrey drink, foolischlie apprehending that the pryce and derth thairof maikis it so much the moir bettir nor the countrey drink. . . .

countrey drink, not rural, but native.   *derth*, scarcity.

22. PLEASE DO NOT SMOKE

In the reign of James VI smoking was still a modern and mildly naughty habit. The first European mention of tobacco appears to be in a Spanish work of 1571, translated into English six years later. By the end of the century it had caught on in both Scotland and England, and one of the King's first literary diversions, after the Union, was his " Counterblaste to Tobacco," published anonymously in London in 1604 but included in the collected works of 1616. James no doubt wrote Scots, but his English printer has translated him.

Shall we that disdain to imitate the manners of our neighbour France (having the style of the first Christian King) and that cannot endure the spirit of the Spaniards (their King being now comparable in largeness of dominions to the great Emperor of Turkey), shall we, I say . . . abase ourselves so far as to imitate those beastly Indians, slaves to the Spaniards, refuse to the world, and as yet aliens from the covenant of God ? Why do we not as well imitate them in walking naked, as they do ? In preferring glasses, feathers, and such toys to gold and precious stones, as they do ? Yea, why do we not defy God and adore the Devil, as they do ?

Smoking at meals comes in for an especial reprobation, and modern smokers with decent table manners may sympathise with His Majesty's fervent wrath.

Is it not both great vanity and uncleanness, that at the table, a place of respect, of cleanliness, of modesty, men should not be ashamed to sit tossing of tobacco pipes and puffing of the smoke of tobacco one to another, making the filthy smoke and stink thereof to exhale athwart the dishes and infect the air, when very often men that abhor it are at their repast ?

In conclusion, the royal opinion on the subject was that it was

A custom loathesome to the eye, hateful to the nose, harmful to the brain, dangerous to the lungs, and in the black stinking fume thereof nearest resembling the horrible Stygian fume of the pit that is bottomless.

Not all James's courtiers agreed with him, however. Here as counter are the views of Sir Robert Aytoun, secretary to James's Queen, Anne of Denmark and Norway, and later to his daughter-in-law Henrietta Maria of France.

> Forsaken of all comforts but these two,
>   My faggot and my pipe, I sit and muse
>   On all my crosses, and almost accuse
> The Heavens for dealing with me as they do.
> Then Hope steps in, and with a smiling brow
>   Such cheerful expectations doth infuse
>   As make me think e'erlong I cannot choose
> But be some grandee, what soe'er I'm now.
>
> But having spent my pipe, I then perceive
> That hopes and dreams are cousins : both deceive.
>   Then make I this conclusion in my mind,
> 'Tis all one thing—both tend into one scope—
> To live upon tobacco and on hope :
>   The one's but smoke, the other is but wind.

IV

MIXTER MAXTER

Made up of odds and ends.
JOHN GALT, *The Annals of the Parish*

23. COPING WITH THE CALENDAR

In 1599 the Privy Council decided that henceforth the year should begin on the 1st January, conform to what already was the custom in most countries of Europe.

The Kingis Majestie and Lordis of his Secreit Counsall, undirstanding that in all uthiris weill governit comoun welthis and countryis the first day of the yeir beginnis yeirlie upoun the first day of Januar, comounlie callit New Yeiris Day, and that this realm onlie is different fra all uthiris [1] in the compt and reckoning of the yeiris, and His Majestie and Counsall willing that thair sall be na disconformitie betwix His Majestie his realm and liegis and uthiris nichtbour countreyis in this particular, bot that they sall conform thaimselffis to the ordour and custom observit be all uthiris countreyis, especiallie seing the course and sesoun of the yeir is maist propir and ansuerabill thairto, and that the alteratioun thairof importis na hurt nor prejudice to onie pairtie : thairfoir His Majestie, with advice of the Lordis of his Secreit Counsall, statutis and ordainis that in all tyme coming, the first day of the yeir sall begin yeirlie upoun the first day of Januar, and thir presentis to taik executioun upoun the first day of Januar nixt to cum, quhilk sall be the first day of them and six hundreth yeir of God. . . .

---

[1] England, in fact, began the year in March, and (apparently considering that a January New Year smelt of Papistry) continued to do so till 1752, to the discomfort of future historians.

24. Rise and Shine

On the 24th November 1574 the Town Council of Aberdeen gave orders to

John Coupar to pas everie day in the morning at four houris and everie nicht at aucht houris at evin throw all the rewis of the toun, playand upoun the Almany quhissil, with ane servand with him playand upoun the tabourine, quhairby the craftismen, thair servandis, and all uthiris laborious folkis, being warnit and excitat, may pas to thair labouris, and fra thair labouris, in dew and convenient tyme: and the said John to haif for his stipend and fee, yeirlie, twa shillingis of everie burges man, and xviij d of everie frie craftisman.

In May 1630 they decided to abolish the custom, considering that it was

ane uncivill form to be usit within sic ane famous burgh, and often fund falt with, alsweill be sindrie nichtbouris of the toun as be strangeris.

But they did pension the piper : and the next year they restored in his place two drummers to go round at four and five in the morning and eight and nine at night.   The forty-hour week is a modern innovation.

rewis, rues, streets.   *Almany quhissil,* the German flute.

25. Civic Pride is Hurt

Town Councils were very properly sensitive about the standing of their burghs.   In 1584, when the young King had newly come to power after his long and dreadful minority, and had set on foot a lively campaign of reforms, including one of procedure in Parliament, the Town Council of Perth sought the chance to deal with a grievance.

Henrie Adamsoun for the Burgh of Perth askit instrumentis

that he producit ane decreit gevin be the Commissionaris of Burrowis anent the placing of thaim in Parliament befoir the burgh of Dundie and nixt Edinburgh. And that albeit the Marischal at command of the King displacit James Hepburn thair Commissionar, that the samyn in na wayis prejuge thair decreit nor richt to be decidit thairanent, and thairupoun askit instrumentis.

He was promptly countered.

Alexander Scrymgeour, Commissiounar of Dundie, protestit that quhat beis done in this caus in na wayis hurt nor prejuge thair burgh nor liberteis of Dundie.

There were quite a number of such petitions, from burghs who thought they had not been given due precedence; and James had to order a Royal Commission, headed by the Lord Lyon and the Earl Marischal, to hear evidence and settle the matter once for all.

26. STRIKES

Touchiness was not confined to Town Councils. In the " Basilikon Doron" James sums up shrewdly the difficulties a government may look for in dealing with the various classes of subjects. After speaking of the nobles and the Kirk, he goes on to the Third Estate.

The craftsmen think we should be content with their work, how bad and dear so ever it be : and if in any thing it be controlled, up goeth the Blue Blanket.[1]

27. THE PHILOSOPHER

The satire of Sir Richard Maitland of Lethington, father of Mary's famous Secretary, was based upon a pretty firm sense of values. Here is the reaction of the blind man of seventy-four when " in tyme of peice quhan nane of that cuntrie lippinit for sic thing "

---

[1] The famous banner of the Trades of Edinburgh.

*the Captain of Wark raided his lands and stole all the furniture of
his House of Blythe and that of his tenants, with four thousand
sheep, two hundred head of cattle, and thirty horses.*

Blind man, be blythe thocht that thow be wrangit.
　Thocht Blythe be herriet, taik no melancolie :
Thow sall be blythe quhen that thay sall be hangit
　That Blythe hes spulziet sa maliciouslie.
　Be blythe and glad, that nane persave in thee
　　That thy blythnes consistis in rychis,
　Bot thow ar blythe that thow eternallie
　　Sall ring with God in eternall blythnes.

thocht, though.　　*ring*, reign.

28. POPULAR WISDOM

Here is a handful of pithy proverbs.

Bettir is man but land na land but man.
He that is weill luvit is nocht puir.
Put mony to the schule, for all will nocht be clarkis.
Ane swyn that is fat is caus of his ain deith.
Still sin maikis loud schame.

29. A WARNING TO HUSBANDS

*This delightful piece of genre-comedy belongs to a tradition that,
unlike the courtly lutanist verse, did not die, or at least was to have
a much earlier resurrection.　It comes from the Bannatyne MS.,
where—though not in Bannatyne's own hand—it is attributed to
one Moffat.*

At Auchtermuchty thair dwelt ane man,
　An husband, as I herd it tauld,
Quha weill could tippil out a can,
　And nather luvit hungir nor cauld :

Quhill anis it fell upoun a day,
 He yokit his pleuch upoun the plain :
Gif it be trew as I herd say,
 The day was foul for wind and rain.

He lousit the pleuch at the landis end
 And draif his ousen hame at ein :
Quhen he cam in he lukit ben,
 And saw the wyf baith dry and clein
Sittand at ane fyr, beik and bauld,
 With ane fat soup, as I herd say.
The man being wearie, weit, and cauld,
 Betwein thay two it was na play.

Quoth he, Quhair is my horsis corn ?
 My ox hes naithir hay nor strae.
Dame, ye maun to the pleuch the morn :
 I sall be hussy, gif I may.
Husband, quoth sche, content am I,
 To taik the pleuch by day about,
Sa ye will reul baith knavis and ky
 And all the hous, baith in and out.

. . . The wyf wes up richt lait at ein—
 I pray God gif hir evil to fair—
Sche kirnit the kirn, and skimd it clein,
 And left the guidman bot the bledoch bair.
Than in the morning, up sche gat,
 And on hir hert laid hir disjune.
Sche put als mekil in hir lap
 As micht haif ser'd thaim baith at nune.

Sayis, Jok, will thow be maister of wark,
 And thow sall hald and I sall call.
I'se promise thee a guid new sark,
 Athir of round claith or of small.

Sche lousit ousen aucht or nyne,
  And hint ane gad-staff in her hand,
And the guidman rais eftir syne,
  And saw the wyf had dune command.

And ca'd the gaislingis furth to feid :
  Thair wes bot sevensum of them all ;
And by thair cumis the greedy gled
  And likkit up five, left him bot twa :
Than out he ran, with all his main,
  How sune he herd the gaislingis cry,
Bot or that he came in again,
  The calvis braik lows and sowkit the ky.

The calvis and ky being met in the loan,
  The man ran with ane rung to redd :
Than by thair cam an ill-willy cow
  And brodit his buttok quhill that it bled.
Than hame he ran to ane rok of tow,
  And he sat doun to say the spinning.
I trow he loutit our neir the lowe.
  Quoth he, This wark hes ane ill beginning.

Than to the kirn that he did stour
  And jumlit at it quhill he swatt.
Quhen he had jumlit a full lang hour
  The sorou crap of buttir he gat.
Albeit na buttir culd he get,
  Yit he wes cummerit with the kirn,
And syne he het the milk our het,
  And sorou spark of it wald yirn.

Than ben thair cum ane greidie sow—
  I trow he kennit hir lithill thank,
For in sche schot hir mekill mou,
  And ay sche winkit and sche drank :

He cleikit up ane crukit club
   And thocht to hit the sow ane rout.
The twa gaislingis the gled had left,
   That straik dang baith thair harnis out.

Than he buir kindling to the kilne,
   Bot sche stert up all in a lowe.
Quhat evir he herd, quhat evir he saw,
   That day he had na will to mow.
Than he yeid to taik up the bairnis,
   Thocht to haif fund thaim fair and clein :
The first that he gat in his armis
   Was all be-dirten to the ein. . . .

Than up he gat on ane know-heid,
   On hir to cry, on hir to schout.
Sche herd him and sche herd him nocht,
   Bot stoutlie steirit the stottis about.
Sche draif the day unto the nicht,
   Sche lowsit the pleuch, and syne cam hame.
Sche fand all wrang that suld bein richt :
   I trow the man had richt greit schame.

Quoth he, Myn office I forsaik
   For all the dayis of my lyf,
For I wald put ane hous to wraik
   Had I bein twenty dayis guidwyfe.
Quoth sche, Weill mot ye bruik your place,
   For trewlie I will ne'er accep it.
Quoth he, Feind fall the lyaris face,
   Bot yit ye may be blyth to get it.

Than up sche gat ane mekill rung,
   And the guidman maid to the door.
Quoth he, Dame, I sall haud my tung
   For an we fecht, I'se get the waur.

Quoth he, Quhen I forsuik my pleuch,
    I trow I bot forsuik my seil,
And I will to my pleuch again,
    For I and this hous woll nevir do weill.

beik, nicely warmed.   *hussy*, housewife.   *bledoch*, buttermilk.   *rok*, distaff.   *say*, assay, attempt.   *yirn*, curdle—for cheese.   *kennit hir litil thank*, was not very grateful.   *na will to mow*, ?.   *be-dirten*, covered with dirt.   *seil*, happiness.

30. Too like Work

If a change of work is not always the best holiday, neither are certain games. In the " Basilikon Doron" James VI goes into minute details of a king's private as well as his public life. Even in his amusements, he must consider his responsibilities, and therefore he had better not play chess, for

It is over wise and philosophic a folly. For where all such light plays are ordained to free men's heads for a time from the fashious thought of their affairs, it by the contrary filleth and troubleth men's heads with as many fashious toys of the play as before it was filled with thoughts on his affairs.

31. A Band of Manrent

This band of manrent, or the formal adoption of a chief, comes a little more than six years after Flodden.

Be it kend til all men be thir present lettiris, me Robert Orrok, son to ane honorabill man Jamis Orrok of that Ilk, bindis and oblisis me be the faith in my bodie to stand for all the dayis of my lyf trew man and servand to ane honorabill man John Melville of the Rayth, knicht, aganis all uthiris, the Kingis Grace, my Lord Governour, my Lord of Sanctandrois, now present, the Abbottis and Convent of Dunfermling and [thair successoris ?] exceptit; and sall taik his aefauld pairt with my personn, freindis, and servandis; And attour I sall nocht heir his skaith or dishonour bot I sall advertise him of the samyn; And I sall gif him my counsall in all mateiris to his weill and honour as to my self;[1] And gif this manrent be nocht sufficiand, it sall be extendit as the said John, knicht, thinkis expedient, and the said Robert, in the best form.

At the Rayth, subscrivit with my hand the secund day of Januar in the yeir of God M^cV^c and xix yeirs, befoir this witnes, William Schevez, Jorge Balfour, William Mailville, with otheris divers.

Robert Orrok, son to umquhill James Orrok of that Ilk, with my hand.

32. ANCIENT MONUMENTS

In 1565 the Lord Treasurer's Accounts contain this item.

To ane boy passand of Edinburgh with ane chairge of the Quenis Grace direct to the baileis of Mussilburgh, chairging thaim to taik diligent heid and attendance that the monument of greit antiquitie now fundin be nocht demolischit nor brokin doun. xij d.

Randolph, the English Ambassador, describes it in a letter to his chief Cecil.

A cave found beside Musselburgh[2] seemeth to be some monument of the Romans, by a stone found there with these words graven upon him: Apollini Granno, Q.L. Sabinianus Proc. Aug. Divers stout pillars set upright in the ground, covered with tile stones large and thick, turning into divers angles, and certain places like unto chines to avoid smoke. That is all that I can gather thereof.

In spite of the Queen's care, by 1593 it had been " utterlie aboloschit," no doubt as savouring of Papistry.

[1] Notice how these two clauses repeat those in the oaths of allegiance given in the preceding volume.

[2] It was in the grounds of Inveresk House.

33. A Pension

This is Calderwood's transcript of the grant made by the General Assembly to Knox's widow. The language is thus not Scots, but Scoto-English of the seventeenth century.

Knox's first wife had been an Englishwoman, and at his death his sons by her were filling charges in England, and were thus self-supporting. The wife here is his second, Margaret Stewart of Ochiltree, whom he married seven years before his death, when he was fifty-two (or, according to some authorities, fifty-nine) and she fifteen. She was now left a widow with three small girls: and Knox, to his credit, had died a comparatively poor man.

The Assembly, remembering the long and faithful travels made in the work of God by umquhile John Knox, minister of Edinburgh, lately departed at the mercy of God, leaving behind him Margaret Stewart his relict, and his three daughters gotten on her, improvided for: And seeing that his long travels and deserts merit to be favourably remembered in his posterity, being also required most earnestly thereunto by my Lord Regent's Grace,[1] as his direct letters thereupon bear, have granted and consented to give, and by the tenour hereof grants, gives, consents, and dispones to the said Margaret Stewart, relict, and her three daughters of the said umquhile John Knox, the pension which he himself had in his time of the Kirk, and that for the year next approaching and following his decease, viz., of the year of God 1573 years, to their education and support, extending to 500 merks money, two chalders of wheat, six chalders bere, two chalders oats, to be uplifted for that year allanerlie, out of the samen assignations and places that he had it in his time. And therefore requires and in the name of God desires the Lords of the Council and Session to grant and give letters at instance of the said relict and bairns of the said umquhile John Knox, to cause them to be answered obeyed and paid of the said pension of the

[1] The Regent, at this time, was that eminent professor, the Earl of Morton.

year foresaid, in the same form, and better if need be, as was granted to himself in his time.

travels, labours.

34. PREVENTION OF CRUELTY

Our ancestors are seldom credited with much tenderness towards the sufferings of animals. It is interesting, therefore, to find that in 1619 the Privy Council, on humanitarian grounds, had forbidden the people of Orkney and Shetland to pluck their sheeps' wool instead of clipping it. The people, however, pointed out that this well-meant decreit was based on misunderstanding.

Althocht the pulling of the woll of scheip heir in the in-countrey may justlie be thocht a barbarous and uncivile form of doing, worthie to be reformit and the abuse removit, yit the cais haldis nocht so in the boundis forsaidis : and gif the compleanaris sould outher pull or clip thair scheip in the ordinar tyme of clipping, thair haill scheip wald perische and die, becaus thay haif verie few pasturis for scheip in the continent and mainland, and upoun their pasturis thay keip sa monie of thair yowis as guidlie thay may hald, fra lambing tyme till harvest be past, at quhilk tyme they maun of necessitie send thair yowis with thair lambis to thair auld pasturis in the ylis, unclippit or pullit, becaus thair in-pasturis ar nocht abill to feid thaim ; and in thair our-pasturis in the ylis, quhair nouther men nor wemen dwellis nor yit dair repair bot in verie fair and sesounabill wedder, all thair scheip remains the haill wintir sesoun and the tyme of Lent, and feidis cheiflie upoun sea wair ; and being thair exposit to the injurie of tempestuous frostie and unsesounabill wintir without onie defens to guard thaim from the injurie of wedder, the compleanaris are constrainit for this caus to keip thaim unpullit or clippit that haill sesoun till the month of Junii, [sa] that the undirgrowth or yong woll cast off the auld groith of the awn accord, without pulling or clipping, and as naturallie as gif the wool wes taen off by industrie or art, seing at that tyme the woll will nocht byd the scheiris, and gif it fall out, as seldom it dois, that sum few scheip will nocht cast thair woll, theis scheip ar clippit or cuttit with scharp knifis.

They repeat that plucking is " nawyse grievous to the puir beastis," and that if they shear at the normal times, they " wald nocht haif ane leivand scheip in the cuntrey." The Privy Council were firm, but reasonable. They sent up a Commission to investigate, with the Bishop of Orkney at its head : the Commission corroborated the statements made above, and the Council thereon rescinded its decreit. To this day sheep in the North Isles are plucked, not shorn.

in-cuntrey, mainland. *ylis*, isles. *unpullit or clippit*, unpulled or unclipped, the prefix governing both nouns.

35. Singing Gossip

That very great thing, " The Bonny Earl o' Moray," was once on a time a street song in Edinburgh ; it nearly dirled a sovereign off his throne, and, by one of the oddest freaks in our strange history, it powerfully helped to establish Andrew Melville as at once the Pope and the Dictator of Scotland.

There seem to have been many such topical ballads. Some were shifted with time into something richer and stranger than their first basis, as when a scandal from the servants' quarters in behind Holyroodhouse grew into the haunting " Marie Hamilton." Here again is one from the Palace, from the very royal bed-chamber itself . . . comedy this time, its heroine one of the Queen's Danish maids of honour, Margaret Vinstar or Twinlace (there are a few more spellings) and its hero, Wemyss of Logie, who in 1592 had been concerned in the dangerous cantrips of Francis, Earl of Bothwell.

I will sing, if ye will hearken,
    If ye will hearken unto me ;
The king has ta'en a poor prisoner,
    The wanton lord o' young Logie.

Young Logie's laid in Edinburgh chapel ;
  Carmichael's [1] the keeper o' the key ;
And May Margaret's lamenting sair,
  A' for the love of young Logie.

" Lament, lament na, May Margaret,
  And of your weeping let me be ;
For ye maun to the King himsell,
  To seek the life of young Logie."

May Margaret has kilted her green cleiding,
  And she has curled back her yellow hair—
" If I canna get young Logie's life,
  Farewell to Scotland for evermair."

When she came before the king,
  She knelit lowly on her knee—
" O what's the matter, May Margaret ?
  And what needs a' this courtesie ? "

" A boon, a boon, my noble liege,
  A boon, a boon, I beg o' thee !
And the first boon that I come to crave,
  Is to grant me the life of young Logie."

" O na, O na, May Margaret,
  Forsooth, and so it mauna be ;
For a' the gowd o' fair Scotland
  Shall not save the life of young Logie."

But she has stown the king's redding kaim,
  Likewise the queen her wedding knife ;
And sent the tokens to Carmichael,
  To cause young Logie get his life.

[1] Sir John Carmichael of that Ilk was Captain of the King's Guard about this time.

E

She sent him a purse of the red gowd,
    Another o' the white monie;
She sent him a pistol for each hand,
    And bade him shoot when he gat free.

When he came to the tolbooth stair,
    There he let his volley flee;
It made the king in his chamber start,
    E'en in the bed where he might be.

" Gae out, gae out, my merrymen a',
    And bid Carmichael come speak to me;
For I'll lay my life to the pledge of that,
    That yon's the shot o' young Logie."

When Carmichael came before the King,
    He fell low down upon his knee;
The very first word that the king spake,
    Was—" Where's the laird of young Logie ? "

Carmichael turned him round about,
    (I wot the tear blinded his eye)
" There came a token frae your grace,
    Has ta'en away the Laird frae me."

" Hast thou played me that, Carmichael ?
    And hast thou played me that ? " quoth he;
" The morn the justice-court's to stand,
    And Logie's place ye maun supplie."

Carmichael's awa to Margaret's bower,
    Even as fast as he may drie—
" O if young Logie be within,
    Tell him to come and speak with me."

May Margaret turned her round about,
   (I wot a loud laugh laughed she)
" The egg is chipped, the bird is flown,
   Ye'll see na mair of young Logie."

The tane is shipped at the pier of Leith,
   The tother at the Queen's Ferrie,
And she's gotten a father to her bairn,
   The wanton laird of young Logie.

Rather unusually for popular gossip, the story is a little watered down. What the plucky Margaret really seems to have done was to get her man out of prison by bringing what purported to be a demand from the King to interview him in the royal chamber. He duly arrived, and Margaret took him past the sleeping monarch and let him down from a convenient window.

36. SIGNS AND WONDERS

Failure to make the most of a promising subject is the last charge that can be brought against David Calderwood. His " Historie of the Kirk of Scotland" is a sort of Left Wing rival to that of the Right Wing Archbishop Spottiswoode. Carstares, the leader of the 1690 Establishment, praises it as " a rich and rare jewel," and Calderwood's Victorian editor declares that he was " qualified in the happiest manner to be an historian of the Kirk of Scotland." He certainly did invaluable work in popularising the Left Wing point of view, for Spottiswoode's calm and judicial sobriety had small appeal beside Calderwood's edifying detail of executions and scandals in high life, his loving descriptions of opponents' death-beds—the Marquis of Hamilton had blisters " of six divers colours "—or such fascinating faits divers as these which follow.[1]

---

[1] He was born in 1575, and his Historie was written towards the end of his life. The Covenanting Assembly of 1648, recognising its value, voted him £800 to finish it. He died two years later, and the book was published in Holland in 1678. The language, so late, is Scoto-English rather than Scots, and has accordingly been given in modern spelling.

1612. In the month of March and April fell furth prodigious works and rare accidents. A cow brought forth fourteen great dog whelps instead of calves. Another after the calving became stark mad, so that the owner was forced to slay her. A third brought forth a calf with two heads. One of the Earl of Argyle's servants being sick, vomited two toads and a serpent, and so convalesced : but vomited after a number of little toads. A man dwelling beside Glascow murthered both his father and his mother. A young man at the plough near Kirkliston killeth his own son accidentally with the throwing of a stone, goeth home and hangeth himself. His wife, lately delivered of a child, running out of the house to seek her husband, before she returned, a sow had eaten the child.

.   .   .   .

1622. Upon Monday the 3rd of June, there was a fiery dragon, both great and long, appeared to come from the south to the north, spouting fire from her, half an hour after the going to of the sun.

This is not Calderwood's only dragon. He took a strong interest also in the more sensational forms of meteorology. Even a lunar rainbow, " whereat many wondered," is carefully set down.

1624. About the midst of Januar, four gentlemen of good credit, having gone out of Stirling some two miles or thereby, to pass their time, heard sensibly like the shots of many muskets, and after that, taking better heed, like the beating upon drums and playing upon piffers, and the sound of trumpets, and last of all the shot of great cannons, so that for fear they went back again to the town, and reported what they had heard.

piffers, pipes.

37. Glasgow is Shocked

The " Diurnal of Occurrents " records in 1570 :

Upoun the ferd day of the moneth of Julii, at ten houris at

nicht, thair wes ane erthquaik in the citie of Glasgow : and lastit bot ane schort space, bot it causit the inhabitantis of the said citie to be in greit terrour and feir.

38. THE LOCH FYNE MONSTER

The same authority also records, for the same year :

In this tyme, thair wes ane monstrous fische in Loch Fyne, havand greit ein in the heid thairof, and at sumtymis wald stand abune the watir as heich as the mast of ane schippe ; and the said had upoun the heid thairof [? two crounis, the ane ?] abuve litel and the dounmaist croun mekill : quhilk wes reportit be wyse men that the same wes ane signe and taikning of ane suddain alteratioun within the realm.

taikning, token.

V

THE RISING GENERATION

O youth, be glaid in to thy flowris grein.
ROBERT HENRYSON, *The Resoun-
ing betwix Age and Youth*

39. THE FOSTER FATHER

*The fairy tales are full of foster brothers : but the relationship
was not confined to the tales.   The son of a great man was very
commonly put out to nurse, and the foster-relationship was as real
as blood-kin and very often nearer.   To foster a chief's son was
a high honour, and we observe that in this Dunvegan contract it is
the foster-father who pays the real one, and that although, excep-
tionally, he is not himself a member of the clan.*

*The original is written, rather hastily, with several erasures and
interlineations, in a bold, clear, and vigorous Erse script, apparently
by the first witness, O'Morrissey.   The other three witnesses write
in Scots, in scholarly hands of some distinction : MacLeod himself
uses a clear Erse script.   The original language, of course, is
Gaelic.   The date is 1614.*

This is the condition and agreement on which MacLeod gives
his son, namely Norman, to John MacKenzie, and this the condition on which he is with John, namely that if so be that John
die first, the child to be with his wife until she get herself a
husband, but the guardianship of the child to belong to Angus
MacKenzie for so long as she is without a husband, and so soon as
a man marries her the child to be with Angus himself from that
time forward during his life ; and if his brother, namely Donald
MacKenzie, be the longer liver after Angus, the child shall be
with Donald in like manner ; and MacLeod has a son's share of
the stock during the life-time of three, namely himself and his
son the heir, namely John MacLeod, and Norman this foster-son

of John MacKenzie, against John and against Angus Mackenzie and against Donald MacKenzie and against the two sons of Donald the son of Murdoch, namely Roderick and Murdoch, and against the two sons of Duncan the son of Donald, namely John and Donald, and against Brian, grandson of Murdoch, and against Gillecallum Macpherson : and this is the stock which John MacKenzie put in possession of the child Norman, namely four mares and other four which MacLeod put in his possession, along with three which he promised him when he took him to his bosom ; and the charge and keeping of these seven mares which MacLeod gave to the child shall be with John MacKenzie, in order to put them to increase for his foster-son ; and the care and keeping of the four mares which John MacKenzie gave to his foster-son shall be with MacLeod to put them to increase for him in like manner. And these are the witnesses to this, namely Master Ewen M'Queen, minister of Duirinish, Donald son of Black Paul, and John MacColgan minister of Bracadale, and Turlough O'Morrissey, now the 8th day of October in the year of Our Lord one thousand six hundred and fourteen.

R. MacLeod.

TURLOUGH O'MORRISSEY,
 as witness.
MR EWEN M'QUEEN,
 as witness.

JOHN McCOLGAN,
 witness.
DONALD MACQUEEN,
 witness.

40. Boys' School

Quite the most likeable of the Scottish Reformers is James Melville, nephew of the great founder of Presbyterianism in Scotland. A charming personality, a fine scholar, and a racy writer, his famous Memoirs are delightful reading. He helped his uncle in the restoration of the University of Glasgow; and in 1580, Andrew, being Principal of St Andrews, was given the St Andrews Chair of Hebrew and Oriental Languages, though he at the time

was only twenty-four.   There was no nepotism in the appointment :
James was a really fine scholar, and did a great deal for the study
of Greek.   He had been in contact with the New Learning from his
boyhood, for his school, which he describes here, was at Montrose,
where Erskine of Dun [1] *had brought the French Grecian Pierre de*
Marsilliers. [2]

My father put my eldest and onlie brother, David, about a
yeir and a half in age above me, and me togidder, to a kinsman
and brother in the ministerie of his, to school, a guid lernit,
kynd man, quham for thankfulness I name, Mr Wilyame Gray,
minister at Logie Montrose. He had a sister, a godlie and
honest matron, reular of his hous, quha often rememberit me of
my mothir, and was a verie loving mothir to me indeed. Thair
wes a guid nombir of gentil and honest mennis bairnis of the
countrey about, weill trainit up baith in letteris, godliness, and
exerceis of honest gamis. Thair we lernit to reid the Catechism,
Prayeris, and Scripture ; to reherse the Catechism and Prayeris
par coeur ; also notis of Scripture eftir the reiding thairof ; and
thair first I fand (blissit be my guid God for it !) that Spreit of
Sanctificatioun beginning to wark sum motiounis in my hart,
evin about the aucht and nynt yeir of my aige ; to pray going
to bed and rysing, and being in the feildis alane to say ower the
prayeris I haid lernit, with a sweit moving in my hairt ; and to
abhor sweiring and rebuik and complein upoun sic as I herd
sweir. Quhairunto the exempil of that godlie matron, seiklie
and giffen to reid and pray in hir bed, did mekil profit me ; for
I lay in hir chalmer and herd hir exerceisis. We lernit thair the

---

[1] One of the first Superintendents of the Reformation Church, and the
Moderator of the General Assembly, which, in 1572, largely through his influence,
made the first move to restore the episcopate.

[2] A Scot had already taught Greek at Cambridge, in succession to Erasmus
himself, and there were a couple more holding Greek chairs in France. By the
early seventeenth century the standard Greek grammar all over western Europe
was that of Alexander Scott, a Scots Catholic exile. In 1553 Aberdeen Grammar
School ruled that its pupils must speak Latin, Greek, Hebrew, French, or Gaelic,
Scots being barred. The status of modern languages shows also in Melville's
description, which deals with a time about ten years later.

Rudimentis of the Latin grammair, with the vocablis in Latin
and French ; also divers speichis in French, with the reiding and
richt pronunciatioun of that toung.   We proceidit furder to the
Etymologie of Lillius and his Syntax, as also litil of the Syntax
of Linacer ; thairwith wer joynit Hunter's Nomenclatura, the
Minora Colloquia of Erasmus, and sum of the Eclogis of Virgil
and Epistolis of Horace ; also Cicero his Epistolis ad Terentiam.
He haid a verie guid and profitabil form of resolving the auctoris ;
he techit grammaticallie, baith according to the Etymologie and
Syntax. . . . Thair also we had the air guid, and feildis reason-
abil far, and be our maistir wer techit to handil the bow for
archerie, the glub for gowff, the batons for fencing, also to rin,
to loup, to swoom, to warsel, to preve pratticks, everie ane
haiffing his matche and antagonist, baith in our lessounis and
play.

A happie and goldin tyme indeid, gif our negligence and
unthankfulness haid nocht movit God to schorten it, pairtlie be
decaying of the number, quhilk causit the maister to wearie, and
pairtlie of a pest quhilk the Lord, for sin and contempt of His
Gospel, send upoun Montrose, distant from Over Logie bot
two mylis ; sa that school skailit, and we wer al sent for and
brocht hame.   I was at that school the space of almost fyve
yeiris, in the quhilk tyme, of publict newis, I remember I herd
of the mariage of Hendrie and Marie, King and Quene of
Scottis, Seignour Davies slauchtir, of the Kingis murdour at the
Kirk of Feild, of the Quenis taking at Carberi, and the Langsyde
feild. . . . Also I remember weill how we passit to the heid of
the muir to sie the fyre of joy burning upoun the stepil heid of
Montrose at the day of the Kingis birth.

preve pratticks, test (by competition).

41. Standard School-books

*Melville's loving list of his old school-books reminds one that,
only a few years after he left his school, a Royal Commission had*

been set up to investigate those in use. It was a formidable body, consisting of the King's Tutors, George Buchanan [1] and Peter Young, with the headmasters of Edinburgh, Stirling, Dunbar, Haddington, Glasgow, and St Andrews. They found that none of the grammars then in use " servit to thair contentment" and set out jointly to compose a new one, which they hoped the Privy Council would make compulsory. The work had been done thoroughly, with meetings (at public expense) for conference and revision.

Now, in December 1593, a decreit of the Privy Council ordered it to be proclaimed at all market-crosses that this joint work must be used throughout the kingdom.

Forsamekil as it is understand to the Kingis Majestie and Lordis of Secreit Counsal, that the maisteris of scholis and pedagogis haif this monie yeiris bygane chosin to thaimselffis sic writtaris of the artis of grammar as hes bein commendit unto thaim be the prentaris or buiksellaris, quhilkis ather thay haif lernit thaimselffis, or ellis hes bein accustomat to teich, or sic as, upoun the occasioun of the tyme and place, nowmer or pryceis, cum reddiest to thair handis : quhairby it cum oft to pas that the best form and maist profitabil for advancing of the studyis of the youth hes nocht bein taucht, bot sic as thay trowit be maist easie for spairing and inhalding of thair travail : and lykewayis als monie divers grammaris ar brocht in and taucht in the countrey as thair is teicharis of that art ; sa that, quhen the scollaris ar changit fra place to place at the arbitrement of thair parentis, thay ar newlingis to begin that art quhairin they haif spendit sum yeiris of befoir, and ar rather chairgit thair to forgett nor repeit that quhilk thay haif lernit, to the greit hindering of their proceidingis and confounding of thair memoreis and ingynis. . . .

forsamekil, forasmuch. *travail,* labour. *arbitrement,* choice. *newlingis,* newly. *ingyne,* ingenium, intelligence. *trowit,* believed.

[1] The famous French scholar-printer Estienne calls Buchanan *Poetarum nostri saeculi facile Princeps,* and the English Camden endorses the opinion.

42. THE KIRK TAKES CONTROL

On the 3rd December of 1567, with Mary in Lochleven, a Commission of the Articles, including Knox, decided

Item, that all scholis, alsweill to burgh as to land, and collegis be reformit, and that nane be permittit nor admittit to haif chairge thairof, or to instruct the youth privatlie or publictlie bot sic as ar or sal be tryit be the Superintendentis and visitatoris of the Kirk, and admittit be thaim to thair chairgis.

43. THE DOMINIE'S VOCATION

This passage, in its setting of vague and formless apprehension, would come home to many teachers in our Europe. It is from the Third Tractate of Ninian Winzet, a pamphlet addressed to the Edinburgh magistrates, defending the Christian observance of Easter.

Winzet had been Rector of the Parish School of Linlithgow and Provost of its collegiate church of St Michael. "Expellit and schot out of that my kindlie toun" for refusing to accept the 1560 Confession of Fayth, he entered into the religious controversies of the time, challenging the triumphant Knox to produce his credentials as a reformer, and incidentally chaffing him for his anglicised speech. Knox preached against him, stating that he had been called like St John Baptist, but declined to answer him in print. An attempt was made to arrest Winzet at his printer's, but the men did not know him by sight : he kept his head and walked calmly out of the shop, to get away, and, after teaching a while at the Sorbonne, died Abbot of the Scots Benedictines in Ratisbon.

Quhen it came to my eris, gentil redar, of the seditious calking of the buith duris of certain Catholikis in Edinburgh at the command of the reularis thairof, on Pasche Mononday last passit, and how at that nicht at een the duris of certain Calvinianis wer calkit also with sum notis of dishonour, I wes penseand how happie ane thing it wes gif everie man micht leve according to his vocatioun, at ane tranquillitie in godliness. And throw that revolvand in mind that maist flourissand pairt of my age, spent in the teiching of the Grammar schule of Linlychtquhow, about the space of ten yeiris, I judgit the teiching of the youthheid in virtew and science nixt after the auctoritie with the ministeris of justice undir it : and efter the angelicall office of godlie pastouris, to obtein the thrid principall place maist commodius and necessar to the Kirk of God. Ye, sa necessar thocht I it, that the dew chairge and office of the prince and prelat, without it, is to them (eftir my jugement) wondrous painful and almost importabil, and yit litil commodius to the comoun welth, til unfenzeit obedience and trew godliness quhen the pepil is rude and ignorant ; and contrair, be the help of it in the youthheid, the office of all potestatis is licht to thaim and pleasand to the subjectis. For the mind of man of ane guid inclinatioun (as ane ancient writtar richt warlie notis) obeyis nocht, nor submittis the self willinglie to ane commandar or teichar, bot to sic quham it is persuadit to command justlie for utiliteis caus, quhilk persuasioun throw ignorance it may nocht weil haif, without the licht of understanding.

calking, chalking.　　*buith duris*, shop doors.　　*penseand*, thinking. *science*, knowledge.　　*ye*, yea.　　*importabil*, insupportable.　　*potestatis*, powers.　　*warlie*, thoughtfully, wisely.

44. Scholars' Diversion

James Melville looks back at his student days at St Andrews, in 1574.

I learnit my music, quhairin I tuik greitar delyt [than in law] of ane Alexander Smithe, servant to the Primarius of our College, quha had bein treinit up amangis the monkis in the Abbay. I lernit of him the gam, plein sang, and monie of the treiblis of the Psalmis, quhairof sum I could weil sing in the Kirk ; bot my naturalitie and eisie lerning be the eir maid me the mair unsolid and unredie to use the form of the art. I luvit singing and playing on instrumentis passing weil, and wald gladlie spend tyme quhair the exercise thairof wes within the College ; for two or thrie of our condiscipulis playit feloun weil on the virginalis, and ane uthir on the lute and githorn. Our Regent had also the pinaldis in his chalmer, and lernit sumthing, and I eftir him ; bot perceiving me ower mekil carryit eftir that, he dishantit and left off. It wes the greit mercie of my God that keipit me from anie greit progres in singing and playing on instrumentis, for gif I had atteinit to anie resonabil messour thairin, I had nevir done guid uthirwayis, in respect of my amorous dispositioun.

gam, gamut.   *naturalitie*, natural turn.   *condiscipulis*, fellow-students. *feloun weill*, frightfully well.   *githorn*, a sort of guitar.   *pinaldis*, spinet. *regent*, university teacher.   *dishantit*, gave up the practice.

45. TECHNICAL TRAINING

In 1587 King James endeavoured to help Scots cloth-making by importing three master weavers from Flanders, which then made the best woollen cloths in Europe. They were offered an elaborate contract, giving them tempting privileges—temporary naturalisation, exemption from taxes, travelling expenses, looms at the city's expense, and a kirk to themselves if enough of them came over. In return, they were to bind themselves not to compete in the market by selling unworked wool, and to take as prentices only " Scottis boyis or madinnis." These were

to be prentissis be the space of fyve yeiris, and that the saidis maisteris sall instruct thaim in the haill pointis of the foirsaid craft within the space of fyve yeiris, and sall hyde na pairt fra thaim, and alswa sall furnische thaim resonablie with meit, drink, cleithing, bedding, wesching, and wringing : for the quhilk causis to be performit be the saidis strangearis to thair prentissis, during the said space of fyve yeiris, the saidis prentissis and ilk ane of thaim sall pay to thair maisteris for ilk ane of their prentissis the soum of forty pundis Scottis money for ilk man child, and twenty pund for ilk madin.

VI

POETS AND LOVERS

Ye your hearts cannot restrain
From sending sighs, feeling a lover's case.
WILLIAM DRUMMOND

" There is a great deal of it," said she, glancing along the paper.
SIR WALTER SCOTT, *Rob Roy*

46. THE LOST POETS

Everyone knows Dunbar's grim poem on the fear of death, with its ghostly catalogue of vanished poets, men whose works were famous, and are sunk without trace. Here are more such ghosts, of a later generation. The man who sang of them has himself survived: he was " Sir David Lindsay of the Mount, Lord Lyon King of Arms, " Scottish Ambassador to the Imperial Court and for many years a member of James V's household.

Anti-clerical and pro-English, with a fine mixture of reforming zeal and frankly scurrilous gusto, he was popular in Scotland and in England, and his works were read into the eighteenth century, while his reputation survived their popularity. His " Thrie Estaitis " is the only whole play, except for the anonymous " Philotus," that survives of the flourishing drama of his age.

In his " Testament of the Papyngo " he calls the roll of the " poetis intil our vulgar toung." First come the men of his youth: he was actually born under James III, in 1486, and was thus twenty-seven at the time of Flodden. There is Dunbar, who had " language at large," and Kennedy, " with termes aureait," and then

Quinting, Mersar, Rowle, Henderson, Hay, and Holland,
Thoch thay be deid, thair libellis bein livand,
Quhilkis to reherce maikis redaris to rejois.

Allace for ane, quhilk lamp wes of this land,
Of eloquens the flowand balmie strand
And in our Inglis rethorik the rois :
As of rubeis the carbunkel bein chois,
And as Phebus dois Cynthia precell,
So Gawane Dowglas, Bischop of Dunkell

Had, quhen he wes into this land on lyve
Abuve vulgare poetis prerogative . . .

And in the court bein present in thir dayis,
That ballatis brevis lustilie, and layis,
Quhilkis til our Prince daylie thay do present.
Quha can say mair than Schir James Inglis sayis,
In ballatis, farsis, and in plesand playis ?
But Culros hes his pen maid impotent.
Kyd, in cunnyng and pratik right prudent,
And Stewart, quhilk desiris ane statlie style,
Ful ornait werkis daylie does compile.

Stewart of Lorne wil carp richt curiuslie :
Galbraith, Kinloch, quhen thay list thaim applie
Into that art, are craftie of ingyne.
Bot now of lait is stert up hastilie
Ane cunning clerk, quhilk werkis craftelie,
Ane plant of poetis, callit Ballentyne. . . .

libellis, books.   *precell*, excel.   *brevis*, write in books.   *carp*, sing.

47. THE LOVER'S LUTE

*Some fragments, possibly, of the work of these men, and of
others who have no memorial even of their names, survive, by sheer
chance, in three MS. collections. The courtly poets of that time,
everywhere, were apt to scorn print : their work was sung to a
select assembly or passed from hand to hand in manuscript.   There*

was a fashion, as with our grandmothers' albums, for collecting and copying down in one's own hand whatever pieces happened to take the fancy.

Of the three Scots collections which have survived, the largest and best known is George Bannatyne's. Its background is not Holyroodhouse, however : the eight hundred pages of its neat close writing, embellished with flourishes of penmanship, were compiled in three months of 1568, when plague in Edinburgh forbade any more sociable diversion.

The compiler, then twenty-three, was the seventh of the twenty-three children of James Bannatyne of Kirkton of Newtyle, near Meigle, in Aberdeenshire.

> Fairweil, my hairt, fairweil baith frend and fo ;
> Fairweil, the weil of sweitest medicyne ;
> Fairweil, my luve, baith lyf and deith also ;
> Fairweill, blythnes, fairweill, sweit leman myne ;
> Fairweill, the flour of colour quhyte and fyne,
> That faidis nocht for weddir, wem, nor weit
> No moir than in the somer sesoun sweit.
>
> How sall I do, quhen I maun yow forgo ?
> How sall I sing, how sall I glad then be ?
> How sall I leif ? I luve yow and na mo.
> Quhat sall I do ? How sall I comfort me ?
> How sall I than thir bitter painis drie,
> Quhair now I haif als mekil as I may
> Of cairis cauld and siching evirie day ?

wem, injury, blemish.   *siching*, sighing.

In this, though the lover is most correctly downcast, the metre has a certain wicked twinkle.

> Quhair luve is kindlit confortles
> Thair is no fevir half so fell.
> Fra Cupid cast his dart be guess,
> I had na hap to saif mysel.

Lyke as my woful hairt can tell
  My inwart painis and siching sair,
For weil I wat, the painis of hell
  Unto my pain can nocht compair.

For onie maladie, ye ken,
  Except puir luve or than stark deid,
Help may be had fra handis of men
  Throw medecyne to maik remeid :
  For harmis of bodie, handis, and heid
    The pottingar will purge the painis :
  But all the membris ar at feid
    Quhair that the law of luve remainis.

As Tantalus in watir standis
  To stanch his thristie appetyte,
Bewailing bodie, heid, and handis,
  The revar flyis him in despyte :
  So dois my lustie ladie quhyte :
    Sche flyis the place quhair I repair.
  To hungrie men is small delyte
    To touch the meit, and eit na mair.

The nar the flamb, the hettar fyre :
  The mair I pyne, yit I persew.
The mair enkindlis my desyr
  Fra I behald hir hevinlie hew.
  Puir Piramus himself he slew—
    Maid saul and bodie to dissever.
  He dyit bot aince.   Fairweill, adieu !
    I daylie de, and dyis nevir.

Yit Jasoun did enjoy Medea
  And Theseus gat Arian ;
Dido dissavit wes with Enea,
  And Demophon to his ladie wan.

F

Gif wemen trowit sic traitoris than,
　　For til enjoy the fruits of luve,
Quhy wald ye slay your sakles man,
　　Quha mindis nevir to remuve ?

The fers Achill, ane worthie knicht,
　　Wes slain for luve, the suth to say.
Leander, on ane stormie nicht,
　　Dyit fleitand the fludis gray.
　　Trew Troyallus, languourit ay,
　　　　Still waitand for his luvis return,
　　Had nocht sic pyne—it wes bot play—
　　　　As daylie dois my bodie burn.

As Poill to pilottis dois appeir
　　Moir brichtar than the starris about,
So dois your visage schyne als cleir
　　As rois amang the rascal rout.
　　Wer Paris levand now, na dout,
　　　　And had the golden ball to serve,
　　I wat he sune wald waill yow out,
　　　　And leif baith Venus and Minerve.

Now papir pas, and at hir speir
　　Gid pleis hir prudence to imprent it ?
My faithfull hairt I send hir heir,
　　In signe of papir I present it.
　　Wald God my bodie wer fornent it,
　　　　That I micht serve hir grace but glamour.
　　To be hir knaif I am contentit,
　　　　Or smallest varlet in hir chalmer.

　　　　　　The hairt did think, the hand did frame,
　　　　　　The bodie send to you the same.

---

siching, sighing.　　*pottingar*, apothecary.　　*feid*, feud.　　*nar*, nearer.
sakles, blameless.　　*Poill*, Pole-star.　　*rout*, mob.　　*but*, without (in
last verse).

*This is again from the Bannatyne MS. George Bannatyne
seems to have written it either from memory or from a very illegible
copy, as one verse—omitted here—has several blanks left in it for
missing words. Other lines limp, or fail to make sense, or both :
but as the whole thing, with its lovely muted internal rhymes, is
too good to leave out, I have ventured on conjectural emendation.*

Luve, quhat art thow, for til allow
    Hes brocht me now into this pain and wo ?
Or yit avow hes gart me trow
    And reft my dow and daliaunce me fro ?
      Fy on the Lord of Luve, set me sa heich abuve,
    And als, but rest or ruif, hes gart me go.

Paris of Troy had nocht mair joy
    Bot til convoy fair Helen, fresch and ying :
Now haif I noy, me to distroy,
    As then at Troy had Menelaus King.
      Sen lost is my delyte and pastyme maist perfyte,
    All erdlie solace quyte heir I resing.

For til discus, I wis, I wes
    As Troylus with Cresseid, trew to tell.
Now am I thus as Piramus,
    Maist dolourous, with Tisby at the well :
      So is becum my cais, as Orpheus did, allais,
    Sekand Euridices fra hevin to hell.

Quhair suld I go now to or fro,
    To seik hir so, my umquhile luve alane ?
Then freind, now fo, then weill, now wo,
    Than mirth but mo, now sche is past and gane.
      Then hoip, now in distres, then joy, now comfortles,
    Then welth and wantonnes quhair now is nane.

O luvaris all, to luve bein thrall,
    Now lat us fall befoir the goddis feit
To clip and call in generall,
    Baith greit and small, that may our balis beit.
      O Venus, Soverane, haif pitie on my pain,
    And grant me now agane my ladie sweit.

Again and nocht let it be thocht
    That sche for ocht will aince return to me.
Sen chance hes socht and weird hes wrocht
    That sche is brocht quhair sche may byde and be,
      Sen fors is I maun want hir, greit gladnes may
        God grant hir,
    And send me als guid anter.   Amen, quod he.

trow, believe.   *daliaunce*, pleasure.   *but*, without.   *noy*, ennui, weary trouble.   *erdlie*, earthly.   *mirth but mo*, mirth with nothing more.   *clip*, embrace.   *anter*, adventure, chance.   *fors is*, needs must.   *weird*, fate.

It was George Bannatyne who saved for us what is left of the work of Alexander Scott—rather more than thirty pieces, of varying kinds. Scott was about the Queen Regent's court, and Mary's, and he wrote satire, topical verse of some shrewdness, and a piece of lively comic manners-painting, but his finest work is in the lyric. Everyone knows his haunting "Rondel of Luve." Here is a snatch of another :

      Oppressit hairt, indure
        In dolour and distress,
      Wappit without recure
        In wo remediless.
        Sen sche is merciless
      And causis all thy smert
        Quhilk suld thy dolour dress,
      Indure, oppressit hairt.

This is Scott's also :

      Hens hairt with her that must depairt,
      And hald thee with thy soverane,

For I had lever want ane hairt
  Nor haif the hairt that dois me pain ;
Thairfoir go, with thy luve remain,
  And lat me lif thus unmolest ;
And see that thow cum nocht again,
  Bot byde with hir thow luvis best.

Sen sche that I haif servit lang
  Is to depairt so suddanlie,
Address thee now, for thow salt gang
  And beir thy ladie cumpanie.
  Fra sche be gane, hairtles am I,
    For quhy, thow art with hir possest ;
Thairfoir, my hairt, go hens in hy,
  And byde with hir thow luvest best.

Thoch this belappit bodie heir
  Be bound to servitude and thrall,
My faithfull hairt is fre inteir
  And mind to serve my ladie at all.
  Wald God that I wer perigall
    Undir that redolent rois to rest !
Yit at the leist, my hairt, thow sall
  Abyde with hir thow luvest best.

Sen in your garth the lillie quhyte
  May nocht remain amang the laif,
Adew, the flour of haill delyte,
  Adew, the succour that may me saif,
  Adew, the fragrant balm suaif,
    And lamp of ladeis lustiest !
My faithfull hairt sche sall it haif,
  To byde with hir it luvis best.

Deploir, ye ladeis cleir of hew,
  Hir absence, sen sche must depairt,

And speciallie ye luvaris trew
That woundit bein with luvis dairt—
For sum of yow sall want ane hairt
As weill as I :   thairfoir at last
Do go with mine, with mind inwart,
And byde with hir thow luvest best.

belappit, wrapped round, smothered.   *at all*, in all things.   *perigall*, equall to, worthy of.   *suaif*, suave, gentle.   *in hy*, in haste.

Scott's characteristic poised and wheeling rhythm shows in a piece of vicarious lover's grieving, " The Lament of the Master of Erskine." The Master loved the Queen Dowager Marie, they say, and, fighting for her and his country, died at Pinkie.

Depairt, depairt, depairt,
Allace, I must depairt
Fra hir that hes my hairt,
    With hairt full soir.
Aganis my will indeid,
And can find na remeid :
I wat the painis of deid
    Can do no moir.

Now must I go, allace,
From sicht of hir sweit face,
The grund of all my grace
    And soverane :
Quhat chance that may fall me
Sall I ner mirrie be
Unto the tyme I see
    My sweit again.

I go, and wat nocht quhair,
I wandir heir and thair,
I weip and sich richt sair,
    With painis smert ;

Now must I pass away, away,
In wildirnes and wilfull way ;
Allace, this wofull day
   We suld depairt !

My spreit dois quaik for dreid,
My thirlit hairt dois bleid,
My painis does exceid :
   Quhat suld I say ?
I wofull wicht alane,
Makand ane pitous mane,
Allace, my hairt is gane
   For evir and ay.

Throw langour of my sweit,
So thirlit is my spreit,
My dayis ar maist compleit
   Throw hir absence.
Christ, sen sche knew my smairt
Ingravit in my hairt,
Becaus I must depairt
   From hir presence.

Adew, my ain sweit thing,
My joy and conforting,
My mirth and sollasing
   Of erdlie gloir.
Fairweill, my ladie bricht
And my remembraunce richt ;
Fairweill, and haif guid nicht.
   I say na moir.

thirlit, pierced.   *ar maist compleit*, are almost at an end.   *sen* (in this verse) if only.

And here is one last sad and nameless lover, not from Bannatyne, now, but from another collection, made at much the same time for old

Sir Richard Maitland of Lethington, the father of Queen Mary's Secretary. It is clearly lute-song, with the sound of the strings— or perhaps harp-song, for our own clarsach was known at Mary's court, beside the instruments that had come overseas.

The day quhenas the fair pairtit me frae
   Plesour me left also.
Quhen that fra hir I sinderit wes away,
   Mischance me hent but ho.
     I waxit wan
     The same hour than.
     Sorou sinsyne
     Dois still me pyne.
   O that guidnicht hes causit mekil wo.

Evin as men may the turtil trew persaif
   Aince having lost hir feir,
On the dry branch, ay faithful to the graif,
   Bewailing perseveir,
     So my desyre,
     Kindlit in fyre,
     Dois sair lament
     My luve absent.
O God, gif amour be ane pain to beir ! . . .

The faithfull messenger quha is the nicht,
   To luvaris languorous,
Augmentis my wo, and als the dayis licht
   Maikis me mair dolourous.
     The day I dwine,
     The nicht I pyne,
     Evin eikis my sorou
     Wors than the morou.
   O God, in luve gif I be malhourous !

And gif that neid to slumber me constrain,
 Faint throu melancolie,
Unrest dois wakin me again,
 To muse my miserie.
  Quhatevir chance
  Dois me outrance,
  Saif fals thinking
  In sweit dreming.
O dreme, maist sweit—gif it were nocht a lie !

In cairfull bed full oft in myne intent
 To tuich I do appeir
Now syde, now breist, now sweit mou redolent
 Of that sweit bodie deir.
  I stretch my hand
  In vain yernand.
  My luve is far
  And nocht found nar.
O scorn of luvaris, Cupid, blind Archeir !

but ho, without quarter. *turtil*, turtle-dove. *eikis*, increases. *out-rance*, a technical term of the tournament : to fight à l'outrance meant with sharpened weapons, to a finish. *malhourous*, malheureux, unhappy.

Mark Alexander Boyd, born in Mary's brief reign and dead in 1601 at thirty-eight, gives the lover who escapes with the smell of the fire still on his garments.   Physician to Henri IV, soldier and scholar, he left some admirable Latin verse, but this is all that remains of his work in Scots.   It is worth noting that he uses the true Italian form of the sonnet—the first time that we find it in work of a British poet.

Fra bank to bank, fra wood to wood I rin,
 Ourhailit with my febil fantasie ;
 Like to a leif that fallis from a tree
Or till a reid ourblawin with the win.
Twa gods guides me ; the ane of them is blin,

Yea, and a bairn brocht up in vanitie ;
The neist a wyfe ingenerit of the sea,
And lichter nor a dauphin with hir fin.
Unhappie is the man for evirmair
That tillis the sand and sawis in the air,
Bot twys unhappier is he, I lern,
That feidis in his hairt a mad desyre
And followis on a woman throw the fyre,
Led by a blind and teichit be a bairn.

ourhailit, overcome.   *ingenerit*, engendered.

48. A Valentine

Here is a valentine, in most graceful and classical Latin elegiacs, for Mary Beaton, the belle of the Four Maries. It was written by, of all men, George Buchanan—no doubt in the days when the Queen, whom later he was to vilify with a quite unscholarly disregard of fact, was making much of him as her Latin tutor and one of the ornaments of a Renaissance court. The poet is careful not to sound too earnest : but one wonders if perhaps Beaton's lively tongue—she was no classicist, and a reigning beauty— pierced his thin skin and made him, later, take refuge in righteous indignation with her and her mistress ? One has come across such processes of the mind in more recent times than the sixteenth century.

Shall I complain, or shall I rather praise the gifts of Fortune, who sets me free from Beton's regiment ? What to me now is that her comely beauty, when no hope is left that she will return my unquiet ? [1] Had Fortune been better to me in better years, and treated me with a more generous hand, I should have turned on a sudden into ash, for life to me would have been short and the pain of death light. Now Chance burns me with slow torch, and gives me neither the joyousness of life, nor the sudden relief of death. But whether life or death remains for

[1] *Cura*, which can have half a dozen senses—like a number of words in these apparently pellucid lines.

me, at all events I may rejoice in this, that my life and death are alike in the choice of my lady.

Another epigram to Mary Beaton, also in elegiacs of singular grace, runs thus :

Winter is fierce, the meadows are not bright nor the gardens with flowers, when I might seek to make ready a sacrificial offering for my lady. So also that garden of my mind and thought, once fertile in the worship of the Muses, is bound by winter in the cold of age. Yet still, if the warm west wind, Betonian airs, should blow on it, there should abound the succour of spring.

49. Late Lovers

All the men quoted above were probably of Mary's court or her parents' : we cannot date their work with certainty, and from 1528, when James broke from his Douglas tutelage, to 1567 when his daughter was discrowned, is not so long a time in the history of letters. After that, though James VI did his best for it, the stream of Scots courtly verse was running thin, and what there is has far less life in it. The Union of Crowns was to take the court to London, and, save for short intervals, to keep it there : none of the Lennox Stewarts was given cause to feel profound affection for this country. English, accordingly, became the court language, and was soon—though it was a definite Scots-English—to be the " curial" speech of all the Lowlands.

Among the work of this transitional time, " the polite and verdant genius" of William Drummond—as Milton's nephew very happily called it—stands out in remembrance. He was born in 1585, and lived to see the death of James's successor, but most of his work belongs to the earlier reign. A courtly poet, he was seldom at court, though he took a hand in the municipal masks in Edinburgh that graced Charles I's belated coronation, with the Muses dancing " in varying taffetas, cloth of silver, and purle."

The cold and fragile beauty of his work has the old grace of form in a new mode, and behind it was the old international outlook : his library ran to seven languages, and, in spite of his use of English and his just admiration for the great English poets, his real kinship is far more with France.

I know that all beneath the moon decays,
And what by mortals in this world is brought
In Time's great periods shall return to nought ;
That fairest states have fatal nights and days ;
I know how all the Muses' heavenly lays,
With toil of sp'rit that are so dearly bought,
As idle sounds, of few or none are sought,
And that nought lighter is than airy praise.
I know frail beauty's like the purple flower
To which one morn oft birth and death affords ;
That love a jarring is of minds' accords,
Where sense and will invassal reason's power.
   Know what I list, this all cannot me move,
   But that, O me, I both must write and love.

His lady died when their wedding-day was set.

O Pan, Pan, winter is fallen in our May,
Turned is in night our day.
Forsake thy pipe, a sceptre take to thee,
Thy looks disgarland : thou black Jove shalt be.
Thy flocks do leave the meads,
And loathing three-leaved grass, hold up their heads :
The streams not glide now with a gentle roar,
   Nor birds sing as before ;
Hills stand with clouds, like mourners, veiled in black,
And owls on cabin roofs foretell our wrack.
   That zephyr every year
So soon was heard to sigh in forests here,

It was for her ; that wrapped in gowns of green
Meads were so early seen ;
That in the saddest months oft sang the merles,
It was for her ; for her the trees dropped pearls,
That proud and stately courts
Did envy those our shades and calm resorts.
It was for her : and she is gone, O woe !
　　Woods cut again do grow,
Bud doth the rose and daisy, winter done,
But we, once dead, no more do see the sun. . . .

*Sir William Alexander, first Earl of Stirling and Viscount
Canada, is strangely mixed up in the queer affair of the first Scottish
overseas colonies. He was poet as well as courtier and politician
and builder of the great town mansion in Stirling that, character-
istically, now bears another man's name. His sequence "Aurora"
was written during his youthful Grand Tour, in his twenties, and
published in the year after the Union : that we have it now in
English rather than Scots may derive from the printer rather than
the poet. This sonnet is to the orthodox cold lady.*

O, if thou knewest how thou thyself dost harm,
And dost prejudge thy bliss and spoil my rest,
Then thou wouldst melt the ice out of thy breast,
And thy relenting heart would kindly warm.
O, if thy pride did not our joys control,
What world of loving wonders shouldst thou see !
For if I saw thee once transformed in me,
Then in thy bosom I would pour my soul.
Then all thy thoughts should in my visage shine,
And if that ought mischanced thou shouldst not moan,
Nor bear the burthen of thy griefs alone.
No, I would have my share in what were thine :
　　And while we thus should make our sorrows one,
　　This happy harmony would make them none.

50. THE LADY'S RETORT

That serious soul, William Drummond of Hawthornden, rather surprisingly sees there is more than one way of regarding the endless poems to cruel ladies. He makes one speak here.

Ye who with curious numbers, sweetest art,
Frame daedal nets our beauty to surprise,
Telling strange castles builded in the skies
And tales of Cupid's bow and Cupid's dart ;
Well howsoe'er ye act your feigned part
Molesting quiet ears with tragic cries,
When you accuse our chastity's best part,
Named cruelty, ye seem not half too wise.
Yea, ye yourselves it deem most worthy praise,
Beauty's best guard, that dragon which doth keep
Hesperian fruit, the spur in you does raise
That Delian wit that otherwise may sleep.
    To cruel nymphs your lines do fame afford :
    Of many pitiful, not one poor word.

51. THE HERETIC

Sir Robert Aytoun, their elder contemporary, was a much less orthodox lover than Drummond and Stirling. He was a younger son of the Laird of Kinaldie, and, after his graduation at St Andrews, was about the court, going as Ambassador to the Emperor and serving Queen Anne, and later Queen Henrietta, as private secretary. As he was thirty-three at the Union of Crowns, the fact that we have his poems in English, not Scots, may perhaps be due to later copying. He wrote also admirable Latin verse, still extant, and more in Greek and French, unluckily lost : one feels he should have been at home in the latter.

There is no worldly pleasure here below
    Which by experience doth not folly prove ;

But among all the follies that I know,
   The sweetest folly in the world is love.

But not that passion which, by fools' consent,
   Above the reason bears imperious sway,
Making their lifetime a perpetual Lent,
   As if a man were born to fast and pray.

No, that is not the humour I approve,
   As either yielding pleasure or promotion :
I like a mild and lukewarm zeal in love,
   Although I do not like it in devotion.

For it hath no coherence with my creed
   To think that lovers die as they pretend.
If all that say they die had died indeed,
   Sure long ere now the world had had an end.

Besides, we need not love but if we please ;
   No destiny can force man's disposition :
And how can any die of that disease
   Whereof himself may be his own physician ?

But some seem so distracted of their wit
   That I would think it but a venial sin
To take some of those innocents that sit
   In Bedlam out, and put some lovers in.

Yet some men, rather than incur the slander
   Of true apostates, will false martyrs prove :
But I am neither Iphis nor Leander—
   I'll neither drown nor hang myself for love.

Methinks a wise man's actions should be such
   As always yield to reason's best advice.

Now, for to love too little or too much
   Are both extremes, and all extremes are vice.

Yet have I been a lover by report—
   Yea, I have died for love, as others do.
But, praised be God, it was in such a sort
   That I revived within an hour or two.

Thus have I lived, thus have I loved, till now,
   And found no reason to repent me yet :
And whosoever otherwise will do,
   His courage is as little as his wit.

Aytoun could wear even rue with a tilt of the lip. Everyone knows the enchanting " I do confess thou'rt smooth and fair "— which is not quite certainly his, though in his voice. This other is in the same key.

I loved thee once, I'll love no more :
   Thine be the grief, as is the blame.
Thou art not what thou wast before,
   What reason should I be the same ?
      He that can love unloved again
      Hath better store of love than brain ;
         God send me love my debts to pay,
         While unthrifts fool their love away.

Nothing could have my love o'erthrown
   If thou hadst still continued mine—
Nay, if thou hadst remained thine own
   I might perchance have still been thine.
      But thou thy freedom did recall
      That it thou mightst elsewhere enthrall,
         And then how could I but disdain
         A captive's captive to remain ?

When new desires had conquered thee
  And changed the object of thy will,
It had been lethargy in me,
  Not constancy, to love thee still.
    Yea, it had been a sin to go
    And prostitute affection so,
      Since we are taught no prayers to say
      To such as must to others pray.

Yet do thou glory in thy choice,
  Thy choice of his good fortune boast.
I'll neither grieve nor yet rejoice
  To see him gain what I have lost.
    The height of my disdain shall be
    To laugh at him, to blush for thee,
      To love thee still, but go no more
      A-begging at a beggar's door.

52. WHAT THEY SANG DOWNSTAIRS

All these are courtly poems, drawing-room verse. But they sang in the kitchen and about the stable, and round the fire of the farm and the cottar-house on a winter evening, and what they sang there in those days was often the ballads. They are forgotten in most accounts of the time, but we shall never begin to understand it unless we recall that they were its popular songs.

There are more kinds than one. A topical one from the Edinburgh streets has been given already. And the Riding Ballads are topical in their way, though they belong to another part of this book. The Riding Ballads are earth between wind and water. Others move to the stir of the wind between the worlds. The greatest of them—Clerk Sanders, the Wife of Usher's Well, and their like—are in every anthology, and have survived even that ; so here, lest the kind should be left out altogether, is a lesser one, less well known, out of Clydesdale . . . though its theme is common to half the

G

nations of Europe. As with the other ballads given in this book,
the version we have is eighteenth century.

" O lady, rock never your young son
    One hour longer for me,
For I have a sweetheart in Garlioch Wells
    I love far better than thee.

The very sole o' that lady's foot
    Than thy face is far mair white."
" But nevertheless, now, Earl Richard,
    Ye will bide in my bower a' night ? "

She birled him wi' the ale and wine
    As they sat down to sup :
A living man he laid him down,
    But I wot he ne'er rose up.

Then up and spake the popinjay,
    That flew aboun her heid.
" Lady, keep weel your gay cleiding
    Frae guid Earl Richard's bleid."

" O better I'll keep my green cleiding
    Frae guid Earl Richard's bleid,
Than thou canst keep thy clattering tongue
    That trattles in thy heid."

She has called upon her bowermaidens,
    She has called them ane by ane.
" There lies a deid man in my bower,
    I wish that he were gane."

They hae booted him and spurred him,
    As he was wont to ride,

A hunting-horn tied round his waist,
   A sharp sword by his side,
And they hae had him to the wan water,
   For a' men call it Clyde.

Then up and spake the popinjay
   That sat upon the tree :
" What hae ye done wi' Earl Richard ?
   Ye were his gay ladie."

" Come down, come down, my bonny bird,
   And sit upon my hand,
And thou sall hae a cage o' gowd,
   Where thou hast but the wand."

" Awa, awa, ye ill woman,
   Nae cage o' gowd for me.
As ye hae dune to Earl Richard,
   Sae wad ye do to me."

She had na crossed a rigg of land,
   A rigg but barely ane,
When she met wi' his auld father,
   Came riding all alane.

" Where hae ye been now, ladie fair,
   Where hae ye been sae late ? "
" We hae been seeking Earl Richard,
   But him we canna get."

" Earl Richard kens a' the fords in Clyde,
   He'll ride them ane by ane,
And though the night was never sae mirk,
   Earl Richard will be hame."

O it fell anes, upon a day,
   The King was boun to ride,
And he has mist him, Earl Richard,
   Should hae ridden on his right side.

The ladie turned her round about,
   Wi' meikle mournfu' din.
" It fears me sair o' Clyde's water,
   That he is drowned therein."

" Gar douk gar douk," the King he cried,
   " Gar douk for gowd and fee.
O wha will douk for Earl Richard's sake,
   Or wha will douk wi' me ? "

They doukit in at ae well-heid
   And out ay at the ither.
" We can douk nae mair for Earl Richard,
   Although he were our brither."

It fell that in that ladie's castle
   The King was bound to bed :
And up and spake the popinjay
   That flew abune his heid :

" Leave aff your douking on the day
   And douk upon the night,
And where that sackless knight lies slain,
   The candles will burn bricht."

" O there's a bird within this bower
   That sings baith sad and sweet :
O there's a bird within your bower
   Keeps me frae my night's sleep."

They left the douking on the day,
   And douked upon the night,
And where that sackless knight lay slain,
   The candles burned bright.

The deepest pot in a' the linn,
   They fand Earl Richard in,
A green turf tied across his breist
   To keep that guid lord doun.

Then up and spake the King himsell
   When he saw the deidly wound,
" O wha has slain my right-hand man,
   That held my hawk and hound ? "

Then up and spake the popinjay,
   Says, " What needs a' this din ?
It was his light leman took his life,
   And hided him in the linn."

She swore her by the grass sae green,
   Sae did she by the corn,
She hadna seen him, Earl Richard,
   Since Mononday at morn.

" Put na the wyte on me," she said,
   " It was my may Catherine."
Then they hae cut baith hay and fern
   To burn that maiden in.

It wadna take upon her cheek
   Nor yet upon her chin,
Nor yet upon her yellow hair
   To cleanse the deidly sin.

The maiden touched the clay-cald corp—
    A drap it never bled.
The ladie laid her hand on him,
    And sune the ground was red.

Out hae they taen her, may Catherine,
    And put her mistress in.
The flame took fast upon her cheek,
    Took fast upon her chin,
Took fast upon her fair bodie—
    She burned like hollins green.

53. INGENIUM SCOTORUM

O river Clyde, baith deep and wide,
    Thy streams are wonder strang.
Make me thy wrack as I come back,
    But spare me as I gang.

VII

THEY PLAY THEIR PAGEANTS

These were decent meetings—but they were a' ae man's bairns that were at them, ilk ane kend ilk ither.
Sir Walter Scott, *St Ronan's Well*

54. Municipal Mirth

In the Middle Ages and the early sixteenth century, Aberdeen was a notable place for plays and pageants. Besides the regular guild-plays, of the type familiar in other towns and countries, and the guild processions on the greater feast-days, its annual spree of the Abbot of Bon Accord was " the auld lovabill consuetud, honor, consolacioun, and plesour of the burgh." The whole burgh took part : in fact absentees were fined, the fines going to the High Kirk of its patron St Nicholas.

By 1508 the place of the Abbot as leader had been taken by Robin Hood and Little John—importations whom Scotland apparently took to its bosom, though soon after Flodden we find them superseded by the more native Lords of Bon Accord. Bon Accord, of course, is the city's famous motto, traditionally the rallying-word of its folk when they fought under Robert Bruce to recover their Castle.

In May 1531—well in advance !—we find the Bailies discussing the order of the procession for the next Corpus Christi and Candlemas.

The said day it wes statut and ordainit by the Provost, Bailzeis, and Consail present for the tyme, conform to the auld honorabill consuetudis and rytis of this burgh, and of the nobill burgh of Edinburgh, of the quhilk ryte and consuetud the foirsaid Provost hes gotten copie in wryte : that is to say, in the honour of God and the Blessit Virgin Marye, the craftismen of this burgh, in thair best array, keip and decore the Processioun on Corpus Christi dayis and Candilmes [1] als honorabillie as thay can, everie craft with thair awin baneir, with the armis of thair craft thairon. And they sall pass, all craft be thaim self, twa and twa, in thair ordour, that is to say, in the first the Fleschearis, and nixt thaim the Barbouris, nixt thaim the Skinneris and Furroweris togidder, nixt thaim the Cordonaris, nixt thaim Tailyouris, efter thaim the Wobsteris and Walcaris togidder, nixt thaim the Baxtaris, and last of all, nerrest the Sacrament, passis all Hammermen, that is to say, smithis, wrichtis, masonis, cuparis, sclateris, goldsmiths, and armouraris. And everie ane of the saidis craftis, in the Candilmes processioun, sal furneis thair Pageane conform to the auld statut maid in the yeir of God 1510.

. . . The Craftis ar chairgit to furneis the Pageanis under-written.

> The Fleschearis, Sanct Bastian and his Tormentouris.
> The Barbouris, Sanct Lowrie and his Tormentouris.
> The Skinnaris, Sanct Steven and his Tormentouris.
> The Cordinaris, Sanct Martin.
> The Tailyouris, The Coronatioun of Our Ladie.
> The Litstaris, Sanct Nicholas.
> The Wobstaris, Walcaris, and Bonet Makaris, Sanct John.
> The Baxtaris, Sanct George.
> The Wrichtis, Masonis, Sclateris and Cuparis, the Resurrectioun.
> The Smithis and Hammermen to furneis the Bearmen of the Croce.

consuetud, custom. *Furroweris*, furriers. *Cordonaris*, shoemakers. *Walcaris*, waulkers. *Bastian and Lowrie*, Sebastian and Lawrence.

It was disciplined fun : disturbances were put down with a firm hand. In 1542, for instance, a lady who had hurled rude

[1] Corpus Christi is the Feast of the Blessed Sacrament, on the Thursday after Trinity Sunday, which is the Sunday after Pentecost. It thus falls normally in June. Candlemas is the Feast of the Presentation of Christ in the Temple and of the Purification of Our Lady.

names at the Lord of Bon Accord, with scathing references to braw slashed hose, was fined by the Town Council, " and that wes gevin for dome." But abuses of another sort crept in : there was too much panis and not enough circenses, and in 1552 the Town Council firmly cut down the " banketting," in which it appears that the givers of the show had been trying " to surmount on thair pre-decessouris," so that

the caus principall and guid institutioun thairof, quhilk wes inhalding of the Guid Toun in gladnes and blythnes with dansis, farsis, playis, and gamis in tymis convenient, wes negleckit and abusit.

Only three years later, however, the scene was clouded. The Estates were in a puritanical mood,[1] and in June 1555

It is statut and ordainit that in all tymis cumming na maneir of persoun be chosin Robert Hude nor Litill John, Abbot of Un-resoun, Quenis of May, nor utherwayis nouther in burgh nor to landwart, in onie tyme to cum. And gif onie Provost, Bailzeis, Counsal and comunitie chesis sic ane persoun . . . [thay] sal tyne thair fredom for the space of fyve yearis. . . . [*And the person elected is to be banished from Scotland.*] And gif onie wemen or utheris about simmer treis singand maikis perturba-tioun to the Quenis leigis in the passage throw burrowis and utheris landwart tounis, the wemen perturbatouris, for skafrie [2] of money or utherwayis, sal be takin, handellit, and put upoun the cukstulis of everie burgh or toun.

The law was very far from popular. Aberdeen persisted in holding its play as usual : and in 1561 there was a famous

---

[1] The same Parliament passed a sumptuary law, ostensibly to help the cloth trade. Except for musicians and royal officials, no one under the degree of a landed gentleman might wear silk, gold or silver embroidery, or fine imported wool. No one under 2000 merks a year was to eat imported drugs or confections, and no one at all to hold a christening feast. But at least the " fraudfull mixioun " of wines was condemned.

[2] Jameson gives " *skaf*, to collect by dishonourable means." Does it survive in the *skoff* of the British Army ?

explosion in Edinburgh, the stronghold of the Saints.   The Diurnal
of Occurrents records that

Upoun the xxi day of Julii, the yeir foirsaid, Archibald
Dowglas of Kilspindie, Provost of Edinburgh,[1] David Symmer
and Adam Foulaston, baileis of the samyn, causit ane cordinare
servand, callit James Killone, to underlie the law in the Tolbuith
of Edinburgh, for the cumin in the toun of Edinburgh and
playing with Robene Hud ; and for that caus thair wes certain
craftismennis servandis put to the horn of befoir, of the quhilk
the said James Killone wes ane, and [the Provost and Baileis]
causit the assisis quham thay had electit of thair assistaris [to]
pass thairon, quha condemnit him to be hangit.   And thaireftir the craftismen maid greit solicitatiounis at the handis of the
said Provost, John Knox minister, and the Bailzeis, to haif
gotten him releivit, promitting that he sould do onything
possibil to be done, salvand his lyfe ; quha wald do nathing bot
haif him hangit.   And quhen the tyme of the puir mannis hanging approchit, and that the puir man was cumand to the gibbet
with the leddar, upoun the quhilk the said cordinar suld haif bein
hangit, the craftismennis childer and servandis passit to armour ;
and first thay housit Alexander Guthrie and [the] Provost and
Bailzeis in the said Alexanderis writing buith, and syne cam
doun again to the Croce, and dang doun the gibbet and braik
it to peicis, and thaireftir passit to the Tolbuith, quhilk wes then
steikit, and quhen thay could nocht apprehend the keyis
thairof, thay brocht foirhammeris, and dang up the said Tolbuith dure perforce, the Provost, Bailzeis, and utheris luikand
thairupoun : and quhen the said dure wes brokin up, ane pairt
of thaim passit in the samyn, and nocht allanerlie brocht the said
condampnit cordonar furth of the said Tolbuith, bot also all the
remenand presonaris being thairintil : and this dune, they
passit doun the Hie Gait, to haif passit furth at the Nether Bow,
quhilk wes then steikit : and becaus thay culd nocht get furth

---

[1] Shortly to be one of Darnley's murderers.

thairat, thay passit up the Hie Gait again, and in the mein tyme
the Provost, Bailzeis, and thair assistaris, being in the writing
buith of Alexander Guthrie, passit to the Tolbuith, and in thair
passing up the said Gait, thay being in the Tolbuith as said is,
schot furth at the said servandis ane dag, and hurt ane servand
of the craftismennis.

That being dune, thair wes nathing bot "Taik and Slay,"
that is, the ane pairt schutand furth and castand stanis, the uthir
pairt schutand hagbuttis in again : swa the craftismennis servandis held thaim continuallie fra thre houris eftirnune quhill
aucht at evin, and nevir ane man of the toun steirit to defend
thair Provost and Bailzeis.   And than they send to the maisteris
of the craftismen to caus thaim, gif thay micht, to stay the saidis
servandis : quha purposit to stay the samyn, bot thay culd
nocht cum to pass, bot the servandis said thay wald haif ane
revenge for the man that wes hurt.   And thaireftir the Provost
send ane messenger to the Constabil of the Castell to cum to
astay the matter, quha came : and he, with the maisteris of the
craftismen, treitit on the maneir, that the Provost and Bailzeis
suld dischairge all maneir of actiounis quhilk thay had againis
the saidis craftis-childer in ony tyme by-gane, and chairgit all
thair maisteris to ressaive thaim in service as thay did of befoir,
and promittit nevir to persew thaim in tyme for to cum for the
samyn.   And this being done, thay skailit, and the Provost and
Bailzeis cam furth of the Tolbuith.

cordinar servand, journeyman shoemaker.   *childer*, in this case prentices.
passit to armour, took arms.   *writing buith*, office.   *astay*, stop.   *treitit
on the maneir*, arranged matters in such fashion.

*The victory must have encouraged Aberdeen, for the next year
John Kello, the Town Bellman, and Alexander Burnet, the Town
Drummer, called out the Braif Toun on the first Sunday of May,
"to pass to the wud to bring in simmer."   There was a violent
row, and they and five burgesses were bidden to ask pardon on their
knees not only from God but from "the congregation."   The*

indomitable Kello was out again in 1565 : and the whole party lost the freedom of the burgh.[1]

Though the City Fathers of the Capital made war on unofficial pageantry, official was still, however, a different story.   The next entry in the Diurnal of Occurrents tells of Mary's arrival on the 19th August, when the prentice lads, mistrusting the Provost's armistice, went to meet her with a petition for royal pardon.   On the 2nd September she made her state entry to her capital, riding round outside the town by the Lang Gait (Princes Street) and " up the castell bank to the castell," where a triumphal arch had been erected for her.   After dining there, she left to shot of guns, and made her entry proper, down the Royal Way, past pageants of Moors and angels, a fiery dragon and the cardinal virtues, she riding under a canopy of purple velvet lined with red taffeta and fringed with gold, borne by sixteen of " the maist honest men of the toun " : and the fountains of the city were running wine.

There was much pageantry on paper too : old Lethington, whose son was soon to do more than most for her ruin, had written for her a stately address in verse which gives the young Queen a good deal of most sound advice . . . although to see the father of Michael Wylie bidding his sovereign choose honest counsellors is one of the grimmer ironies of our history, all the more because there is no doubt the old man meant it.

> Excelland Princes potent and preclair,
>   Prudent, peirles in bontie and bewtie,
> Maist nobil Quene of bluid undir the air,
>   With all my hairt and micht I welcum thee
> Hame to thy native pepil and countrie,
>   Beseikand God to give thee grace to haif
> Of thy leigis the hairtis faythfullie,
>   And thaim in luve and favour to ressaive.

[1] Even in 1602, when Episcopacy had the upper hand, Helen Hay, Countess of Linlithgow, was in trouble with Linlithgow Presbytery for " bigging of midsummer fyris."   That was, however, a Presbyterian district.

Now sen thow art arrivit in this land,
    Our native Princes and illustre Quene,
I traist to God this regioun sall stand
    An auld fre realm as it lang tyme hes bein,
    Quhairin richt sune thair sal be herd and sein
        Greit joy, justice, guid peice and policie,
    All cair and cummer banist quyte and clein,
        And ilk mannis lyf in guid tranquillitie.

cummer, tiresomeness.

But before long he was to write of sad times of confusion, where there were " No guisaris all the yeir, Bot kirkmen cled lyk men of weir," and ask

Quhair is the blythnes that hes bein,
Baith in burgh and landwart sein
Amang lordis and ladyis schein,
    Dancing, singing, game, and play ?
Bot now I wat nocht quhat thay mein :
    All mirrines is worn away.

guisaris, maskers, especially at New Year.   *landwart*, in the country.

55. Wedding Festivities

Old Lethington exaggerated somewhat. There could still be pageantry if its ideas were sound. Here are wedding delights under saintly patronage . . . though one does wonder what the bride thought about it. James Melville records them in 1571.

This yeir, in the moneth of Julii, Mr John Davidson, ane of our Regentis, maid a play at the mariage of Mr John Colvin, quhilk I saw playit in Mr Knox presence : quhairin, according to Mr Knox doctrine, the castell of Edinburgh wes besiegit, takin, and the Captain, with ane or two with him, hangit in effigie.

The representation is the more interesting in that the Castle was still holding out for the Queen, and did not fall for another couple

*of years, when its captain was duly hanged in his own proper
person.*

56. DIVERGENCE ON DRAMA

*There was a good deal of difference among the Reformers on the
subject of dramatic representation. 1574–5 brought a considerable controversy. In the former year, the St Andrews Kirk
Session records that*

Anent the supplicatioun gevin be Maister Patrick Auchinlek for
procuring licence to play the comedie mentionit in Sanct Lucas
Evangel, of the Forlorn Soul, upoun Sunday the first day of
August nixt to cum, the Seat hes decernit, first the play to be
revisit be my Lord Rectour, minister, M. John Rutherfurd,
Provost of Sanct Salvatoris College, and M. James Wilkie,
Principal of Sanct Leonardis College ; and gif thay find na fault
thairintil, the same to be playit upoun the said Sunday the first
of August, swa that the playing theirof be nocht occasioun to
withdraw the pepil fra heiring of the preiching, at the hour
appointit alsweill eftirnune as befoir nune.

seat, session.

*The piece was duly played, by the boys of the Grammar School :
but next year, when the General Assembly met, there was a terrific
row in consequence, and finally*

It [wes] thocht meit and concludit that na clerk playis,
comedeis, or tragedeis be maid of the Canonicall Scripturis,
alsweill New as Old, on Sabbath nor wark day, in tyme coming :
the contraveinaris heirof, if thay be ministeris, to be secludit fra
thair functioun, and if thay be utheris to be punischit be the
discipline of the Kirk. . . .

. . . That for uthir playis, comedeis or tragedeis or utheris
profane playis as ar not maid upoun authentick pairtis of the
Scripture may be considerit befoir thay be proponit publictlie,
and that thay be nocht playit upoun the Sabbath dayis.

Even fifteen years later, pageants might still decore the streets of the capital. When the young Queen was brought home in 1590 —in a coach and eight with a canopy over her of purple velvet, borne by a number of eminent citizens—she was greeted by no less than six separate masques: and the Latin oratory interspersed included a long speech by Andrew Melville in person, which was much admired by the scholar King and the foreign ambassadors. There was only one sermon, and it but of half an hour.

In 1599, however, when Shakespeare's company came on tour to Scotland and were patronised by the King, there was violent trouble, and the Left Wing ministers informed their sovereign that " not a man of honour in England would give these fellows their countenance."

VIII

THE GODLY

> I hae kend a minister wad be fair gude day and fair guid e'en wi'
> ilka man in the parochine, and hing jist as quiet as a rocket on a stick, till
> ye mentioned the word abjuration-oath, or patronage, or sic-like ; and
> then, whiz, he was off, and left in the air a hundred miles beyond common
> manners, common sense, and common comprehensions.
>
> SIR WALTER SCOTT, *Heart of Midlothian*

57. THE COMMON BASIS

*Catholics, Episcopalians, and Presbyterians might differ widely
in theology ; but as they were only too prone to forget, they all
accepted the Apostles' Creed. Here is a " popular " rhymed
version of it, from the famous " Gude and Godlie Ballatis."*

> We trow in God allanerlie,
> Full of all micht and majestie,
> Maker of hevin and erd sa braid,
> Quhilk hes himself our Fader maid :
> And we his sonnis are in deid,
> He will us keip in all our neid,
> Baith saul and bodie to defend,
> That na mischance sall us offend.
> He takis cure, baith day and nicht,
> To save us throw his godlie micht,
> Fra Satanis subteltie and slight.

> We trow in Jesus Christ his Son,
> God, lyke in gloir, our Lord alone,
> Quhilk, for his mercy and his grace
> Wald man be born to maik our peace ;
> Of Mary Mother, Virgin chaist,
> Consavit be the Haly Ghaist ;
> And for our saik on croce did de,

Fra sin and hell to maik us fre,
And rais from deith, throw his Godheid,
Our Mediatour and our remeid,
Sall cum to judge baith quik and deid.

   We trow in God the Halie Spreit,
In all distress our comfort sweit.
We trow the Kirk Catholick be
And faithful Christian companie
Throw all the warld with ane accord.
Remissioun of our sin we trow :
And this same flesche that livis now
Sall stand up at the lattir day
And bruik eternall lyfe for ay.

slight, sleight, trickery.   *bruik*, possess fully.

58. PRAYER

The best of James VI's complex character went into the " Basil-ikon Doron," the Royal gift, the treatise on kingcraft he wrote for his small son Henry. As not seldom happens in counsel of fathers to sons, the advice is often better than his own practice : but the book shows what is by no means a base conception of a King's arduous and intricate duty, expressed in terms that are sane and practical, and coloured now and then by a shrewd humour.

The book was written in 1599, in a very forcible and racy Scots. When a limited edition, for a few intimates, was published soon after, the printer, being an exiled Englishman, considerably angli-cised the text. On his assumption of the English crown, James sought, perhaps, to reassure his new subjects by producing a public version of it, in English. The extracts here are from the English version.

[Faith] must be nourished by prayer, which is nothing else but a friendly talking with God.

H

As for teaching you the form of your prayer, the Psalms of David are the meetest schoolmaster that ye can be acquaint with (next the prayer of Our Saviour, which is the only rule of prayer) whereout of, as of most rich and pure fountains, ye may learn all forms of prayer necessary for your comfort at all occasions. . . .

In your prayer, be neither over strange with God, like the ignorant common sort, that prayeth but out of books ; nor yet over homely with Him, like some of the vain Pharisaical Puritans, that think they rule Him upon their fingers. The former way will breed an uncouth coldness in you towards Him, the other will breed in you a contempt of Him. But in your prayer to God speak with all reverence. . . .

When ye obtain your prayer, thank Him joyfully therefor : if otherways, then bear patiently, pressing to win Him with importunity . . . and if notwithstanding thereof ye be not heard, assure yourself God foreseeth that which ye ask is not for your weal : and learn in time so to interpret all the adversities that God shall send unto you : so shall ye in the midst of them not only be armed with patience, but joyfully lift up your eyes from the present trouble to the happy end that God will turn it to. And when ye find it once so fall out by proof, arm yourself with the experience thereof against the next trouble, assuring yourself, though ye cannot in time of the shower see through the cloud, yet in the end shall ye find God sent it for your weal, as ye found in the former.

59. Prayer before Work

This " Prayer to be said before a man begin his work " comes from the 1565 edition of the " Form of Prayer and Administration of the Sacrament used in the English Church at Geneva, approved and received by the Church of Scotland," otherwise known as " the Book of Common Order," and as " Knox's Liturgy." It was published in 1561 at Geneva, with Calvin's imprimatur. Next

*year the printer Lekprevik published an edition in Scotland, adding
the Geneva Confession. This 1565 edition is also Lekprevik's,
with various new prayers added, this among them.*

O Lord God, most merciful Father and Saviour, seeing it
hath pleased thee to command us to travail that we may relieve
our need, we beseech thee of thy grace so to bless our labour,
that thy blessing may extend unto us, without the which we are
not able to continue, and this great favour may be a witness
unto us of thy bountifulness and assistance, so that thereby we
may know the fatherly care thou hast over us. Moreover, O
Lord, we beseech thee that thou wouldst strengthen us with thy
Holy Spirit, that we may faithfully travail in our state and
vocation without fraud or deceit : and that we may endeavour
ourselves to follow thine holy ordinance rather than seek to
satisfy our greedy affections or desires to gain. And if it
please thee, O Lord, to prosper our labour, give us a mind also
to help them that have need, according to that ability that thou
of thy mercy shalt give us ; and knowing that all things come of
thee, grant that we may humble ourselves to our neighbours
and not by any means lift ourselves up above those which have
not received so liberal a portion as of thy mercy thou hast given
unto us. And if it please thee to try and exercise us by greater
poverty and need than our flesh would desire, that thou wouldest
yet, O Lord God, grant us grace to know that thou wilt nourish
us continually through thy bountiful liberality, that we be not
so tempted that we fall into distrust : but that we may patiently
wait till thou fill us, not only with corporal graces and benefits,
but chiefly with thine heavenly spiritual treasures, to the intent
that we always have more ample occasion to give thee thanks
and wholly to rest upon thy mercies. Hear us, O Lord of
Mercy, through Jesus Christ thy Son our Lord. Amen.

*It is a fine prayer, but certain of its implications seem rather to
foreshadow the conception of work, as earning rather than as making
or doing, which made the Industrial Revolution what it was.*

60. Lighting the Fire

These Gaelic prayers, and the other Gaelic prayers and carols which follow, were recently in use in the Catholic Isles, and no doubt are still : but since they are old, and may be very old, they may fittingly enough find a place in this book.

This first is a prayer at the lighting of the fire that is the heart and centre of the house.   The original is an intricate verse, whose delicate pattern of subtly balanced phrasing is impossible to give in a translation.

> I will kindle my fire this morning
> Before the holy angels of Heaven,
> Before Ariel the most fair,
> Before Uriel the most lovely,
>> Without spite, without jealousy, without envy,
>> Without fear or dread of any under the sun,
>>> But with the holy Son of God to guard me.

> God, kindle in my heart within
> A flame of love to my neighbour,
> To my foe, to my friend, to my kin,
> To the brave, to the base, to the slave,
>> From the lowliest living
>> To the Name that is highest,
>>> O son of most sweet Mary.

61. A Night Prayer

This again is a Gaelic prayer from the Isles.

> O God, shield house and fire and beast
> And all that dwell herein tonight.
> Shield me and my beloved household
>> From cruel hands.

And save us from our enemies tonight
For the sake of the Son of Mary Mother,
Here and wherever they may be tonight,
Tonight and every night.

62. AN ACT OF THE PRESENCE OF GOD

This again is Gaelic.

I bend my knee
In the sight of the Father Who created me,
In the sight of the Son Who redeemed me,
In the sight of the Spirit Who cleansed me,
In love of friends.
Through thine Anointed, O God,
Give us that we need :
Love to our God,
Kindness of God,
Smile of God,
Wisdom of God,
Grace of God,
Fear of God,
And will of God
Be done of the Three on the world
As on saints and angels in Heaven.

In all shadow and brightness,
In all day and night,
Ever in kindness,
Grant us thy Spirit.

63. A PRAYER FOR THE DYING

This again is Gaelic, with an echo of the " Proficiscere anima."

This soul be in thy hand, O Christ,
O King of the City of Heaven.
Amen.

Since thou, O Christ, hast purchased this soul,
May its peace be in thy keeping,

Amen.

May the mighty Michael, High King of the Angels,
Make the way before this soul, O God,

Amen.

O Mighty Michael at peace with thee, soul,
And making thy way to the kingdom of God's Son.

High King is Ard-righ in the original—the old Gaelic title for the chief of the nation, as distinct from the chiefs of provinces or clans.

64. THE GODLY AND GAELIC

The first book to be printed in Gaelic was a translation of the Liturgy of the English Congregation at Geneva, made by John Carswell, Superintendent of Argyll—and made, apparently, somewhat against his will, for in his introduction he declares :

Great the blindness and the sinful darkness and ignorance and evil will of those who teach, write, and foster the Gaelic speech ; for to win for themselves the empty rewards of the world, they both choose more and use more to make vain and misleading tales, lying and worldly, of the Tuath De Danann, of fighting men and champions, of Fionn MacCumhal and his heroes, and many more whom now I will not number.

65. SONGS OF THE REFORMERS

The famous collection commonly called the " Gude and Godlie Ballatis " is fairly well known by name, and in one of the less unquotable verses of one of its more unquotable songs, which Scott included in " The Monastery." We have it in an edition of 1567 : but it actually belongs to the first movement of the Reformation, before Calvin's influence superseded Luther's. Some of its pieces

are translations of German Lutheran hymns. Others are pious
adaptations of popular secular songs, to be sung to their tunes.
Others are based on a principle still not unknown—that anything
can be considered Gude and Godlie so long as it is fervently anti-
Catholic : they have the combination of righteous indignation with
gusto in lechery that still makes best-sellers. And yet others have
real and strong religious feeling, nobly expressed.

Here is a scrap of one of the less fortunate adaptations :

> John, cum kis me now,
> John, cum kis me now,
> John, cum kis me by and by,
> And mak no moir ado.
>
> The Lord thy God I am,
> That John dois the call :
> John representis man
> By grace celestiall . . .

and so on for twenty-six verses. But other adaptations were
happier, as here :

> My Luve murnis for me, for me,
>   My Luve that murnis for me ;
> I am nocht kynd, hes nocht in mynd
>   My Luve that murnis for me.
>
> Quha is my luve, bot God abuve,
>   Quhilk all this warld hes wrocht ?
> The King of Blis, my luve he is,
>   Full deir he hes me bocht.
>
> His precius bluid he sched on rude,
>   That wes to maik us fre :
> This sall I prove, be Goddis leve
>   That sair my luve murnis for me.

This my luve cumis from abuve,
    And born wes of ane Maid,
For til fulfill his Fatheris will,
    To fill furth that He said.

Man, haif in mind, and thow be kynd,
    Thy Luve that murnis for the,
How he on rude did sched his blude
    From Sathan to maik the free.

Here is a fine version of the Thirteenth Psalm :

O Lord, how lang forevir wil thow forget
    And hyde thy face fra me ?   Or yit how lang
Sall I rehers thy counsell in my hairt ?
    Quhen sall my hairt ceis of this sorie sang ?
      O Lord, behald, help me, and licht my ein,
      That suddand sleip of deid do me na tein.

Or ellis quhen my enemies seis my fall,
    We did prevaill, sone will they say on me :
And gif thay se me be thaim brocht in thrall
    They will rejois into thair tyrannie.
      Bot I in God hes hoip, and traist to se
      His godlie help : then sall I luve the Lord
      Quhilk did me save fra thaim that had me schord.

          schord, threatened.

66. CHRISTMAS

Mediaeval Scotland kept Christmas heartily : even the early Reformers saw nothing blasphemous in rejoicing over the Incarnation of God.   This charming macaronic carol is from the " Gude and Godlie Ballatis " itself.

In dulci jubilo, now let us sing with mirth and jo,
Our hairtis consolatioun lyis *in praesepio,*
And schynis as the sone, *Matris in gremio.*
Alpha es et O, Alpha es et O.

O Jesu parvule, I thirst soir eftir the,
Confort my hairt and mynd, *O Puer optime*.
God of all grace sa kind, *et Princeps gloriae*,
Trahe me post te, trahe me post te.

Ubi sunt gaudia in any place bot thair
Quhair that the angellis sing *nova cantica?*
Bot an the bellis ring *in Regis curia*,
God gif I war thair, God gif I war thair !

jo, joy.

*By very old custom in the Outer Isles, the boats would put to
sea on Christmas day, and the whole of the catch would be given to
those folk of the township who were in need.   This is the Gaelic
hymn traditionally sung as the men were on their way to the grounds.
The 707 strokes are the number given by legend to St Peter, when
he rowed out to catch the fish with the tribute money.*

The day of light is upon us,
Christ is born of the Maid.

In His name I sprinkle the water
Over all in my close.

I will sit to the oar,
I will row seven hundred and seven.

I will cast my hook :
The first fish that I catch,

In the name of Christ, King of the Elements,
The poor shall have for his need,

And the King of Fishers, Saint Peter,
Will give me his blessing.

Ariel, Gabriel, John,
Kind Raphael and Paul,

Columcille, kind in trouble,
Bright gentle Mary, full of grace,

Be about us till we reach the bank
And quiet for us the breaking waves.

The King of Kings at the end of our way
Of long life and long-lasting happiness.

Crown of the King from the Three on High,
Cross of Christ, bowing down to shield us.
   Crown of the King from the Three on High,
   Cross of Christ, bowing down to shield us.

*And this is a Gaelic carol.   As in the noble Scots one which
follows it, the Incarnation is seen in the Johannine terms of light—
the true imagery for our Northern country.*

Hoire, hoire, blessed is He,
Hoire, hoire, blessed is He,
Blessed the King of Whom we sing,
   Ho rò, ho rò, rejoice !

This is the night of the mighty Noel,
Born is the Son of Mary Virgin.
He has set His feet on the earth,
Son of Glory from on high.
Heaven and earth all light for Him,
   Ho rò, ho rò, rejoice !

Peace of earth to Him, joy of Heaven to Him,
Behold, He has set His feet to the earth.
King's homage to Him, a lamb's welcome to Him,
King of Victories, Lamb of Glory,
Earth and sea all light for Him,
   Ho rò, ho rò, rejoice !

Mountains alight for Him, plains alight for Him,
Voice of the waves and song of the shore
Bring word to men that Christ is born.
High King's Son from the Land of Salvation,
The sun shone on the high hills for Him,
      Ho rò, ho rò, rejoice !

Earth and the spheres all light for him,
God the Lord has opened a Door.
Son of Maid Mary, haste to shield us,
O Christ of hope and Door of joy,
Golden sun of hill and mountain,
      Ho rò, ho rò, rejoice !
Hoire, hoire, blessed is He,
Hoire, hoire, blessed is He,
Blessed the King of Whom we sing,
      Ho rò, ho rò, rejoice !

*And here is a Scots carol from the Bannatyne MS.   One can
hear the voices crash in its refrain in the chapel of Stirling, high in
face of the hills.*

    Jerusalem, rejois for joy !
      Jesus, the sterne of maist bewté
    In the is risin, as richtous roy,
      Fra derknes to illumine the :
      With glorius sound of angell gle
        The Prince is born in Bethlehem
        Quhilk sall the maik of thraldom fre,
        Illuminare Jerusalem.

    With angellis licht, in legiounis,
      Thow art illuminit all about ;
    Thre Kingis of strange regiounis
      To the ar cumin with lustie rout,

All dressit with dyamantis bot dout,
    Revest with gold in everie hem,
Sounding attonis with ane schout,
    Illuminare Jerusalem.

The rageand tirant that in the rang,
    Herod, is exilit and his offspring,
The land of Juda, that chosit wrang,
    And risin is the richtus King.
    So He, so michtie is and ding,
      Quhen men His glorious name doth nem,
    Hevin, erd, and hell maik inclining,
      Illuminare Jerusalem.

His cuming knew all element.
    The air be sterne did Him persaif ;
The watir, quhen dry He on it went ;
    The sun, quhen he na lichtis gaif,
    The erd, that trimlit all and raif ;
      The crois, quhen it wes done contemn ;
    The stanis, quhen thay in peicis claif,
      Illuminare Jerusalem.

The deid Him knew that rais upricht,
    Quhilk lang tyme had the erd lain undir.
Cruikit and blind declairit His micht
    That heilit of thaim sa monie hunder ;
    Nature Him knew, and had greit wondir
      Quhen He of Virgen wes born but wem ;
    Hell, quhen thair yettis wer brokin in sundir,
      Illuminare Jerusalem.

---

sterne, star.   *roy*, king.   *bot dout*, without doubt.   *rang*, reigned.
raif, split asunder.   *ding*, digne, worthy.   *but wem*, without blemish.

67. Carols come Expensive

Before the young King James VI was of age to rule, the Parliament of 1581 had made it penal to sing such things as the foregoing.

Forsamekil as pairt for want of doctrine and raretie of ministeris [1] and pairtlie throw the pervers inclinatioun of mannis ingyne to superstitioun, the dreggis of idolatrie yit reignis in divers pairtis of the realm, be using of pilgrimmage to sum chappellis, wellis, crocis, and sic monumentis of idolatrie, as also be observing the festuall dayis of the sanctis sumtyme thair patronis, in setting furth of banfyris, singing of carolis within and about kirkis at certain sesounis of the yeir, and observing of sic uthir superstitius and papisticall rytis to the dishonour of God, contempt of the trew religioun, and fostering of greit errour amang the pepill : for remeid quhairof it is statut and ordinit be our Soverane Lord with advise of his thre Estaitis in this present Parliament, That nane of His Hienes leigis presume or taik upoun hand in tyme cuming to frequent or use the saidis pilgrimmagis or utheris the foirnamit superstitiunis and papisticall rytis, undir the painis following : videlicet, ilk gentilman or woman landit, or wyf of the gentilman landit, ane hundred pundis, the unlandit ane hundred merkis, and the yeman fourtie pundis for the first falt, and for the second falt the offendaris to suffer the pain of deid as idolatoris.

68. Christmas dies Hard

A special war was made against Christmas : but it took a lot of killing. Calderwood, the Left Wing historian of the Reformation Church, records that in 1575,

The town of Dumfries, at Christmas-day last by-past, seeing that neither [the minister] nor the reader would neither teach

[1] The Reformation, like so many seizures of power in our own time, was effected by a minority body, and, even fourteen years after the Reformed Church had been by law established, it could find ministers for only about one parish in every four.

nor read upon these days, brought a reader of their own, with tabret and whistle, and caused him read the prayers, which exercise they used all the days of Yule.

A few days later, St Andrews Kirk Session were dealing with other culprits.

The said day, James Clunie, cultellar, and Waltir Younger [wer] accusit for violating of the Sabbat day be superstitius keiping of Yuill-day haly-day, and absteining fra thair wark and labour that day . . . James Thomsoun, masoun, being dilatit and accusit for superstitius keiping of Yuill-day last wes halie day, and that he said that quha wald or wald nocht, he wald nocht wark on Yuill day, and was nocht in use of the samen ; and being again askit quhethir he wald stand be that or nocht, promittit that in tyme cuming, during his remaining in this citie, he sould nevir keip the said Yuill day haly-day, bot sould wark on that day . . . to onie man that wald offer him wark . . . and gif na man chairgis him with wark, he sall wark sum rigging-stanis of his ain.

Dumfries, however, was still obdurate, even ten years later. This is from a MS. report by Father Crichton, chaplain to Mary's faithful adherent, Lord Seton.   The original is in Latin.

In spite of the persecution of the Catholics, which at that time was of considerable violence, Father Dury resolved to sing the whole of the Office of the Feast of the Nativity of Our Lord, together with the three masses, solemnly, in a monastery which is outside the town on the far side of the river, guards being placed on the bridge to make sure that none crossed without a written order.   But the people were so eager to hear him preach, and to be present at that solemn duty, that those who were not allowed to cross the bridge forded the water, though it was up to the waist : and thus, wet through, they passed the night of Christmas, hearing the office in the church.

In 1609, when the Right Wing of the Church had been " in "

for fifteen years, a gentle attempt was made to restore some observ-
ance of Christmas.   David Calderwood records the reactions : by
" the ministers," he means of course those of his own party, the Left.

. . . The Session should rise the 25th day of December and
not to sit down till the eighth of January.   This was the first
Christmas vacance of the Session kept since the Reformation.
The ministers threatened that the men who devised the novelty [1]
for their own advancement might receive at God's hand their
reward to their overthrow, for troubling the people of God
with beggarly ceremonies long since abolished with Popery.
Christmas was not so well kept by feasting and abstinence from
work in Edinburgh these thirty years, an evil example to the rest
of the country.

cultellar, cutler.   *dilatit*, reported to the authorities.

69. Good Friday

The war of the Kirk against the Church's Year was waged most
bitterly against the feasts, but the fasts were also under ban : and
as with the feasts, the fight was a long and hard one.   The Bishop
of London writes to Sir William Cecil, at some time when English
troops had been sent to Scotland as allies of the Reformers :

Our men are all returned out of Scotland. . . . One of them,
named Evans . . . hath reported (as I am credibly informed)
that at Dunbar on Good Friday they saw certain persons go
barefoot and barelegged to the church to creep to the Cross.
If it be so, the Church of Scotland will not be pure enough for
our men.   They are a wilful company.   God keep you humble
spirits.

8º Maii.   From my house at Paul's.
                   Yours in Christ.
                              Edmund London.

[1] Rather an odd word, as Christmas had been regularly kept in Scotland
for some nine hundred years before an attempt was made to abolish it—an attempt
which was then but forty-nine years old, and as Calderwood implies, far from
successful.

Creeping to the Cross was the popular name for the old devotion of Good Friday, when the crucifix was taken from the altar and laid in the chancel, and the people, approaching it on their knees, bent to kiss the pierced feet.

70. EASTER

In his " Tractates " of 1563, the Catholic Reformer, Ninian Winzet, throws out this challenge to the Sabbatarians who yet abolish Easter.

I misknaw nocht sum of you to object the command chairge-and *sex dayis to labour, and the sevint to sanctifie the Lord* ; thairfoir I desire the doutsum man to caus his doctor and propheit [*Knox*] . . . to ansuer in wreit, quhat Scripture hes he, or uthir auctoritie, by [*beyond*] the consent of the haly Kirk Universall, to sanctifie the Sunday to be the sevint day ? And gif he abolischis, with us, the Setterday, as ceremonial and nocht requirit in the law of the Evangel, quhat hes he, by [*beyond*] the consent of Goddis Kirk, to sanctifie onie day of the sevin, and nicht to labour all the sevin dayis ? . . . [*This being so*] Quhy abolischis he nocht the Sunday, as he dois Yuill, Pasch, and the rest ?

misknaw nocht, know well, ne pas ignorer.

71. WHISTLING ON THE SABBATH

In 1593 the Kirk Session of Glasgow records :

The Presbiterie of Glasgow statutis and ordainis that gif Mungo Craig sal play on his pypes on the Sonday fra the sun rising quhill the sun going to, in onie place within the boundis of the Presbiterie, that he incontinent thaireftir sall be summarilie excommunicat.

72. MONUMENTS OF IDOLATRY

In 1561 the Abbot of Crossraguel addressed a tract to the Lords of the Congregation, who had just seized control of the Government, and abolished the Old Kirk to establish the New.

The Abbot was Quentin Kennedy, son of the Earl of Cassillis, one of the chief men among the " Reformers Within," who sought to reform the Old Kirk without abolishing it. He was an austere and very learned scholar, who had challenged Knox to open debate at Maybole. As at Jutland, both sides claimed the victory : but the Abbot kept his temper and made his opponent lose his very badly, so we may perhaps assign him a win on points.

It is writen in the Scripture of Almichtie God, how the Lord commandit to destroy the idolatouris and all placis quhair thair idolis wer had in reverens and honorit as the leving God : quhairwith hes Knox and divers utheris malheureux prechouris to the Congregatioun, steirit up with zeil but [*without*] knaw-lege, to wrak ane greit pairt of the policie of this realm. . . .

He agrees that it is right that idolators and their temples should be destroyed, but goes on :

Be the contrair, I am mair nor assurit that thair wes never Cristen man quhilk evir biggit ane tempill or kirk, or onie uthir placis of prayeris, bot to the intent that the leving God sould be deulie worschippit thairinto : quhairfoir it wes the dewtie of all Christian men to quhom it appertainis to taik order in mateiris concerning religioun, in cais thair wes abusion, to correct the abusioun conform to the practeis of the Evangell, and nocht to maik ane plain destructioun misorderlie, as men dois in thir dayis. Did nocht Our Saviour correct the abusiounis quhilk He fand into the tempill dedicat to honour of God, without destructioun of the samen ? Quhairby we are manifestlie instructit, that al tempillis and placis, biggit be Christian men to the honour of God (in cais thay are abusit) are to be correctit, and nocht uttirlie destroyit as placis biggit be the idolatouris to

I

idolis. Thus may we cleirlie persaive quhat abominatioun and wiketnes, quhat furie and wodnes, ofttymis proceidis of thrawin interpretatioun and impropir applicatioun of the Scripturis of Almichtie God.

policie, culture, civilisation.   *thrawin*, thrawn, twisted.

73. DISCIPLINE

These two extracts from the Kirk Session records of Glasgow belong to the spring of 1593, during the religious and political dominance of the Left or Presbyterian Wing of the Kirk.

The Presbiterie hes found William Craig at Walkmill of Partik to haif bein absent fra his kirk this lang tyme by-gone, and thairby to haif contravenit his obligatiounis quhairin he obligit him, undir the pain of ten merkis, to keip his kirk on Sonday to heir Goddis Word. Is decernit to pay to the Theasaurer of his kirk the said ten merkis, and to maik his repentance in his kirk for absence fra his kirk the twa Sondayis nixt to cum, and that he be nocht absolvit quhill he schew evident takennis of his repentance ; and that he find suretie undir the pain of ten pundis to be present to heir Goddis Word on the Sonday in tymis coming.

The discipline was not confined to layfolk. A few weeks later one of the ministers has evidently been unsound on the Sacraments.

The brethren ar nocht satisfyit with the doctrine teichit be Mr Ninian Drew, minister at Leinzie this present day, and finds him to haif bein als unprofitabill in handling the text prescrivit to him als of befoir : and now the brethren ordainis the said Mr Ninian to teich in the first Epistill of Paull to the Corinthianis, the xi chaptour, beginnand at the 24 vers, upon the thrid day of April nixt to cum, befoir the Synodall Assemblie or those to be appointit be the said Assemblie to be his auditouris.

This has no date, but the language is Scoto-English rather than Scots. It comes from a collection of papers made by David Calder-

wood, the historian of the Prebyterian party in the Reformation Kirk.

King James had produced a metrical version of the psalms, which some loyal subjects have taken to using in church. The Saints objected, not only to the breach of uniformity, but because

the very private use ought to be suppressed. First because some perhaps will labour to have them by heart, who should rather labour to have those in memory which are sung in the church ; for who will study to both ? And therefore a metaphrase of the Psalms different from that which is usual in the church is the most unprofitable work that may be ; yea, prejudicial to that which is publicly received, unless it be in Greek or Latin, which are not nor cannot be used in public. . . .

Ye see the like doth not occur in any other reformed church, French, Dutch, or Italian. A learned paraphrase upon the Psalms is permitted to any that hath the gift, and is commendable. But another metaphrase is never convenient, but prejudicial to that which is used in the Kirk,[1] and serveth to make people glaik. Next, the allowing of it to be read in private importeth allowance of the error above mentioned. Thirdly, it may justly be feared that in short process of time it may pass from private use to public. For have not some already used this new metaphrase when the congregation were singing the old ? A door should not be opened to such light heads and profane hearts.

74. STANDARDS OF JUDGMENT

We are used today to accepting a man's conduct as right and proper if he happens to hold the right abstract principles. It was even so in the sixteenth century.

In 1541 Sir Thomas Wharton writes to Henry VIII to

---

[1] The present-day or Westminster version of the Psalms in Metre had not yet come in, and the one used was still that of Thomas Sternhold, Groom of the Robes to Henry VIII and his son, and John Hopkins, Rector of Great Waldingfield, Suffolk.

recommend to him Douglas of Drumlanrig, who has jinked south out of reach of his country's law :

His offence was very little, being only accused as accessory of a murder :

While twenty-odd years later Knox, finding his best friends banished from the country for nothing more than murdering the Queen's Secretary and almost killing her and her unborn child, shows a natural resentment at the injustice :

That poltron and vile knave Davie was justlie punished . . . by the counsall and handis of James Dowglas, Erle of Morton, Patrik Lord Lyndesay, and the Lord Ruthven, with otheris assistaris in thare cumpany, who all, for thare just act and most worthy of all praise, arr now unworthely left of thare brethrein, and suffer the bitterness of banischement and exyle.

Some years earlier, about the time when Knox was telling those who were shocked by the personal lives of certain ardent Reformers that goodness of life was no test of true religion, old Sir Richard Maitland took another view. A vigorous satirist, he did not spare the corruptions of the Old Kirk, but saw some leading lights of the New one with a vision that was somewhat disillusioned.

> Thay think it weill, an thay the Pape do call
>   The Antichrist and Mess idolatrie
> And syne eit flesche upoun the Frydayis all,
>   That thay serve God richt than accordinglie,
>   Thoch in all thing thay leve maist wikkitlie :
>   Bot God commandit us His law to keip—
>   First honour Him, and syne heif charitie
>   With our nichtbour, and for our sinnis weip.

IX

THE UNGODLY

The deevil's peats, I trow, hard to ken whilk deserves the hettest
corner o' his ingle-side.

SIR WALTER SCOTT, *Heart of Midlothian*

75. BLACK MARKET

*There were saints in Scotland in the sixteenth century, in all
the three conflicting ways of thought. But there was also a thriving growth of sinners. Some of them we still have with us. Others
. . . grow less remote than they would have felt to, say, our grand-
parents. Here are two worthies of 1529, from the records of the
Edinburgh Town Council.*

We do yow to wit, Forsamekil as John Giechan and Don
Paterson hes brokin the statutis of the toun in the bying of
buttir in the greit in the mercat to regreit again till our Soverain
Lordis legis befoir the hour limit thairto, Quhairfoir the Provost,
Baileis and Counsall hes banischit the said John and Don this
toun, induring thair willis, and to devoid within xxiiij houris.

in the greit, in bulk, wholesale.   *regreit,* to buy up the available supply of
a commodity, so as to sell again at an unfair profit.

76. INFECTIOUS DISEASES

*One of the perpetual headaches of local government all over
Europe was the problem of infectious diseases, notably plague,
epidemics of which, in those rat-ridden days, might break out at
any time. In 1530 the Town Council of Edinburgh record this
case.*

The quhilk day, Forsamekil as it wes perfitlie understand
and kend that David Duly, tailyeour, hes haldin his wyf seik
in the contagius seiknes of pestilens ij dayis in his hous, and
wald nocht reveil the samen to the officiaris of the toun quhill

sche wes deid in the said seiknes, And in the mein tyme the said
David passit to Sanct Gelis kirk quhilk wes Sonday, and thair
said [sic] mess amangis the clein pepil, his wyf beand in extremis
in the said seiknes, doand that wes in him til haif infeckit all the
toun, For the quhilk causis he wes adjugit to be hangit on ane
gebat befoir his ain dure ; and that wes gevin for dome.

*This was evidently considered an especially serious case, for the
usual penalty for concealing cases of infectious illness was branding
on the cheek and banishment from the town, after going through
some kind of disinfection. (The Cleansing Station was on the
Borough Muir.) The case, however, had a sequel.*

The quhilk day, Forsamekil as David Duly wes decernit
this day befoir nune for his demeritis to be hangit upoun ane
gebat befoir his dure quhair he dwellis, Nochtwithstanding
becaus at the will of God he hes eschapit, and the raip brokin
and fallen off the gebat, and is ane puir man with small bairnis,
and for pitie of him the Provost Baileis and Counsall banischis
the said David this toun for all the dayis of his lyf, and nocht
to cum thairintill in the mein tyme undir the pain of deid.

77. PROFANITY

*In the fifteen-fifties reform was in the air, both within and without
the Old Kirk. The Parliament took a hand over manners and
morals, and in February 1551, in Edinburgh, they passed this act.
The sliding scale of fines, with the penalty in proportion to privilege,
is a common Scots practice. Incidentally, the Act shows more sense
of human nature than is common in puritanic legislation : the
framers had clearly realised that profanity is very largely a habit,
and time was given to get out of it.*

Item becaus nochtwithstanding the oft and frequent pre-
chingis in detestatioun of the grevous and abominabill execratiounis and blasphematiounis of the name of God, sweirand in
vain be His precius bluid, bodie, passioun, and woundis, Devill

stick, Cummer gar roist or ryse thaim, and sic utheris ugsome aithis and execratiounis againis the command of God, yit the samyn is cum in sic ane ungodlie use amangis the pepil of this realm, baith of greit and small estaitis, that dailie and hourlie may be herd amang thaim opin blasphematiounis of Goddis name and majestie, to the greit contemptioun thairof and bringing of the ire and wrath of God upoun the pepil thairfoir : and for eschewing of sic inconvenientis in tyme cuming, it is statut and ordainit that quhatsumevir persoun or persounis sweiris sic abominabill aithis and destestabill execratiounis as is afoir rehersit sall incur the painis eftir following, als oft als thay failzie, respective :

That is to say, ane Prelat of Kirk, Erl, or Lord, for everie fault to be committit for the space of thrie monethis nixt to cum, that is to say unto the first day of May exclusive, xij d. Ane baroun or beneficit man constitut in dignitie ecclesiastik, iiij d. Ane landit man, frehalder, vassall, fewar, burges, and small beneficit man, ij d. Ane craftsman, yeman, a servand man, and all utheris, j d. Item, the puir folkis that hes na geir to pay the pain foirsaid to be put in the stokkis or presonit for the space of four houris, and wemen to be weyit and considderit conform to the bluid or estatit of thair parteis that thay ar cuplit with. And this pain to be dublit upoun everie committar efter the outrunning of the saidis thrie monethis, for the space of uthir thrie monethis thaireftir.

Three months later it was to be tripled, and three months later again, " quhilk maikis the yeir compleit," to be quadrupled.

And fra the compleiting of the said yeir, the first falt of ane prelat, erl, or Lord, to be iiij s, the second falt viij s, and the third falt xvi s, and for the ferd falt to be banist or put in ward for the space of yeir and day, at the will of the Prince, and siclyk of all uthir estaitis, eftir thair qualitie foirsaid, to be punischit effeirandlie.

estaitis, rank, condition. *inconvenientis,* unbefitting. *effeirandlie,* suitably.

78. Gambling

In 1621 *this anti-betting act was passed by the Estates. One observes that it carefully does not interfere with individual liberty. A man may bet if he wants to : but he is not to make a living at it, or to set an example of gambling to the public.*

By this time the language was in a transition state between classical literary Scots and the fine strong Scoto-English of the later century. It is still uncertain, the new and the old forms appearing side by side in the same sentence : it has therefore been given in the modern spelling.

Our Sovereign Lord and Estates of Parliament, considering the manifold evils and inconvenients which ensue upon carding and dicing and horse-races, which are now over much frequented in this country, to the great prejudice of the lieges : and because honest men ought not to expect that any winning had at any of the games above-written can do them good or prosper, have therefore statute and ordained that no man shall play at cards or dice in any common house, town, ostlery, or cook's house, under the pain of forty pounds, money of this realm. To be exacted of the keeper of the said inns and common houses for the first fault, and loss of their liberties [1] for the next. Moreover that it shall not be lawful to play in any other private man's house, but where the master of the family plays himself. And if it shall happen any man to win any sums of money at carding or dicing, attour the sum of an hundred merks within the space of twenty-four hours, or to gain in wagers upon horse races any sum attour the said sum of an hundred merks, the superplus shall be consigned within twenty-four hours thereafter in the hands of the Treasurer for the Kirk, if it be in Edinburgh, or in the hands of such of the Kirk session, in the country parochines, as collects and distributes money for the poor of the same, to be employed always upon the poor of the parish where such winning shall happen to fall out.

[1] Licences.

79. THAE WEEMEN

Knox, like many men dependent on women's admiration, intensely resented the fact of his dependence . . . and still more those women on whom he could not depend.   In an age when women were ruling, or had just ruled, France, Spain, England, the Netherlands, and Scotland, he fiercely denounced their Monstrous Regiment. The book was printed (in English, not Scots), at Geneva in 1558. Here is its exordium : it is a good specimen of Knox's prose and his method of reasoning.

To promote a woman to bear rule, superiority, dominion, or empire above any realm, nation, or city, is repugnant to nature, contumely to God, a thing most contrarious to His revealed will and approved ordinance, and finally it is the subversion of good order, of all equity and justice. . . .

First, where that I affirm the empire of a woman to be a thing repugnant to nature, I mean not only that God, by the order of His creation, hath spoiled woman of authority and dominion, but also that man hath seen, proved, and pronounced just causes why that it should be.   Man, I say, in many other cases blind, doth in this behalf see very clearly.   For the causes be so manifest that they can not be hid.   For who can deny that it repugneth to nature that the blind shall be appointed to lead and conduct such as do see ?   That the weak, the sick, and impotent persons shall nourish and keep the whole and strong ? And finally, that the foolish, mad, and phrenetic shall govern the discreet and give counsel to such as are sober of mind ? And such be all women compared unto man in bearing of authority.   For their sight in civil regiment is but blindness ; their strength weakness ; their counsel foolishness ; and judgment phrenzy, if it be rightly considered.

The book got poor Knox into a deal of trouble.   Mary of England, against whom it was chiefly directed, died soon after it appeared ; and her sister, for whose favour Knox was anxious,

was direly offended by it.   When, a couple of months after Eliza-
beth's accession, Knox applied for a passport through England, he
did not get it . . . and when Calvin, a little later in the year,
dedicated to her his book upon Isaiah, she held him art and part in
his pupil's work, and refused the compliment.   Calvin's remarks
upon Knox, in his letters to Cecil, are distinctly irate.

Poor Knox himself regretted his indiscretion.   He needed
Elizabeth's favour rather badly : and she needed him.   Both, in
fact, were to succeed through each other's help.   So here he is
attempting reconcilement, some fortnight before his own Queen's
arrival in Scotland.[1]

Grace from God the Father through Our Lord Jesus Christ
with perpetual increase of His Holy Spirit.

May it please Your Majesty, that it is here certainly spoken
that the Queen of Scotland travaileth earnestly to have a treatise
entitled The First Blast of the Trumpet [2] [con]futed by the
censure of the learned in divers realms, and farther that she
laboureth to inflame the hearts of princes against the writer, and
because that it may appear that Your Majesty hath interest, that
she mindeth to travail with Your Grace, Your Grace's Council,
and learned men for judgment against such a common enemy
to women, and to their regiment.   It were but foolishness in me
to prescrive unto Your Majesty what is to be done in any thing,
but especially in such things as men do suppose do touch myself.
But of one thing I think myself assured, and therefore I dare not
conceal it.   To wit that neither doth our Sovereign so greatly
fear her own state by reason of that book, neither yet doth she
so greatly favour the tranquillity of Your Majesty's reign and
realm that she would take so great and earnest pains, unless that

---

[1] Both handwriting and spelling are of interest.   The letter is more strongly
anglicised than the text of his Historie—in fact, its greater part is completely
English : but in one sentence, where his emotions are getting the better of him,
he suddenly drops back into " the auld kind Scottis that his mither lernit him "
(as Ninian Winzet had advised him to do) returning to English as he remembers
himself.   The letter begins in neat deliberate writing, but sweeps suddenly into
a violent scrawl.

[2] *The First Blast of the Trumpet against the Monstrous Regiment of Women.*

her crafty counsel shot at a farther mark. [*Then he drops into Scots.*] Two years ago [*at Elizabeth's accession*] I wrote to Your Majesty my full declaration touching that work : experience since hath shown that I am not desirous of innovation, so that Christ Jesus be not in His members openly trodden under the feet of the ungodly. [*The spelling now returns to English.*] With farther purgation I will not trouble Your Majesty for the present, beseeching the Eternal so to assist Your Highness in all affairs that in His sight ye may be found acceptable, your regiment profitable to your commonweal, and your facts to be such that justly they may be praised of all godly unto the coming of the Lord Jesus, to Whose mighty protection I unfeignedly commit Your Majesty, from Edinburgh the 6 of August 1561.

Your Majesty's servant to command in godliness,

JOHN KNOX.

To the Mighty and Excellent Princess,
    Elizabeth the Queen's Majesty of England,
        be these delivered.

It was not only women rulers—or those of the wrong creed at any rate—who were apt to have a rough passage with the godly. In 1564 one James Gilmour, burgess of St Andrews, tried to desert Bessie Beveridge his wife. The Kirk Session stopped him. Being a man of resource, he then accused her of adultery with his nephew, and demanded a divorce. The case being heard, the lady cleared herself : and the Kirk Session settled matters thus :

Finalie, upoun the xxiiij of Maii, anno quo supra, the parteis being movit to concord, the said Besse Bawerage, in presens of James [Gilmour] and haill Sessioun of Superintendent and ministeris, purgis hir of the said allegit adulterie aganis hir, and acknawlegis and confessis in tymis past nocht to haif bein sa obedient to James hir husband as becaim hir of dewtie toward hir husband and heid, quhairby sche understandis him to haif takin occasioun to intent and propone the exceptioun of adulterie aganis hir, tending to divorcement ; and at desyr of James, on hir kneis askit him forgifnes, and hes maid promis nevir to be sein in companie with John Simson in prevy nor in [publict] pairt, and to serve and obey hir husband as becomes hir of dewtie. And Robert Bawerege, hir father, is becomen cautioun for James that Bess sal be ane guid and faithfull wyf and servand to the said James hir husband ; and gif at ony tyme sche failzies, he nevir sall assist hir with ony help, and heirupoun hes gevin his hand to James.

And James Gilmour remittis all caus of offence to Bess, and resavis hir in his favour, and is finallie reconcillit with hir.

80. WITCHES

James Melville, in his delightful Diary, gives us this queerly vivid little picture :

. . . The first execution that evir I saw . . . of a witch in Sanct Androis, aganis the quhilk Mr Knox delt fra the pulpit, sche being set up at a pillar befoir him.

That most worthy advocate, James Boswell of Auchinleck, is so much a man of the eighteenth century that it is rather difficult to remember that he had ancestors. Here is one of them in 1591, in difficulties with the Privy Council.

[John Boiswell of Auchinlek] nocht onlie hes oft and divers tymis consultit with witcheis, bot alswa be himself practisit witchecraft, sorcerie, inchantment, and utheris divilische practiseis, to the dishonour of God, sklander of His Word, and greit contempt of His Hienes his auctoritie and lawis.

Richie Graham, the most notorious wizard of his day, who was mixed up in the Tranent and North Berwick cases (both these villages were nests of witches), admitted to having raised the Devil in Auchinleck's own house . . . and in the Lord Justice Clerk's Canongate back-yard. So no wonder Auchinleck, instead of

*compearing, promptly fled and was put to the horn for con-
tumacy.*

*Here is a case in 1576, the first of which a detailed record
remains. The witch here was admittedly a " white " one, and the
background is not the Satanic cult of the covens, but the fairy world
of True Thomas and Tamlane. Bessie Dunlop, wife of Andrew
Jack in Lyne, Ayrshire, being examined by Douglas of Whit-
tinghame and a jury of small tenants, on charges of curing illness
and finding lost property by supernatural means,*

answerit and declairit that sche herself had na kind of art nor
science swa to do ; bot divers tymis, quhen ony sic persounis
come . . . to hir, sche wald inquire at ane Thom Reid, quha
dyit at Pinkie [1] as he himself affirmit, quha wald tell hir quhenevir
sche askit.

Item. Sche being inquirit, quhat kynd of man this Thom
Reid wes. Declairit, he wes ane honest weil elderlie man, gray
berdit, and had ane gray coit with Lumbart slevis of the auld
fassioun, ane pair of gray breikis and quhyte schankis, gartarit
about the kne ; ane blak bonet on his heid, clois behind and
plain befoir, with silkin lacis drawen throw the lippis thairof ;
and ane quhyte wand in his hand. Item, being interrogat, how
and in quhat maneir of place the said Thom Reid cum to hir ?
Answerit, as sche wes gangand betuix hir awin hous and the
yard of Monkcastel, drivand hir ky to the pasture and maikand
hevie sair dule with hirself, greitand verie fast for hir kow that
wes deid, hir husband and child that were lyand seik in the land-
ill, and sche new rissen out of gissane.[2] The foirsaid Thom met
hir be the way, halsit [3] hir, and said Guid day, Bessie, and sche said,
God speid yow, guidman. Sanct Marie, said he, Bessie, quhy
maikis thow sa greir dule and sair greiting for ony warldlie
thing ?

Poor Bessie tells her troubles, and is answered :

[1] 1547.　　　[2] Childbed.　　　[3] Embraced

Bessie, thow hes craibit God, and askit sumthing yow suld nocht haif done ; and thairfoir I counsell thee to mend to Him : for I tell thee thy bairn sal dye, and the seik kow, or yow cum hame ; thy two scheip sal dye to : bot thy husband sal mend, and be als haill and feir [1] as evir he wes. And then wes I sumthing blythe, fra he tauld me my guidman wald mend. Then Thom Reid went away fra me, in throw the yard of Monk-castel, and I thocht he gaed in at a narrowar hoill of the dyk nor ony erdlie man culd haif gane throw, and swa I wes sumthing fleyit.

At a later meeting, he asked her,

gif sche wald nocht trow in him ?   Sche said, Sche wald trow in ony body did hir guid.   And Thom promisit hir baith geir, horsis and ky and uthir graith, gif sche wald deny hir Christen-dom and the faith sche tuik at the font-stane.   Quhairunto sche answerit, That gif sche suld be revin at horsis taillis, sche suld nevir do that ; bot promisit to be leill and trew to him in ony thing sche culd do.   And fordar, he wes sumthing angrie with hir that [sche] wald nocht grant to do that quhilk he spaik.

At his next appearance, he arrived in her house at noon,

quhair thair wes sittand thrie tailzeouris and hir awin guidman ; and he tuik hir apperoun and led hir to the dure with him, and sche followit and yeid up with him to the kiln-end, quhair he forbaid hir to speik or feir for ony thing sche herd or say, and quhen thay had gane a litill peice fordward, sche saw twelf personnis, aucht wemen and four men.   The men wer cled in gentilmennis cleithing, and the wemen had all plaiddis round about thaim, and wer verie semelie lyk to sie ; and Thom wes with thaim. . . . Demandit, Quhat thay said to hir.   Answerit, Thay baid hir sit doun, and said Welcum, Bessie, will thow go with us ?   Bot sche answerit nocht, because Thom had for-bidden hir.   And forder declairit, that sche knew nocht quhat

[1] Able.

purpois [1] thay had amang thaimselffis, onlie sche saw thair lippis muve : and within a schort space thay pairtit all away, and ane hideus uglie souch of wind followit thaim : and sche lay seik quhill Thom cam again bak fra thaim. Item, sche being demandit, Gif sche speirit at Thom quhat persounis thay wer ? Answerit that thay wer the Guid Wichtis that wonnit in the Court of Elfame ; quha cum thair to desyr hir to go with thaim : and forder, Thom desirit hir to do the same, quha answerit, sche saw no profit to gang that kind of gaittis, unles sche kend quhairfoir. Thom said, Seis thow nocht me, baith meit-worth, claith-worth, and guid aneuch lyk in persoun : and suld maik hir far better nor evir sche war ? Sche answerit that sche dwelt with hir awin husband and bairnis, and culd nocht leif thaim. And swa Thom began to be verie craibit with hir, and sayit, Gif swa sche thocht, sche wald get litill guid at him.

Notwithstanding this tiff, she was in the habit of consulting Thom when people asked her advice, and he gave her herbs and told her how to use them as medicine.

The Lady Johnstoun, elder, send to hir ane servand of the said ladeis, callit Catherine Dunlop, to help ane young gentil-woman, hir dochtir, now mareit on the young Laird of Stanlie ; and I thairfoir askit counsall at Thom. And he said to me, That her seiknes wes ane cauld bluid, that gaed about hir hairt, that causit hir dwam and vigous away ; and Thom bad hir taik ane pairt of ginger, clovis, annetseidis, licorese, and sum stark aill, and seill thaim togidder, and schyre [2] it.

Lady Stanley was to drink a mutchkin of this potent mixture before breakfast, with sugar : and Bessie was rewarded with meat and cheese. Lady Kilbowie, elder, then demanded the cure of a crooked leg. Thom, consulted, said :

Sche wald nevir mend, becaus the merch [3] of the bane wes consumit and the bluid dosinit, and gif sche socht ony furder help, it wald be the waur with hir.

[1] Talk.   [2] Strain.   [3] Marrow.

Other activities included finding stolen goods. In one case, Thom sent her to a girl to tell her that if she married the man to whom her family were trying to betroth her he would go mad or die a shameful death : whereat the match was broken off, and the putative bridegroom married her younger sister. Asked how she knew it was Thom Reid who died at Pinkie, she answered :

That sche suld nocht dout that it wes he, he bade hir gang to Thom Reid his sone, now officiar in his place to the Laird of Blair, and to certain utheris his kinnismen and freindis thair, quham he namit, and bade theim restoir certain guidis and mend uthir offencis that thay had done.

Asked what she thought of " the new law,"

answerit, that sche had spokin with Thom about that mateir, bot Thom answerit that thir new law wes nocht guid, and that the auld faith suld cum hame again, bot nocht sic as it wes befoir.

To further pressing questions, she affirmed that her relations with Thom were purely Platonic : she commonly saw him at noon. Asked if she had seen him going up and down the world, she declared that she had once seen him in the Kirkyard of Dalry, among the people, but did not speak to him, as he had told her that she must never do that unless he spoke first.

Item, sche saw him gangand up and doun on the gait of Edinburgh, upoun ane mercat day, quhair he leuch upon hir and gaid up and doun amangis the pepill.

Being asked the rather interesting question if she had ever spoken to him at the loch or water side, she

answerit, nevir, save anis that sche had gane afield with hir husband to Leith, for hame-bringing of meil, and ganging afield to teddir his naig at Restalrig-loch, quhair thair cum ane cumpanie of ridaris by, that maid sic ane dinn as Hevin and Erd had gane togidder, and incontinent thay raid into the loch, with

monie ane hiddous rumbil.   But Thom tauld, it wes the Guid
Wichtis, that wer rydand in Middel-Erd.

*It sounds innocent enough, but the luckless Bessie was " convict
and brint."   Often enough it was far less innocent, and the fires had
behind them some black and sulphurous smoke.   There is no doubt
of the existence of a sort of organised Kirk of Satan, an ugly and
decadent inversion of Christianity.   It may go back to ancient
fertility cults, but the antinomianism that shadowed the doctrine of
predestinate election gave it a fresh hold.   If one was damned whatever one should do, it was mere common sense to make terms with
the authorities of Hell.   If one was saved whatever one should do,
then it also could appear merely rational to make the best of all
three worlds in the by-going . . . and the greater the sinner, the
greater the glory of God in being able to save him.*

*Not all the many women who were burnt were innocent house-
wives wrongfully accused.   But the deepest horror of the thing,
none the less, is what it caused to hang over the innocent.   Archbishop Spottiswoode gives a grim glimpse of this side, in the case of
Margaret Aitken, " the great witch of Balwearie."* [1]

Being examined touching her associates in that trade, she
named a few, and perceiving her delations found credit, made
offer to detect all of that sort, and to purge the country of them,
so that she might have her life granted.   For the reason of her
knowledge, she said that they had a secret mark, all of that sort,
in their eyes, whereby she could surely tell, how soon she looked
upon any, whether they were witches or not ; and in this she
was so readily believed that for the space of three or four months
she was carried from town to town to make discoveries of that

[1] The Archbishop was, so to speak, the good Calderwood's opposite number
as the contemporary historian of the Right.   His rival History of the Church
was finished in the unpropitious year 1639, and remained unpublished till 1655.
Scotland owes him a debt, for it was he who sought to put in practice Knox's
admirable scheme for parish schools, which up to his time had remained on
paper.   As historian, however, he could not compete with Calderwood, for his
temper is too critical to admit the latter's fascinating marvels, and his death-bed
details are far less ornate.

K

kind. Many were brought to question [1] by her delations, especially at Glasgow, where divers innocent women, through the credulity of the minister, Mr John Cowper, were condemned and put to death. In end [sic] she was found to be a mere deceiver (for the same persons that the one day she had declared guilty, the next day, when presented in another habit, she cleansed) and sent back to Fife, where first she was apprehended. At her trial she affirmed all to be false that she had confessed either of her self or others, and persisted in this to her death.

When an innocent woman had the knowledge, and the courage, to demand a proper legal trial, she might win free. The Privy Council came down very heavily on that pet of the Kirk authorities, the witch-pricker : and both the Council and the Court of Justiciary were on the alert against false or interested accusations. In one instance we see the Council defending a couple of poor women accused by the Earl and Countess of Athol, in another intervening in a case in Lasswade, where the pannel has claimed that the charge is maliciously brought by a pursuer who wants her property, and demanding a full investigation. The hideous tortures inflicted on accused witches were, in fact, illegal. Legally, torture could not be used save on the order of the Privy Council and in the presence of a full meeting of it.

In too many cases, however, there was no chance of an appeal, or the vindication was too late to save the victim. In 1596 the unpleasant Patrick Stewart, Earl of Orkney, accused his brother John Stewart, Master of Orkney, of plotting his murder in conjunction with a witch named Alison Balfour. The unhappy Mrs Balfour was dead already, but the Master produced her dying declaration.

Apud Kirkwall, upoun the Heding-hill of the same, saxtein day of Dec. 1594. In presens of Thomas Swinton, Minister at Kirkwall, John Stewart, Reidar thair, Mr Gilbert Bodie Minister at Holm, Alexander Somerville in Denness, John Mackenzie,

[1] Torture.

David Moncrieff, servitour to my Lord Erl of Orkney, and Gilbert Pacock, with sindrie uthiris. The quhilk day, in presens of the notar public undirwritten and witnes foirsaidis, Alesoun Balfour, being condampnit for hir alledgeit poyntis of witchcraft and led to the hill to the place of executioun ; sche, in presens of me and witnesses foirsaidis, declairit and tuik upoun hir saul and conscience as sche wald answer at the day of Judgment, quhen the secreitis of all hairtis sal be disclosit, that sche wes als innocent and wald die als innocent of onie point of wichcraft as ane bairn new born : And als being inquyrit upoun hir saul and conscience to declair quhat sche knew of the Laird of Stenhous and to quhat effect he gaif to hir the wax that wes fund in hir purs ?   Quha then presentlie declairit, be hir pairt of Paradys, and als sche wald answer to the leving Lord, that sche knew nathing to the auld Laird of Stenhous bot honestie, and that his Lady, being subiect to the colick, notour to hir, willit the Laird to gif hir ane peice wax, a four yeir bygane syne, to maik ane implaistir, to be imployit be hir to his Lady, for remeidie of hir said diseis, and na uthirwayis, as sche wald answer to the leving God of Hevin and Airth : and said then plainlie, that sche wald die with the same confessioun : lykeas, sche then dyit constantlie thairwith.

And siclyk, being inquirit and accusit be the Persoun of Ropher, gif sche wald abyd be hir first depositioun, maid in the Castell of Kirkwall upoun the   day of December instant : Quha answerit, that the tyme of hir first depositioun, sche wes tortourit divers and several tymis in the caschelawis, and sindrie tymis takin out of thaim deid and out of al remembraunce aithir of guid or evill ; as lykwayis hir guidman being in the stokis,[1] hir sone tortourit in the buitis, and hir dochtir [*aged seven*] put in the pilniewinkis, quhairwith sche and thay wer vexit and tormentit, that pairtlie to eschew ane greitar torment and punischement, and upoun promeis of hir lyf and guid deid be the said Persoun, falslie againis hir saul and conscience, sche

[1] Elsewhere described as " the lang irnis of fiftie stane wecht."

maid that confessioun, and na uthirwayis ; for the quhilk, sche askit at the Lord mercy and forgivenes, and constantlie dyit thairat.

The Master was acquitted by the Court : but it was too late to do much for poor Alison Balfour.

81. DUELS

The sixteenth century everywhere was violent : in Scotland, indeed, there were times when it was very little quieter than, say, in Chicago under Prohibition. The unfortunate authorities did their best. Here is an act of the year 1600.

Our Soverain Lord and Estaitis of this present Parliament, considering the greit libertie that sindrie personis takis in provoking utheris to singular combattis upoun suddein and frivole querrellis, quhilk hes engenderit greit inconvenientis within this Realm : Thairfoir statutis and ordainis that na persoun in tyme cuming, without His Hienes licence, fecht onie singular combat undir the pain of deid, and his movabill geir escheit to His Hienes use : and the provocar to be punischit with ane mair ignominius deid nor the defendar, at the plesour of His Majestie.

singular, single.   *deid*, death.

82. HIS MAJESTY'S REBELS

In 1594 the Privy Council Register gives an enlightening picture of what the unlucky young King had to contend with. This is the record of his cousin Francis, Earl of Bothwell, sister's son to his stepfather by his mother's half-brother, Lord John Stewart.

First breiking ward out of the castell of Edinburgh ; invading His Majestie undir cloud of nicht at his palaceis of Halirudhous and Falkland ; awaiting on His Majestie at his overpassing at the ferryis of Leith and Kinghorn ; seiking at sindrie tymis, besyde the burrowis of Edinburgh and Lynlithgu, to haif seasit on His Hienes persoun at the hunting ; entering in his presens in maist irreverent and barbarous maneir the xxiii day of Julii the yeir of God j^{m}v^c lxxxxiii yeiris at his palace of Halirudhous foirsaid ; clengeing himself of the odius cryme of witchecraft in a jugement quhair he wes baith juge and pairtie ; pressing His Majestie (yea, almaist compelling him aganis his hairt, gif he had nocht preferrit his honour and libertie of his croun to his ain lyfe) to capitulat with him in mateiris maist foul and ignominius ; and the thryd of Aprile last, in his dispyt of His Majestie, cuming with displayit baneiris in sicht of strangearis, and in His Hienes ain presens committing presumptuous insolence upoun His Hienes guid subjectis. . . .

We know from other sources that these charges were true enough, though they tactfully omit the further fact that Bothwell was petted and bribed by the English Government, who hoped that he might disembarrass them of James. The King contrived to hold his own, however, and the dangerous Bothwell died at last in Naples, " past doing any harm, though he want not malice."

83. STREET SCENES

Habakkuk Bisset was luckless in his christening. He was the son of Queen Mary's caterer, who begged his mistress to find the child a name. Mary, on her way to mass, was in something of a hurry, and picking up a Bible said she would choose the first name that turned up when she opened it. He grew up to be a Writer to the Signet, and the author of a famous digest of Scots laws and legal process called the " Rolment of Courtis." He does not seem to have been popular, as he brought no less than three actions for assault, in one of which he was " verie shairplie " admonished for malicious prosecution.

In this case, however, before the Privy Council, he won his case by default, as the defenders in it refused to compear, and were accordingly put to the horn. The date is 1587.

Robert Hamilton, younger of Preston, had " consavit ane

deidlie feid and haitrent" against Habakkuk, *who had acted as agent for a creditor. He swore to get even.*

Nevirtheles, the said Abacuck, having committed na cryme that deservit the samyn, and supponing that the said injurius bosting, consavit without just caus, eftir proces of tyme had bein foryett, behavit himself in peacabil and quiet maneir, as become ane man of his vocatioun, quhill at last, upoun the xxiiii day of Julii instant, the saidis Maister Patrik Hammiltoun and Robert Hammiltoun, appeirand of Preston . . . cam to Sanct Gelis Kirk in Edinburgh, boden in feir of weir, with swerdis, pistolettis, and utheris weponis invasive, and thair, finding the said Abacuck gangand in peceabil and quiet maneir a litill befoir fyve houris at evin, awaiting upoun the ringing of the fyve houris bell to the evening prayeris, and quhair he was mindfull to haif said his prayeris to God, conform to his accustomat use, having na swerd, weponis, nor armour, bot purposing to haif levit undir Goddis peax and His Majesteis . . . then the said Robert Hammiltoun appeirand of Preston, and the said Mr Patrick sett upoun the said compleinar in the said kirk, and braik his heid first with the plumbattis of ane of thair swords, to the effusion of his bluid, and thaireftir he fleand away from thaim furth at the West Kirk dure of the said kirk, thay followit him and in the portche or throwgang of the said West Kirk dure, invadit and struck him with drawen swerdis, quhairthrow thay or either of thaim, concurrent togidder, cruellie woundit him in the left hand, and hes mutilat and dismemberit him of the haill four fingeris of the left hand. . . .

appeirand (heir) apparent.   *boden in feir of weir*, arrayed in warlike manner —the technical legal and military term.   *plumbattis*, pommel.   *throwgang*, passage.

Here is another street row, from Dundee, which again was brought before the Privy Council.

David Flescheour in Dundie persewit the Young Constabill [*i.e., the eldest son of the High Constable of Scotland*] that he, beiring grudge at him, had cum off the Hie Streit of Dundie to the syde of the gait quhair the said David wes conferrand with Mr Andro Lamb, and had taen aff his hat, cassin it to the erd undir his feit, and bostit to naill it to his heid with ane quhinger ; and sinsyne of new again had met him upoun the calsay of Dundie, and had riven aff his hat aff his heid, and callit him knaif.

The Young Constable compeared, and admitted the fact. A solemn debate established provocation, and in the end both parties were roundly admonished, and told to mend their manners for the future.

   calsay, causeway.   *quhinger*, whinger, dagger.

Our Whig propagandists have left the Scots Privy Council with a quite undeserved repute for subservience. In fact, both in legislation and administration, they were apt to show considerable vigour, and quite remarkably little respect of persons. In 1607 we find them upholding the case of an Aberdeen plumber against the Earl Marischal, and, a few years later, they heavily fined their own colleague the Earl of Lothian, for maltreating a humble burgess of Edinburgh. Their major function was keeping the King's peace—or trying to do so. Between 1607 and 1610 they had to cope with a round dozen private wars, from one between the Earls of Caithness and Orkney to an internecine one in the clan of Scott.

84. Atreidae in the Isles

The great age of the clan feud, Highland and Lowland, begins in the fifteenth century and reaches its height in the early seventeenth. Here is a Highland case, though within a clan. It comes from a MS., " The Ewill Trowbles of the Lewes," in the National Library. It is written in a hand of the first half of the seventeenth century, and the language is Scoto-English rather than Scots. The events took place between the fifteen-forties and the fifteen-nineties.

Rorie Macleod of the Lews married Barbara Stewart, daughter to the Lord Methven, by whom he had Torquil Oighre, a valiant gentleman. After the death of Barbara Stewart, Rorie MacLeod married MacKenzie his daughter,[1] by whom he had Torquil Conanach of the Coigeach. Then Rorie MacLeod, having repudiate MacKenzie his daughter for her adultery with the Brieve of the Lews [2] who was said to be the father of Torquil Conanach. Then he married MacLean his daughter, by whom he had Torquil Dubh MacLeod and Norman MacLeod, both sufficient and gallant gentlemen. Besides these, Rorie MacLeod begat divers bastards, to wit, Tormod Ongach, Murdo, Neil, Donald, and Rorie Og. This Brieve of whom mention is made is a kind of judge among the islanders, who hath an absolute judicatory, unto whose authority and censure the people willingly submit themselves, and never appeal from his sentence when he determineth any debateable question in controversy between party and party.

Torquil Oighre sailing from the Lews to Trotternish in the Isle of Skye, with a hundred men, perished with all his company by an extraordinary storm and tempest. Then Torquil Conanach, coming to perfect age, married Glengarry's daughter, by whom he had John, Neil, and divers daughters. This Torquil Conanach was never acknowledged by Rorie MacLeod of the Lewes to be his lawful son, being indeed the Brieve his son ; which moved Torquil Conanach to take arms against his reputed father Rorie MacLeod, being assisted by his base brothers Tormod Ongach and Murdo : so they invaded their father Rorie MacLeod, and took him and detained him two or three years in captivity. In end he was released upon promise that he should henceforth acknowledge Torquil Conanach as his

[1] Actually she was his first wife, and natural daughter of Kintail.
[2] The Brieve was the hereditary judge. By tradition he is said to have rebuked Rorie—who had five acknowledged bastards—for his morals, and the accusation against the Brieve and Janet was Rorie's revenge. Tradition also makes Rorie expose the latter on a half-tide rock : another and rather more probable version—though neither is impossible—is that the birlinn on which she sailed home to her father was deliberately run down, and she was drowned.

lawful son. Then was Tormod Ongach slain by his brother Donald, whereupon Torquil Conanach, being assisted by his brother Murdo, took Donald and carried him prisoner to Coigeach ; from thence he escaped and came again to the Lews to his father Rorie MacLeod, who then again was offended with Torquil Conanach for taking his brother Donald, and presently thereafter he caused his son Donald to apprehend Murdo, whom Donald delivered to their father Rorie MacLeod, who imprisoned his son Murdo at Stornoway, who moved Torquil Conanach to come hither and invade that fort.[1] After a short siege he took it and relieved his brother Murdo, apprehended again the father Rorie MacLeod, killed a number of his men, and conveyed away all the evidence, writs, charters, and old infeftments of Lewis, which he gave in custody to MacKenzie.

Then did Torquil Conanach send for his son John (who was then bred in the Earl of Huntly his company) and left him in the castle of Stornoway to keep the fort, together with his grandfather as prisoner. John MacLeod being in possession of the Lews, and acknowledged as master and superior of it, he went about to banish his uncles out of the Lews, to wit, Rorie Oig and Donald, which moved Rorie Oig to invade his nephew John MacLeod, where John was slain and old Rorie relieved. Then was old Rorie MacLeod made again commander of the island, which he did possess during the rest of his troublesome days. Then was Donald apprehended and executed without law at Dingwall in Ross by his brother Torquil Conanach, who was assisted and advised by the Clan Kenzie. . . .

But that is only the beginning of it. There was then fresh feud, involving Torquil Dubh, who married a daughter of Harris and contrived to get some kind of control of the Lews. The episode of the Fife Adventurers—an attempt at a Crown Colony in the Lews—made things still more elaborate, as the Lews people, of whatever

[1] Under the pier where the mailboat ties up today. The present Editor was born within a few hundred yards of it.

*faction, agreed at least in resenting the Lowlanders; and the re-
sentment took an active form. Eventually, Norman MacLeod,
captured and imprisoned in Edinburgh but set free in 1615, went
over to Holland, and died there in the service of Maurice of Nassau.
The feud itself trailed on into the 'twenties, and most of the family
who did not go into Dutch service came to sticky ends, leaving
Kintail, as decimus gaudens or thereby, the pleasant task of pacify-
ing the island, which the King by that time had handed over to him.
He was, by the way, a lineal ancestor of this book's Editor.*

85. The Forms of Sound Business

*Feuds were by no means confined to the Highlands, however.
This formal band belongs to one in Ayrshire. Sir Thomas Kennedy
of Culzean had been murdered by Thomas Kennedy of Drum-
marchie, at the instigation of that very ripe scoundrel, John Mure of
Auchendrayne, whose full career Mr Roughead has told in rich
detail. The murderer and his accomplices had, to be sure, been
forfeited by the Estates: but the Earl of Cassillis, head of the
Kennedy name, decided that more adequate action was called for.*

We John Erl of Cassillis, Lord Kennedy, etc., bandis and
obligis us that how soun our broder, Hew Kennedy of Bronns-
toun, with his complices, taikis the Laird of Auchendraynis
lyf, that we sall maik guid and thankfull payment to him and
thaim, of the soum of twelff hundreth merkis yeirlie, togidder
with corn to six horsis ay and quhill we reseave thaim in household with ourselff, beginning the first payment immediatlie
eftir thair committing of the said deid. Attour, howsoun we
resave thaim in houshold, we sall pay to the two serving gentlemen the feis yeirlie as our ain houshald servandis; and heirto
we obligis us upoun our honour.

Subscrivit with our hand at Maybole, the ferd day of September 1602.

                                    JOHN ERL OF CASSILLIS.

86. The High Seats of the Synagogue

A quite surprising number of feuds broke out over the peaceful matter of sittings in church. Here is one which came before the Privy Council so late as February 1622.

It begins as a case brought by Andrew Fraser, younger of Muchalls in Buchan, his miller, and the King's Advocate, against Sir William Keith of Ludquharn and his two uncles. The pursuers averred that Young Muchalls and his wife had gone to spend Christmas with her father, leaving their children " in his place of Faichfeild." The Keiths, with eighteen or twenty men, all "with lang wepponis and uthir prohibit armour," arrived there on Christmas night, guided by a masked man. They came to the miller's house, dragged him out in his nightshirt, and made him guide them to Faichfeild. There they

straik at the outir yett of his clois with foirhammeris, and seing that thay culd nocht [braik thaim], sum of thaim clam in ovir the wallis of the clois [and] straik aff the lokkis of the said Andro his yettis, and having oppinit the samyn, the haill rest of thair compliceis cum within the clois, and cum directlie to his hall dure, and with the foirsaid hammeris thay straik at the samyn ane hour and a half or the lok maid up ; and in end, eftir ane lang and furius stryking at the hall dure, thay braik and dang up the samyn, and enterit thairin, being fullie persuadit to haif fund the said Andro . . . [*Not finding him*] with axis and swerdis thay cuttit and hewit doun his hall burd of wainscott, and sew the branderis thairof with sawis, and thaireftir thay cuttit, hew doun, and braik in peicis his dressoir, and braik his silver wark within the same, with the haill remenaunt moveabillis within his hous.

One of the Keith uncles was assoilzied for lack of evidence, but there was enough to have the other men warded pending investigation. On the 4th June, after some trouble in laying hold of the defenders, the case was heard, and we learn how the matter started.

Young Muchalls averred that a new kirk had been built in the parish of Peterhead, a third of which parish was the property of his father, who had given liberally to the building fund. Once the outer walls were up, there came the business of appointing places to

gentilmen and utheris of the paroche, for accomodating of thaim with deskis and seattis. Amangis utheris, thair wes ane pairt appointit and designit unto the said complenar for bigging of ane desk, seat, and roume for him and his familie, with ane entrie to the said seat throw the side wall of the kirk, for the said complenar his mair commodius entrie to his seat, untroubling the kirk.

So far so good. He and the other parishioners then brought contributions in kind—beams and joists to make a bridge, for the more convenient access to the kirkyard. These were left to lie till the men should get round to the job, and the sight, it appears, was too much for the worthy Ludquharn, who

mellit and intromittit with ane of the best of the saidis treis, and affixit the same betuix the side wallis of the kirk, directlie above the dure designit and appointit for the entrie of the said complenar his seat . . . [*Thus Ludquharn*] tuik up the thrid pairt of the kirk, quhilk he intendis to appropriat to himself, to the prejudice of the rest of the parochinaris, althocht the tenth pairt of the paroche pertainis nocht to him ; and this place appointit be him to him self will contein sevin or aucht hundred men, and the pairt quhair he hes fixit the joist to uphald the foirsyde of his seat is twenty-sax foot distant fra the east gavel of the kirk, quhilk haill boundis he mindis to taik up for his seat.

Young Muchalls, accordingly, moved his private door to a place eight feet west of the joist : but there was still a good deal of resentment over the proposed gallery. Muchalls now put temporary stools into his place. Ludquharn did the same, and for a time there was peace. Then, however, Ludquharn, arriving with armed men, threw Muchalls' form and stools outside his door.

This edifying evidence duly led, the Council bound both parties to keep the peace, with a bond of 10,000 merks.   But then they were faced with a counter-claim from Ludquharn.   His story bears that it was he who had first got the patron's permission to build a new kirk at all, and that he gave it a hundred merks every year, besides his teinds.   Yet in spite of these benefactions, the kirk was no sooner built than Young Muchalls demanded

the first and chief place in the said kirk, being in the middest of the kirk on the south side thairof [*while the pursuer, with true Christian meekness, contented himself with*] the east gavel of the kirk, for edifying of ane loft to him and his familie,

for which he made " greit preparatioun of hewin wark."   The joist is mentioned, but not its originally appointed function as part of the kirkyard brig.   Then Ludquharn's tale proceeds to the temporary seating of the two antagonists, side by side.   But this time that scandalous personage, Young Muchalls, removed the pious Ludquharn's stools and forms, and put his own in their place.   They were decorously " reponit in peaceabil maneir, but onie challeng of injurie " :   and this time it was Muchalls, still with armed men, who flung them into the kirkyard and broke them up, and in addition broke the famous joist, leaving

nathing aither side of the kirk bot the twa stumpis thairof, to be ane spectakil to the haill parochine,

who had, not unnaturally, come to " gaise and behald."

More evidence was led.   Young Muchalls was found guilty of cutting the joist, and the joist was decerned to have been lawfully lent to Ludquharn by the Master of Works.   Muchalls was committed to the Tolbooth, though his father was assoilzied altogether. As for Ludquharn, he joined his antagonist behind the bars, on the grounds of his " insolence " to Muchalls.

Eventually, Ludquharn's Christmas visit to Faichfeild cost him £3000 in damages :   and both parties were impartially admonished and commanded frielie and fra thair hairtis to forgive all rancor, haitrent, and displesour, greif and malice, that onie of thaim hes consavit aganis utheris for onie caus or occasioun . . . and to observe His Majesteis peace, keip guid rulis and quietnes ilk ane of thaim with utheris, and to live togidder in tyme cuming as becomis guid Cristian dewtiful subjectis and peaceabil nichtbouris,

all which they " promittit faithfullie to do," and the Bishop of Aberdeen was thereon appointed to redd the original question of the pews. The sermon of the Right Reverend Patrick Forbes on his next official visit to Peterhead must have been rather eagerly awaited.

yett, probably here has the specific meaning of an iron grille.   *maid up*, gave way.   *sew*, sawed.   *branderis*, cross-bars.   *burd*, here table. *mellit*, meddled.

KINGS, QUEENS, AND PRINCES

Fall quhat may fall,
The Lyoun sal be lord of all.
On a Jewel of Queen Mary.

87. THE KING AND THE PAGE

The Lord Treasurer's accounts for 1537 give a pleasant hint of James V's relation with his servants.

Item, for ane cord to the child that braik his leg, to turn him in his bed with, xij d.

Item, for ane reid bonet to the page that braik his leg, iij s viij d.

Item, to the wyf that keipit the lad that braik his leg, xx s.

88. ROYAL TOILETTE

The same records, four years later, give a glimpse of royalty very much in undress.

Gevin to John Mosman for ane clamb schell of silver to put tuith pulder in, weyand thrie uncis, price of the unce xvj s and for the warkmanschip, xiiij s.　Summa iij li ij s.

li, libri, punds.

89. JAMES V ENTERS PARIS

Here is King James on a much more public occasion.　On the last day of 1536 he made his state entry into Paris, to marry Madame Madeleine de France.　King Francis had ordered the Parlement to receive him in scarlet : the Parlement, however, considered this a breach of protocol, claiming that they only wore scarlet for their own royalty, but were told that as James was in

*point of becoming one of the family, the protocol in fact demanded
scarlet. This is the official minute, in very legal French.*

This day, assembled the Court at the Palais [de Justice]
about an hour after noon, to meet the King of Scotland, for whom
the King had ordained a formal entry into this city of Paris, as
for his proper person : and it left, after two o'clock, the said
Palais on horseback in the customary order : to wit, the ushers
first, holding each their rods ; after them the four Notaries, two by
two, and the Registrars of the Presentation and the Criminal
Court together, the said Registrars and Notaries clad in robes
and hoods of scarlet ; after them myself alone, clad in robe and
gown of furred scarlet ; the first usher after, clad in scarlet robe,
having his cap furred and a rod in his hand ; then Messieurs the
Presidents, two by two, clad in robes and mantles of scarlet
and bearing their velvet hats ; the Councillors two by two,
according to their rank ; and after them the Advocates and the
King's Procurator General, all in robes of scarlet and hoods of
the same, furred with miniver ; then the Advocates of the said
court, two by two, clad in seemly manner in robes other than
scarlet, with their caps furred. After the said Advocates, the
Procurators, also two by two, clad in seemly wise according to
their rank, having their hoods with padded edges. . . .

And after making their reverences to the said King of Scotland, Monsieur the First President addressed him in the name of
the said Court : which ended, the King of Scotland embraced
my said lords the Presidents, without saying to them anything
at all, because he knew no French.

*James's education, carefully provided for in the beginning, had
in fact been badly neglected by the usurping Angus : but he did
write French fluently enough, if not always very grammatically.
He may have felt self-conscious about his accent . . . or merely
thought there had been enough oratory for that one morning.*

90. ROSE OF MAY

Here is Bishop Lesley's description of the bride whom James was on his way to marry. It comes from the Scots version of "De Origine, Moribus, et Rebus Gestis Scotorum," written at Burton-on-Trent during Mary's imprisonment and printed in Rome in 1578. Lesley is a cool and objective writer, speaking with notable moderation on the thorny points of the religious divisions; but there is genuine pity in his account of the little Queen Magdalen, who died, still in her honeymoon, at sixteen.

. . . Ane young ladie of plesand bewtie, guidlie favour, luving countenance, and cumlie maneiris, above all utheris within the realm of France.

James, rejecting her father's offer of other brides—for Francis knew how the match was likely to end—married her in Notre Dame, with great splendour.

And they baith tuik thair leif of the King of France at Paris at the lattir end of Aprill, and passit thairfra to Rowan, quhair thay wer ressavit with greit triumph, and wer conveyit doun the revar of Sane to the New Havin,[1] quhair thay schippit : being accumpanyit be the Admirall of France and monie utheris nobill men of France, send be the King to convoy thaim to Scotland, and saillit with plesand windis and prosperous voyage throw the seis, and landit at the peir of the Havin of Leith, the xix day of May 1537 ; quhair thair wes monie erlis, bischoppis, lordis, barounis, and utheris of Scotland, quha ressavit thaim with exceding greit blythnes, and with greit triumph wes convoyit to the Abbay of Halirudhous.

This guid ladie, throw hir luving countenance and cumlie behaviour at hir first arryving, conquest the luve and hertlie guid will of the nobillis of the realm, and of the pepill alswa, and plesit the King sa weill in all sortis, quhairthrow thair wes nevir

---

[1] Le Havre.

greittar hoip and appeirance of welth [1] and all kind of pro-speritie within the realm nor did appeir than.

Bot fortune, invying thair felicitie, wald nocht suffer thaim to byd lang togidder, and thairfoir causit Atropos to cut hir threid : swa that about the moneth of Junii, sche wes vexit with seiknes of ane vehement fevir, quhairof sche decessit the Xth day of Julii, and wes buryit in the Abbay Kirk of Halirud-hous, quhairof the King tuik greit displesour, and thairfoir keipit him quiet a lang tyme eftir.

It is interesting to speculate what would have happened if she had lived, or had James, as their father wanted him to do, married her sister Marguérite. Marguérite lived, so there would have been no Queen Mary, and the Union of Crowns would have come about differently. And since there would also have been no Marie de Guise, Henry VIII might possibly have conquered Scotland.

91. THE QUEEN'S RING

Queen Magdalen did die. James had to remarry. He could not marry his deceased wife's sister, so the young widowed Duchesse de Longueville, of the great fighting house of Guise-Lorraine, was given honorary status as a Daughter of France, and offered to him. Henry VIII of England, then no more than thrice a widower, courted her also, but the lady remarked that she had a slender neck ; and within a year of the death of Queen Magdalen the Lord Treasurer's accounts record the item

Gevin for ane greit diamond sett in tabill for the Queinis spousing ring, j^{m}j^{c} crounis.

92 THE KING TO THE QUEEN

This second marriage lasted not so much longer than their brief first ones had done—from June 1538 to December 1542, and was

[1] Well-being.

*shadowed by the death of their two sons; but there is a friendly
affection in this scribbled note, written by James in a flying, untidy
scrawl.*

Obeying your command, I send you by the present bearer
the gown and *?lvʒie* which I promised you, with my most
humble commendations to your good favour, praying of you
the occasion to do well by you, and to keep the promise which
you have made me, as a good wife should to him who always
deserves and will all my life deserve it, by God's help.   Praying
our Lord to give you good life and long,
Your most humble husband,
JAMES R.

*This other note, again in the King's own hand, suggests that
someone has been trying to make trouble.*

I have received the letter which it has pleased you to write
me, for which I humbly thank you : but those who have said to
you that I wished not to go from this place have falsely lied,
because I never thought but to be on Sunday where you are.
And touching my mother's business, I will not forget, begging
you not to be so amazed till you shall hear the truth.   Praying
you to make good cheer until my return, which will be on
Sunday.   Praying Our Lord to give you good life and long,
Your humble husband,
JAMES R.

93. STEPSON OF SCOTLAND

*Royal motherhood has often been tragic enough, but seldom
more than for Marie de Guise.   Married at eighteen to Louis
d'Orléans, Duc de Longueville, of the Blood Royal of France, she
had two sons.   One died as a baby, the other, a lovable bairn not
three years old, she had to leave in France on her Scottish marriage.
In the brief four years of that she bore and lost two more, and then
was left widowed with a daughter not a week old, born to queenship*

of a bitterly troubled and assaulted kingdom. From this child also she was to be parted, for the little Queen was not yet six years old when she had to be sent, for her own safety, to France. When Queen Marie saw her children again, the boy was fifteen and the child Queen eight.

The boy was brought up by his very charming grandmother, Antoinette de Bourbon, Duchesse de Guise, who kept his mother's memory alive for him, and encouraged him to write to her and to his small step-sister. The letters make one wonder if Mary's tragic life might have been different had this other, lawful, half-brother lived to serve her.

This is a passage from a long letter of family gossip written by the Duchesse de Guise to her daughter Queen Marie, apparently soon after the latter had gone to Scotland. It is in French, in a delicate graceful hand.

. . . I cannot hear enough from Mademoiselle de Curel of the King's kindness to you. His picture, which has been brought to me, gives me more desire than ever to see him, for in truth he is a handsome prince. He has sent me a gift, which I assure you I like well, and will keep all my life in his honour. . . . I keep the best till the last, to tell you of our grandson, who will very soon be a man. There lacks but a painter, that you may see how bonny he is. He is the best child I have ever seen. He is tall and healthy, thank God. I hope he will give you joy, if it please the Lord to permit him and vouchsafe to you, Madame, such joy, health, and long life as for you desires,

Your humble and good mother,

ANTOINETTE DE BOURBON

Written this 18th November, at Joinville.

To the Queen of Scots.

In August of 1538, a couple of months after Queen Marie's wedding at St Andrews, her mother had written news of the small François, who was evidently excited by tales of his mother's wedding festivities.

And to return to what I fancy you most desire to hear, I tell you that our grandson is as well as can be, and you never saw him so fat. His grandfather has looked after him so well, and there is such a friendship between the two of them, that there is no separating them without tears on both sides : he is so pleased with him that he has lost some of his illness. . . . For three days [little François] has never stopped talking about *la Reine Madame*.

The next year the adoring grandmother writes :

We have found our grandson as pretty and plump as a child can be. . . . He is big and grown so sturdy his dress will not meet on him by the breadth of three fingers, and his face so round and bonny you cannot get enough of looking at him. Monsieur your father is so crazy about him that he does not half see him.[1] He has the prettiest chatter possible.

Soon he was able to dictate letters of his own, with a little prompting, and to sign them in a large round childish scrawl.

I commend myself to *la Reine Madame*, who so well has commended her to me. You have not written to me and I am very sorry and I play games and grandpapa has given me a horse and I take it hunting and will you send me a Scots horse to carry me and Maman Tétault who will carry me behind me [*sic*] and *la Reine Madame* come to see me and bring the King and my Dear [2] and Madame Grandmamma, who comes to see me in bed and gives me cordial and good black bread, and Ma'selle my aunt who has shown her fine cabinet to Monsieur, and adieu.

FRANÇOIS D'ORLÉANS.

In this letter again, the secretary who took it down has had the kind thought of making a shorthand report of the child's chatter, in his own words.

---

[1] This is a literal translation of the Duchess's phrase.
[2] His aunt Louise, later Princesse de Chimay.

To la Reine Madame.

I commend me to *la Reine Madame*. I put on my green gown on Sunday at Our Lady's feast, and was in the litter with my aunt and the nuns,[1] and a little silver litter which is broken it must be mended to go and see you, *Reine Madame*, in the big litter, and a little friend I found at Joinville, Marie Crustande, who dances with me. Our donkey is dead. Write, Jean, write to *la Reine Madame* that I have had a sore head and hands, and Dear who cropped me and didn't cut my ear but she did cut my hair. And I have hunted the stag and Gilbert was him and that little silly De Joisine was the hound and barked wow wow wow, and I was on my little horse who cried henny henny. And Madame Grandmamma who takes me into the garden and Grandpapa who gave me a great horse with a tail behind, and it will charge Monsieur my uncle and René Monsieur and Monsieur will say " Look out, René Monsieur, look out, he will ride you down," and I will spur him and I will sing when I am on the big horse. And say to *la Reine Madame*, Jean, that I need a pony, it is to be black, write, write, Jean, and mules, one which shall be in front and the other behind. And adieu *Reine Madame* and the King too, and I will go to see him to-morrow. Let me see, Jean, have you not finished ?

François.

In 1545, having reached the mature age of nine, he can write for himself, very much under the eye of his tutor, whom his mother probably found a poor substitute for his old amanuensis, Jean of the shorthand.

To the Queen,

Madame, since the means to write to you from here presents itself, although Madame my grandmother writes to you all news, as she has told me, yet I should be very sorry, for the duty and obedience which I owe you, Madame, to fail to send

---

[1] Possibly his other aunts, both of whom were nuns.

you mine. Which is, thanks to our very good Lord, continuing to be well, and according to those to whom I belong I begin to be tall, which is a thing I greatly desire, obeying first of all, Madame, the orders it has pleased you to give me, whom all my life I shall obey, being always in that firm will and resolution to go and see you, and meantime, so that you may know just how tall I am, I send you my exact height by the length of the string that you will find enclosed.

Assuring you, Madame, that Monsieur et Dame and Messieurs my uncles are well, and commending me most humbly to your good Grace and the little Queen, Madame my good sister. Praying God, Madame, to give you always most happy prosperity, good health, and long life. From Joinville, this 22nd day of March,

Your most humble and most obedient son
FRANÇOIS D'ORLÉANS.

Some two years later, being then about eleven, he writes to his little half-sister, then rising five. Apparently she had sent him some baby scrawl.

TO THE QUEEN,

Madame, I have received the letter it has pleased you to write to me by Monsieur d'Auzel, and have been very glad to have your news, and following the prayer you make me to come to your succour, I practise every day wearing armour and riding at the ring, so that after I may do you the succour and service that are possible to me, against all those who would hurt you. And in this good will, Madame, I remain all my life, with God's help, of Whom I beg, Madame, to send you good life and long, after humbly commending myself to your good Grace.

From Fontainebleau this xii January,

Your most humble and most obedient brother,
FRANÇOIS D'ORLÉANS.

In 1549, in his fourteenth year, the boy made his first public appearance as hereditary Lord Chamberlain of France. At the end of the year, when his sister had been in France since the summer of the previous one, he writes to his mother. By this time he could use a beautiful print script, though he has not a solitary punctuation mark.

Madame, the bearer has gone so suddenly that I have not had the means of writing to you, save to inform you of the coming of Madame the Princess of Ferrara to this court, who is one of the fairest and most gracious princesses that one could see. Monsieur d'Aumale my uncle [1] will marry her in a week. I would not forget, Madame, to tell you that the little Queen of Scotland is thought so pretty in this company that the King is delighted with her. I design, Madame, to do her as much service as is possible for me, and that, Madame, with as good heart as I commend myself, Madame, most humbly to your good favour, and beg the Creator, Madame, to give you a most good and long life.

From St Germain en Laye, this 19th day of December.

Your most humble and obedient son,

FRANÇOIS D'ORLÉANS.

The next year but one, the long looked-for meeting of mother and children took place, and his mother was with him when, in September of that year, he died, only a few weeks before his sixteenth birthday.

94. THE RIVAL EARLS

The Queen Dowager Marie had troubles enough in Scotland, though this one had more than a touch of comedy in it. The story is told by that inveterate and lively gossip, Robert Lindsay of Pitscottie. A Fifer, living near Falkland, the King's new summer palace, he was a cousin of David Lindsay the poet and of Mary's brutal opponent, Lindsay of the Byres.

[1] Queen Marie's youngest brother.

This story belongs to the time just after the death of James V. The marriage of the Earl of Angus to Margaret of England, the widowed Queen-Mother of the preceding reign, had stirred the ambitions of the Earls of Lennox and Bothwell . . . though, as Sir George Mackenzie observed later, " kindness to widow Queens" was a characteristic of the House of Hepburn, one of whom had already courted James V's great-grandmother, the young Marie de Gueldres. The son of one suitor and the grandson of the other married, to her misfortune, Queen Marie's daughter.

And thairfoir dailie thir two lordis persewit the court and the Quene with brawetie, with dauncing, singing, and playing on instrumentis, and arayit everie day in sundrie abulziementis, and prydit everie ane of thaim quha suld be mair galliard in thair cleithing and behaif thaimselffis in the Quenis presens, sumtyme in dauncing, sumtyme in schuting, sumtyme in singing and justing and rinning of greit hors at the listis, with all uthir knichtlie gamis that micht satisfie the Quene or do hir plesour. Bot the Erl of Lennox warstit evir the uthir at all gamis, becaus he wes bettir practisit in weir nor the Erl of Bothwell wes, be resoun he wes brocht up in France with his onkil Monser Daubony,[1] quho lernit him in feit of armes and daylie exercessit him thairto, quhill he becam practisit in the samyn. Forder he wes ane strang man of personage, weill schapin in portratour, that is to say weill brent in leggis and armis, weill schoulderit, fair pleasand facit, with ane guid and manlie countenance, and

---

[1] Robert Stuart d'Aubigny, Marshal of France, cousin and son-in-law of the even more famous Bernard Stuart d'Aubigny, Duke of Terra Nova and Père de la Guerre of the Italian wars. Brantôme writes of him, " The great King [Louis XII] had under him very great captains, whom he trained and made among others M. d'Aubigny, a Scot and a grand seigneur, who did his nation much honour : so that certain French annalists have called him ' Grand seigneur sans reproche,' as indeed he showed himself in many actions. . . . He died in the reign of King Francis [I], very old and broken, more by combats and victories than through too great age." The two houses of Stewart of Lennox in Scotland and Stuart d'Aubigny in France were both descended from the famous John Stewart of Darnley of Charles VII's wars, Seigneur d'Aubigny et de Concressault and Comte d'Évreux ; and for five generations were very closely connected, the French lordships going to a younger brother or first cousin of the reigning Lennox.

yeid brent and upricht in his passage. Thairfoir in that tyme
he wes maist plesand for ane ladie. As for the Erl Bothwell,
he wes fair and quhitelie, and sumthing hingand schulderit, and
yeid sumthing fordwart, with ane gentill and humane countenance, bot yit he wes nocht thocht to do ane gentilwoman sa
greit plesour as the uthir.

Thir two lordis daylie exercessit thaimselffis in this maneir,
as I haif schawin to you, everie ane of thaim believand to obtein
his purpois at the Quenis hand. Bot nevirtheles, sche did
nathing bot gaif thaim fair wordis, to the intent that thay suld
serve hir quhile sche saw hir tyme expedient to gif thaim ane
answer.

> *brawetie*, roughly, finery, with untranslatable overtones.　　*abulziementis*,
> habillements, one's whole " get up," with a suggestion of full dress.　　*brent*,
> straight.　　*yeid*, goed, went.　　*yeid fordwart*, stooped.

95. A Queen's Face gives Grace

*A formal letter from Marie as Regent to the Lords of the
Session commends to them the case of a poor widow bigamously
married by a burgess of Glasgow, who has tangled her in a law-
plea and declines to answer. The letter is written by the Queen's
secretary in the old-fashioned " Gothic " hand, in Scots. Marie,
signing it, has added a French postscript in her own swift Italic.*

Do justice to this poor woman, for they do her great wrong.
The small [flies] are caught in the spider's web, while the big
fly goes through.

MARIE R.

96. A Queen's Passport

*In the year after the peace of 1550, Queen Marie permitted
herself a holiday in France, where she was entertained " like a
goddess." Relying on the peace, she ventured on her return to
make the short sea crossing and come home through England,
paying a state visit to the boy Edward VI at Hampton Court.*

This is her passport through England. One observes the tactful and courteous elision of the King's titles : until 1801 *the Kings of England persisted in calling themselves the Kings of France, but on this occasion it seems to have been felt that it would not do.*

Edward the Sixth, etc. to all dukes, marquises, earls, viscounts, barons, admirals, wardens or keepers of our Marches, to all captains, keepers of our castles or bulwarks or their lieutenants, to all customars, comptrollers and searchers, mayors, sheriffs, bailiffs, constables, and to all other our officers, ministers, and subjects, as well by land as by sea and fresh waters within our realm of England and Ireland or any other our dominions or any our islands belonging to the same, to whom these our letters shall come, Greeting.

Whereas the Right Excellent Princess, Mary Queen Dowager of Scotland, minding to make her repair from France into Scotland, hath determined to pass by sea,

Know ye that we, at the earnest desire and request of our dearest brother the French King, by the advice of our Council are contented and pleased and have permitted and do permit that the said Right Excellent Princess Mary Queen Dowager of Scotland, in this her passage into Scotland to be made before the feast of Michaelmas ensuing next, with all ladies, earls, bishops, lords, abbots, knights, and all other persons spiritual and temporal, of what estate or degree soever they be, and such number of ships, galleys, and other vessels as she shall have with her and avow to be hers and of her said company, may surely and safely and freely for their relief or necessity or if she shall think so good, to repair unto any port, haven, town, or other place within any of our said realms of England or Ireland, the realm of Scotland, or any of our said islands upon the sea coasts of any of the said realms of England, Ireland, or Scotland, at their pleasure,

And there to land, if they shall think good, with mules and horses as well stoned as geldings, budgets, fardels, coffers, jewels, money, old silver, coined and uncoined, letters close and open, and all other their bags and baggages, reposing and refreshing themselves and their horses for a convenient time or two or three days after that the wind or weather may serve them again to pass by sea into the parts of Scotland without any search, arrest, trouble, or impediment to be made or done to them or any of them in their entering or remaining within any our said realms of England or Ireland or other our dominions, or any our islands belonging to any of the same, during this our present safe conduct.

Wherefore we will and command you and every of you not only to receive the said Right Excellent Princess with her train in form aforesaid, but also during their abode there to help and relieve them for their reasonable money with all such things as they shall have need of, and otherwise entreat them in all their lawful requests gently and comely, as to every of their estates shall appertain,

Provided always that the said Right Excellent Princess and her train and every of them do well behave themselves towards us and our subjects, without doing or attempting anything in our prejudice or contempt,

Foreseeing nevertheless that if it happen any of them to break this our safe conduct, we will not that any displeasure or hurt be therefore done or executed upon any other that hath not offended, but only upon such as shall infringe or break this our safe conduct, accordingly, notwithstanding any ordinances, customs, and defences made to the contrary.

In witness whereof, etc.

Witness ourself, at Westminster, xii Die Maii.

97. MARY'S MOTHER-IN-LAW

James V's half-sister, Lady Margaret Douglas, later Countess of Lennox and mother of Henry, Lord Darnley, was Red Douglas on the father's side and Tudor on the mother's, and as legitimate

niece of Henry VIII, stood high in the order of succession to England . . . and within the dangers incumbent on that position. She had been born in England, just after her parents had fled there on the detection of their plot to bring about an English invasion and the kidnapping to England of the child King.

In 1536, *when Lady Margaret was twenty-one, the English antiquary Stow records :*

In the month of July, Lord Thomas Howard, youngest brother of the Duke of Norfolk, was sent to the Tower of London for making a privy contract of marriage with the Lady Margaret Douglas, daughter to the Queen of Scots by the Earl of Angus and niece to King Henry of England : the said Lord Thomas was attainted by Parliament, and also the said Lady Margaret Douglas was after committed to the Tower for the same.

In the next year comes this :

On Allhallows Eve, Lord Thomas Howard, brother to the Duke of Norfolk, died prisoner in the Tower of London, and was buried at Thetford, and then the Lady Margaret Douglas was pardoned and released from the Tower.

She was still, however, under open arrest, and, soon after, she writes to an unnamed lord, anxiously explaining that her two new servants

Indeed were my Lord Thomas's servants, and the cause that I took them for was the poverty that I saw them in, and for no cause else.   But seeing, my lord, that it is your pleasure that I shall keep none that did belong to my Lord Thomas, I will put them from me.

And she anxiously explains that indeed and truly she does not love Lord Thomas any more.   It would have made some difference to our history had she married him instead of the Earl of Lennox.

98. The Boy Darnley

Lady Margaret did marry Lennox, however, he being exiled, like her father, as a quisling : and since her formidable uncle, Henry, was anxious to make him a satisfactory one, she married him with that monarch's consent.

Here is a letter from their eldest son, Henry, Lord Darnley, then a boy of eight, to his mother's first cousin, Mary, Queen of England. It is exquisitely written in a beautiful Italian print script. The writing is probably the boy's own, but the letter itself was no doubt composed by his tutor, a Scottish quisling of the name of Elder, who soon after this was writing pro-English propaganda for distribution among his countrymen. He made the most of this chance of eloquence.

Like as the monuments of ancient authors (most triumphant, most victorious, and most gracious Princess) declare how that a certain musician named Timotheus Musicus was wont with his sweet proportioned and melodious harmony to inflame Alexander the great conqueror and King of Macedonia to civil wars with a most fervent desire, even so I, remembering with myself oftentimes how that (over and besides such manifold benefits as Your Highness heretofore hath bestowed on me) it hath pleased Your most Excellent Majesty lately to accept a little plot of my simple penning which I termed Utopia Nova, for the which, it being base, vile, and maimed, Your Majesty hath given me a rich chain of gold. The noise (I say) of such instruments as I hear, now and then (although their melody differeth much from the sweet strokes and sounds of King Alexander's Timotheus) do not only persuade and move, yea, prick and spur me forward, to endeavour my wits daily (all vanities set apart) to virtuous learning and study, being thereto encouraged so oftentimes by Your Majesty's manifold benefits, gifts, and rewards. But I am also inflamed and stirred, even now, my tender age notwithstanding, to be serving Your Grace, wishing every hair in my head to be a worthy soldier, of the self same heart, mind, and stomach that I am of. But whereas I conceive that neither my power, nor years are (at this present) corresponding unto my good will, this shall be therefore (most gracious Princess) most humbly rendering to Your Majesty immortal thanks for your rich chain and other Your Highness' sundry gifts, given unto me, without any my deserving, from time to time. Trusting in God one day, of my most bounden duty, to endeavour myself, with my faithful hearty service, to remember the same, and being afraid, with these my superfluous words, to interturb (God forfend) Your Highness, whose most Excellent Majesty is always, and specially now,[1] occupied with weighty matters, thus I make an end, praying unto Almighty God most humbly and faithfully to preserve, keep, and defend Your Majesty's long reigning over us, all your true and faithful subjects, a most victorious and triumphant Princess, Amen.

From Temple Newsam, the xxviij of March, 1554.

Your Majesty's most bounden and obedient subject and servant,

HENRY DARNLEY.

99. BIRTH AND DEATH

In 1542 *the Diurnal of Occurrents records laconically :*

Upoun the aucht day of December, Marie Quene of Scottis wes lichtir of ane virgen, namit Marie, Princes of Scotland. And upoun the xiiij day of the said moneth, the Kingis Grace decessit in Falkland, quhairfoir thair wes greit murning in Scotland.

100. THE LITTLE QUEEN

In 1548, *when the Queen was five, a young French officer, Jean de Beaugué, was attached to the staff of Monsieur d'Essé, commanding the French troops fighting in Scotland. His position*

---

[1] Mary at this time was deep in the preparations for her ill-starred marriage, which took place in the following July.

brought him in contact with the Queen Dowager, and this is how her little daughter struck him :

One of the most perfect creatures that ever was seen, and such that from that young age, with wonderful and praiseworthy beginnings, she has given so great an expectation of her that it is not possible to hope for more from any princess of the earth.

101. THE QUEEN'S DOCTOR

In December 1548 Giovanni Ferrerio writes, in Latin, to his patron, Bishop Reid of Orkney, concerning the appointment of a physician for the six-year-old Queen, who, a few months before, had been sent to the French court.

Bishop Reid was one of the best of the Catholic Reformers. He was a diplomat who had represented Scotland at the courts of France and England and those of Italy, and a scholar who had founded Kirkwall High School, and taken the first steps towards the founding of a university in the capital. Ferrerio was a Piedmontese scholar whom he had brought to Scotland, and who had written the lives of the abbots of Reid's former abbey of Kinloss.

Above all, we must have a care of the little lass your Queen. I foretell for her, and much desire, that she may one day fill the place of both her parents, to the great advantage of both France and Scotland. Inquiries are being made here about a doctor, such as princes are wont to appoint, who after the manner of courts shall have care of her health. Many Frenchmen desire the post, but it seems to me not very sensible, nor much to the convenience of the Queen. Most of them do not take their art seriously, or are little fit to understand the Scottish constitution, and are likely to do more harm than good to the little Queen. One only is a Scot, William Boig, M.D. In learning he will bear comparison with any Frenchman, and he is easily the first of them when it comes to understanding a Scottish constitution. All the Scots at court are eager that he should be appointed :

but the man, being modest, hesitates to accept so grave a charge until he has the Queen-Mother's consent. But as he cannot easily find a man well-known and of authority to procure it for him, he has begged me to ask you not to fail him—rather, not to fail the small Queen—in the matter.

I know well that the Queen-Mother holds you in such esteem that she will not refuse any favour that has your backing. A most important point is that Lady Fleming [1] could not conveniently explain the little Queen's ailments, should she have any, except in her own language to a Scotsman : and to ensure good health it is necessary to diagnose the condition of the body.

But perhaps I am needlessly prolix. You are not unaware what a difference there is between foreign physicians and those of one's own country. And beyond being of your nation, [Dr Boig] is a skilled physician and apothecary, and above all a lover of religion and of his own country's freedom. What you do for him, I count as done for me. Farewell.

The good Dr Boig, however, was not appointed.

102. THE CHILD QUEEN GROWS

This letter is from Anne d'Este, Duchesse d'Aumale (the Princess of Ferrara of the little Duc de Longueville's letter on p. 154) to her sister-in-law the Queen Dowager of Scots. It seems to have been written some time after the latter's visit to France in 1551, when Mary was eight.

Madame, Monsieur de Glasgow going towards you, I would not neglect to recall myself to your good grace and remembrance. Monseigneur the Cardinal is so much wont to send you all news that I will send you none—also because I do not really know

---

[1] Lady Fleming, Mary's governess, was also her aunt by the half-blood, being a daughter, on the wrong side of the blanket, of James IV. Her mother was a granddaughter of Queen Joan Beaufort, her daughter one of the Four Maries . . . and she herself was a half-sister of Bothwell, her mother having married the Fair Earl, who had once courted Marie de Guise. It is a queer tangle of relationships.

any !—and will assure you only, Madame, that you have the most lovely and charming little Queen that I think can be in all the world.   I believe you would have great happiness if you saw her, for one must think no longer of treating her as a child.   Her talk and behaviour have nothing childish in them.   I wish well that my daughter were older, to have the honour of being in her suite to serve her, and also, as she has assured me that she will be as good as she can, in order that when you come again you may find her a good girl, and that she may better be able to serve you when she is with you.   I would much desire that she and my son might have the honour soon of being in your company, as you have ever been pleased to promise me.

Madame your mother says that she consents for you, but there is no other person to whom she would give them up.   In expectancy of that happy time, I beg you, Madame, to hold the children's father and mother in your good grace, to which, Madame, I beg you to receive my very humble commendations, praying God to give you as good and long life as I desire for you.

Your most humble and obedient sister,

ANNE D'ESTE.

103. MARY'S FIRST COMMUNION

This letter is from the child Mary to her mother.   It is in French, in a clear, beautiful, and careful hand, very like that of her young fiancé the Dauphin : no doubt the children had the same writing-master.   It is apparently written in 1554, when the elder Queen had just been appointed Regent : the " Governor " is the dubiously loyal Earl of Arran, her predecessor in the office.   Mary was then no more than eleven, but her elders seem to have done their best to explain to her what went on in her kingdom.

Madame, I am very pleased to have the means of being able to write you my news, being much distressed at having been so long without hearing yours.   Madame, I have heard that the Governor has submitted himself to your will, and has put into your hands the chief places of the kingdom, for which I am very pleased, and praise God daily for it, and also for that all the princes and great lords have returned to you.   I have come to Meudon to Madame my grandmother's, to keep Easter, because she and my uncle Monsieur the Cardinal are agreed that I should receive God, to Whom I pray humbly to give me the grace of a good beginning.[1]   I will not forget to tell you that the bearer of this letter has done good and pleasing service to the King.

Madame, in this place I will offer you my most humble recommendation to your good grace, praying the Creator to give you in long health a most happy life.

Your very humble and very obedient daughter,

MARIE.

104. The Crowd at the Queen's Wedding

In the binding of a 1559 *edition of Lindsay's " Monarchie " there was found a torn scrap of printed paper, apparently part of an eye-witness account of the Paris festivities at Mary's wedding to the Dauphin.   The writer may perhaps have been a Scots student, turning an honest penny by acting as " special correspondent " to some Edinburgh printer-publisher.*

. . . gold and silver amang the pepil on everie side of the scaffald within the kirk.   Quhair, with *potest capere captat*, was sic yelping and yelling, sic calling and crying, as the lyke, I think wes nevir herd.   Thair gentilmen tint thair clokis, gentil-wemen thair fartingalis, merchant men thair gownis, maisteris in art thair hudis, studentis thair cornet cappis, and religius men had thair scapularis violentlie rivin fra thair schulderis. . . . It wes ane merie sport for him that tint nathing.   And then to heir thair lamentatiounis, it wes na les sport.   Sum saying, " I haif tint my cloke worth x crounis, and gat but a teston."   Ane uthir sayis, " Alace, my goun wes plukkit fra my bak, worth vj crounis, and gat but v sous.   " The thrid sayis, " My purs is

---

[1] This phrase seems to echo Mary's personal motto, *En ma Fin est mon Commencement.*

gane, and l crounis in it, and gat nathing." "I haif gottin,"
quoth ane uthir, " a cuppill of guid crounis of the sun, and tint
nathing." Quhairfoir I, heiring and seing theis guid fellowis
having sic greit tinsal for greidines in getting of a few peicis of
money. . . . I wes forcit, not allanerlie, to say with the poet
Virgill, *Quid non mortalia pectora cogis, auri sacra fames?* Bot
also I did wish sic ane merrie companioun as Plautus wes to be
thair present, to maik a merrie clark play of thair happie
speidingis. Quhair at the beginning . . . wes also sumquhat
besie amang the rest, almaist . . . for in catching of iij soussis
. . . for a . . . king my nebouris round about me with a scharp
preen, my fortune wes (I thank God) to scaip cleir with my iij
soussis, and tint nathing, bidding thaim " Fairweill, Messieurs,
I cum na mair thair."

tinsal, loss.   *preen*, pin.

105. BRANTÔME ON MARY

*Brantôme, that chronicler of the scandals of courts, who does
not spare his own country's royal ladies, has nothing but good to
say about Queen Mary. He saw her as a girl at the French Court,
came to Scotland with her in 1561, and lived to hear of her death
at Fotheringay. This is how he writes of her in his " Dames
Illustres."*

Those who will ever write of that most illustrious Queen of
Scots will have two most ample subjects, the one that of her
life, the other that of her death : the one and the other most ill
accompanied by good fortune. . . . [Having come to France
for her greater safety] where truly that ill luck, not being able
to cross the sea with her, or not daring for the time to attack her
in France, left her so long as that kind [nurse] held her hand.
And as her fair age grew, so she was seen in her great beauty
and her great virtues, increasing in such sort that, coming to
fifteen years, her beauty began to show its fair light in the full
fair noon, and darken the sun when he shone forth most

strongly, so fair was the beauty of her body.   And as for that
of her mind, it was even the same, for she was very learned in
Latin . . . which she understood and spoke very well . . .
and was at pains to cause Antoine Fochain, of Channay in
Vermandois, to draw up for her a Rhetoric in French, which we
still have in light, so that she should better understand French
and be more eloquent in it ; as she was, and better than if she
had been born in France.   So it did one good to watch her
speak, whether to the highest or the lowest.   And so long as
she was in France, she kept always two hours a day to study
and read.[1] . . . Above all she loved poetry and poets, but
above all Monsieur de Ronsard,[2] Monsieur du Bellay, and
Monsieur de Maison-Fleur, who have made fine poems and
elegies for her . . . which I have seen her often read to herself
in France and in Scotland, tears in her eyes and sighs at her
heart.

She concerned herself to be a poet, and made verses, of
which I have seen some that were good and very well made,
and not in the least like those put on her as made on the love of
the Earl of Bothwell : [3]   these are too rude and ill-polished to
have come from her fair workshop.   Monsieur de Ronsard was
strongly of my opinion in that, as we read and discussed them
one day.[4] . . . Always, when she spoke with anyone, she used
a very gentle, dainty, and attractive speech, mingled at times
with a most discreet and modest intimacy, and especially with a
most lovely grace. . . .

Being dressed (as I have seen her) in the barbaric fashion of

[1] Even in Scotland, where she worked hard at her profession of queenship,
she read Latin regularly with George Buchanan, the greatest Latinist of Scotland,
or of Europe, to whom she showed much favour.

[2] Ronsard and Du Bellay were the chief French poets of the day, the leaders
of the famous Pléïade.   Ronsard had been in Scotland as guest of James V, and
Mary continued the friendship.

[3] These are the French poems in the Casket Letters.   Mr Robert Gore-
Browne has shown good cause to believe that they were actually the work of
Bothwell's blue-stocking Norwegian mistress, Anna Throndsen.

[4] Ronsard was the foremost critic of his day, as well as its leading poet, so
this testimony of his has a good deal of weight.

the savages of her country,[1] she seemed in a mortal body and a rude and barbaric dress, a true goddess.   Those who have seen her so dressed can confirm it in all truth, and those who have not can have seen her portrait so attired ; so that I have seen it said to the Queen Mother and the King that she showed herself still in that more fair, charming, and desirable than in any other.   How then would she appear in state, in her fair and rich adornments, whether in the French or the Spanish fashion, or with an Italian cap, or in her other gear of the full white mourning, in which it was most fair to see her, for the white of her face warred with the white of her veil which should be victor.

She had yet more, that perfection to fire the world, a voice very sweet and good, for she sang very well, according her voice with the lute, which she touched so daintily with that fair white hand.

. . . Ah, Kingdom of Scotland, I think that your days are now shorter than they were, and your nights longer, since you have lost that princess who was your light.

106. MARY'S HOLYROOD

Our Holyrood, of course, save for Mary's Tower, was rebuilt for Charles II by Sir William Bruce, and never really completed till our own time, when George V and another Queen Mary took it in hand, and made it again a stately and habitable palace.

Much is made of its shabbiness on Mary's arrival, though the historians who insist upon it seldom remark that the palace had been sacked in Mary's childhood, not so long before, by Hertford's English and Spanish and German troops.   Even its library had been effectively looted.[2]   The Queen Dowager had made no attempt

---

[1] i.e., in the Highland dress described by Bishop Lesley in § 15.

[2] Scots libraries of the day—like those of the Highland gentry in Dr Johnson's time—appear to have been fairly polyglot.   The Bishop of Orkney who married the Queen to Bothwell had (unlike his predecessor, good Bishop Reid) no special repute as a scholar: but his library included a considerable number of Latin,

to restore it—for lack of money, very probably—but had built a small lodging on the Castle Hill. Mary, with her large private means as Queen Dowager of France and Duchess of Touraine, was able to restore its dignity, so that it held its own with the houses of her nobles.[1]

The great frontal range of the palace, planned by James IV (of which Mary's Tower is the only part remaining) had never been finished : but we may assume that the palace as Hollar shows it some ninety years later, in his minutely detailed prospect of Edinburgh, is much the Holyrood of Mary's time. One can count a row of thirty-five windows in its long façade—half as many again as it has today—with a mass of irregular buildings huddled behind, out of sight of the great cour d'honneur *(which seems to be much larger than that of today), and four-storeyed, counting the row of very Scottish dormers in the roof. The Abbey Kirk stands well behind one end, its low spire still rising, while another springs from an angle of the palace courtyard, and perhaps is the belfry of the Chapel Royal. There is a huge fore-court, and, opening from it, left and right, are formal gardens, enclosed in high walls after the Scottish fashion. The larger has a gate of some stateliness and apparently a fountain in the middle : that to the south, towards Arthur's Seat, is smaller, probably the Privy Garden. The front of the Palace looks west, across the long range of formal tree-shaded gardens behind the great noble houses of the Canongate. Hollar*

Spanish, Italian, and French books, with a Hebrew Bible, which may have been ornamental. Their contents included not only theology but architecture, botany, agriculture, medicine, and law, and a couple of cookery books, in French and Latin. Bothwell himself, though essentially a man of action, cared enough for his books to have them finely bound, with his arms on the covers, and though he read his classics, it seems, in translation, he had education enough, in his stormy boyhood, to write a delicate fastidious hand of the new Italian mode, like Mary's own.

[1] We know that when Huntly's goods were forfeited after Corrichie, his possessions went to the Queen and the Earl of Moray : and, from what we know of both Moray and his wife, it is hardly likely the Queen had the pick of the basket. Yet her share included nine gorgeous beds, one hung with cloth of gold, one of crimson velvet with gold embroidery, one of black figured velvet, and others of plain velvet, violet and black, or of green, tawny, and yellow damask, or of yellow and blue taffeta silk, while there was also a good deal of fine glass, and such decorative details as statuettes.

*draws these, within their high walls, in loving detail : ana north-
ward, beyond the walls of the royal garden, is open country, lightly
wooded, with fields and the tall ships anchored in Leith Roads :
one sees Leith Walk running down through the open fields.
Hollar's foreground, to the southward of the palace, has a glimpse
of the wild rocks of Arthur's Seat : it is clear enough that the
artist felt very strongly that peculiar strangeness and magic of
Edinburgh, the urban stateliness of streets and buildings, the rich
and fertile Lothian country round it, and the wild bone of rock and
hill underlying all of it in the salt sea wind.   Hollar's drawing
tells us much of the city—and of Scotland : and though it is
actually the Edinburgh of the Covenant dictatorship, in its last
years before Cromwell shattered it, it is still substantially Mary's
Edinburgh.*[1]

*Mr J. S. Richardson, presently His Majesty's Inspector of
Ancient Monuments for Scotland, thinks that the State Apart-
ments ran across the James IV façade—the Bedchamber, with its
ante-room behind, surviving in the still surviving tower, the Privy
Chamber, Presence Chamber, Guard-hall, and Chapel running across
the front, over the main gate of entry to the courtyard, to what
should have been the corresponding tower.*

*We can visualise these rooms holding tall canopies—the mark
of royalty—in cloth of gold and silver, cloth of gold with orfrays
of cramoisie or of violet and green, one of black velvet, one of cramoisie brown and silver, and one of embroidered black satin—
though that, with its matching bed, went to the Castle.   There
were eighteen gorgeous beds, cloth of gold worked with red, cloth of
gold and silver worked with violet and grey, black velvet and cloth
of gold with little pots of flowers worked on medallions, satin of
red, blue, yellow, and white, scarlet velvet appliqué, black velvet,
gold embroidered with classical legends, white velvet with gold and
damask, incarnate damask, and a number more " not enrichit with*

---

[1] The Hollar drawing belongs to His Majesty the King, and is at Windsor,
but there is a magnificent reproduction of it in Cosmo Innes's *National Manuscripts
of Scotland.*

ony thing" but of white, green, or violet damask or red, yellow, and blue velvet. The beds, of course, were the major furniture, and in all that splendour but one chair is listed, and a few stools. People sat on carreaux—big square heavy cushions, as gorgeous as the many gorgeous table-cloths. There was much tapestry and Turkey carpets, specifically mentioned as " for the flure "—a great luxury still.

107. Queen's Braws

The Queen's wardrobe lists help us to people the rooms of the palace. She was still in mourning when she arrived in Scotland, but by the next year etiquette gave her leave to wear colours again, and though many of her dresses were still either white or cloth of silver, there are others of cramoisie, blue, grey, carnation, or yellow, while one is cloth of gold . . . though several are of a practical serge or stamming (the etamine or thin ribbed woollen stuff of our mothers) that would be suitable for a hard-riding Queen whose profession took her about the country in all weathers. There is a great royal mantle, bordered with ermine, several masking dresses—a Picard, two Spanish, and a fanciful one of carnation, white, and blue—and a warm dressing-gown of chestnut velvet trimmed with silver cord.

The gorgeous materials were, of course, but a background for the jewels that made a great lady—or lord—in full dress glitter from head to foot like an Eastern idol. A " parure " in those days was no mere necklace, earrings, and pair of bracelets. There would be a belt with long end, borders for the open-fronted skirt and bodice, another across the stiff edge of the corsage, broad chains from shoulder to shoulder, brooches, clasps, the jewelled cap-border, and the " tour," the arches that (as in the Lothian portrait of the Queen) held the veil above the shoulders in great gauze wings : in that portrait the tour is set with huge pear-shaped pearls. Mary's pearls (like those of her ancestor Alexander I) were famous : Moray sold them, when she was in Lochleven, to Elizabeth for something like £60,000 of our money, and that was a good deal below their value. A portrait in the Victoria and Albert Museum, London, shows her wearing a rope of great black ones, as big as grapes. She had also a number of " accoutrements," full sets with the pieces matched, of various stones—three of diamonds, one of rubies and diamonds, one of great rubies and pierced pearls, one of rubies, diamonds, and pearls, one of ruby roses, one of rubies, emeralds, and sapphires, and various others, down to a couple of pierced gold filigree filled with some solid scent.

In the will made before her confinement she left most of her best jewels to the Crown, specifying that some were to be worn by the Queens of Scots. They included a cross with seven large diamonds, a great table diamond in a ring, two cabochon rubies, and the Great Harry diamond—a huge faceted stone set, with a large cabochon ruby, in an H, which had been a wedding gift from her father-in-law Henri II. She had it inserted in the Scottish Crown, but years afterwards Parliament had very hard work to get it out of the clutches of Moray's widow. James VI had it mounted in a great royal jewel, called the Mirror of Britain : it disappeared under the Commonwealth, and has never been traced.

108. Mary hopes for Peace

The core of traditional Scots foreign policy was alliance with France and peace—so far as that might be compatible with freedom and independence of the country—with England. It was Mary's obvious duty to carry it on, for the French Alliance was—as her childhood had proved—essential if her Kingdom was to be saved from England's recurrent attempts at annexation ; while an English peace was equally essential if Scotland's whole energies were not to be spent in the mere securing of her national freedom. The English menace had lately become much greater through the development of artillery : but Mary, as certainly rightful heir to England, had a better chance than any predecessor of ending the war by a peaceful federation. The policy of friendship with

*two countries which themselves cordially disliked each other was a
difficult one to carry out, and the young Queen had her hands full
from the start.*

*Here she is trying to explain her position in a very long private
letter to her uncle, the Duke of Guise. It was written in January
1565, five months after her arrival in Scotland; and it rather
quaintly recalls another young Queen's correspondence with "Uncle
Leopold"—though Mary was a less submissive niece.*

*After speaking of the official French diplomats and the news of
the French court, she tells him she is enclosing copies of the letters
which have passed between Elizabeth and herself.*

She shows herself most desirous of my friendship. . . . The
Sieur de Foix, in talking to me one day (for he came once every
day without formal notice) attacked me [about this, saying]
that peace would never be as secure between two [neighbours]
so near as she and I as between the King [of France] and me ;
for not counting the Auld Alliance, he could win nothing by
making war on me ; and [Foix] told me plainly that I ought
not to forget France for my old enemy England, and said to
Du Croc that if I did I would rue it. I assured him well that
I would never do so, but that I desired her friendship as secure
as I could, seeing that she and the king [of France] were at
peace, and that she sought mine by so many good offices as
she was doing me ; and that the Queen herself had counselled
me to it, telling me that she had no means of doing anything
for me at this time, but that it would in nowise harm that which
for so many reasons I held the better. Also that all my kin,
whoever they were, urged me too much, and that they alone
were [those ?] from whom I received most : and indeed I did
not bind myself to anything. You will see by what is between
us that it comes more of good will than anything else.

*Pollen translates the last sentence as " More talk of good
wishes than anything else," but the French can hardly be made to
bear this sense, even in Mary's flying and rather ungrammatical*

scribble.   The young Queen seems to have had no suspicion that Elizabeth was doing all she could to make her position impossible in Scotland, and that not only her avowed enemies, but her most trusted counsellor, her brother, were in Elizabeth's pay—and earning it.

109. Enemy Testimony

Here are three glimpses of Mary, through the eyes of enemies who saw her daily for hours, at work and play.   The first comes from William Maitland of Lethington, the Chamaeleon, a type-figure of that Machiavellian time—a man of grace, scholarship, and courtly accomplishments, fine enough to see and value fineness in others, and completely pitiless in dragging it down if it happened to conflict with his own purpose.   Through all the reign he was in close and secret correspondence with Cecil, his opposite number at the English Court : and it is he who writes, and to Cecil himself, in the November of 1562, that his Queen is

A princesse so gentle and bening and whose behaviour hath bene always soche towards all her subjectis and every one in particular that wonder it is that any one could be found so ongracious as ones to think evill against her.[1]

This is from the English Ambassador, Randolph, one of Mary's most inveterate and skilful enemies, and one of the most fervent of her admirers.   He is writing to Cecil, about a month later.

The Queen herself, how well soever she favour her uncles, that yet she loveth better her own subjects.

And a month later again, here is Randolph once more, on a fellow-enemy whom he was using skilfully as a tool.

[Knox] is so full of mistrust in all [the Queen's] doings, words, and sayings, as though he were either of God's Privy

---

[1] The spelling is Lethington's own, and is interesting.   Not only is it—apart from the one word *subjectis*—purely English, but it is very much nearer modern English than that of most Englishmen of the time.

Council, that know how He had determined of her from the beginning, or that he knew the secrets of her heart so well that neither she did nor could have forever one good thought of God or of His true religion. Of these matters we commune oft. I yield as much as in conscience I may unto him.

110. ELIZABETH AND THE HOUSEKEEPING EXPENSES

Among the English Foreign State Papers there is a memorandum in Cecil's hand, dated the 7th October 1564, which makes one wonder just what that worthy statesman thought and felt when he took it down from his mistress's dictation. Elizabeth had at last made up her mind to put forward Lord Robert Dudley as a possible husband for Mary, and the paper begins by a definite offer of him as "meet to be bestowed in the company of Kings or princes." Mary is to be told that as she and Elizabeth cannot marry each other, it will best conserve the amity between them if Mary shall marry one whom Elizabeth loves as her brother—which was not quite how Europe saw their relation! Mary is to be assured that it is the most advantageous match she could make, as she will find no one greater "for the nobility of his house," [1] *while acceptance of it will incline Elizabeth to name Mary her heir, seeing that if it lay in her power, Elizabeth would make Lord Robert "owner or heir of her own kingdom." Finally,*

If they shall require of what sufficiency she will make Lord Robert for his private estate, they shall say she has already begun to advance him in honour and livelihood, and therein means not to deal sparingly with him. And this also shall most content her that if she, Mary, shall be conversant with her,

---

[1] Elizabeth was on the point of making Lord Robert Earl of Leicester. He was the son of a Duke, and the brother-in-law of a rather shaky claimant to the throne : but his grandfather had been a shyster lawyer whom Elizabeth's had found a convenient tool for his extortions. Mary had eleven centuries of royal descent, and at the moment was being courted by most of the sovereigns of Europe, or their heirs.

The relations, in fact, of Mary and Bothwell and of Elizabeth and Leicester, as seen by most Scots and English historians, are one of the finest illustrations extant of a certain proverb about a horse and a hedge.

Elizabeth, in this realm, and living with her, she will gladly bear the charges of the family, both of the Earl of Leicester and her, as shall be meet for one sister to do for another.

Poor Cecil, when his audience came to an end, must certainly have needed a stiff drink!

III. ENCHANTMENTS

Michel de Castelnau, who had come with the Queen to Scotland in 1561, returned three years later as envoy to press the suit of the Duc d'Anjou. He found the Queen " in the flower of her age, esteemed and adored by her subjects and courted by all her neighbours," but stayed long enough to see the Darnley marriage that began her ruin. He declares that Elizabeth " made a present " of Darnley to the Queen, but, more pardonably than a number of later historians, he does not grasp the political implications that made the match seem such an excellent stroke of statecraft, while he could and did judge the man, and did not like him.

[Darnley] sought me out as much as he could, to be favourable to his love, seeing the access I had long possessed to that princess, who did me the honour to hide nothing from me of what was proposed for her marriage, my audiences lasting from morning till evening.

It was not, all the same, my intention to sway her to that side, although I realised that the business was so far advanced that it would have been very difficult to get her out of it—whether she was urged to it, as some have seen fit to say, by magic, artificial or natural, or by the constant solicitations of the Earl of Moray and the Secretary Lethington, and others of that party, who lost no time in bringing about this marriage.

112. QUEENS' COMPLEXIONS

This letter of Mary to Elizabeth was written a couple of months after Rizzio's murder and about a month before the birth of the future James VI—that is to say, in May 1566. *Mary, thanks first to her own courage and resource and then to Bothwell's, had saved herself and her child, and ridden back to Edinburgh through cheering streets. Elizabeth had just had smallpox, and evidently wanted to know how Mary had preserved her complexion when she had had it in childhood.*

I can only congratulate myself, my good sister, on my fortune, which has not permitted that I should have more tiresomeness [*ennui*] than it has given me strength and power to bear it. So good has mingled so closely with evil that the occasion has been the sooner given me, on receipt of your letters, written with your own hand, to praise God for your health than time to regret your illness ; which I do with my whole heart, and chiefly since I have heard the great danger you were in, and how you came off so cheaply that that fair face will lose nothing of its perfection.

Randolph begged me to send you some recipe to keep it from showing, which I could not have done as I would wish, for he who dressed me is dead, and was called Fernel, First Physician to the King : and he would never tell me the recipe for the water which he put on my face, after having opened it all with a lancet : and after all, it would be too late to use it. What they did for me after, you will see in this memoir. I am very sorry I did not know it sooner, for I would have sent you him whom I consider most excellent for this, who was my man, assuring you that I would never know of anything that would serve you, but that I would do it as a good sister should, so long as I know my love rewarded by such affection.

I have no doubt of this, trusting your promises and the constancy of that heart which you have given me in exchange for mine, which I think so well employed. And on this conclusion, not to trouble you with too long discourse, I will make an end, having informed you, by the same means, of the quieting of those disturbances which for a short time have troubled me—more for pity of those whom God has so far abandoned than from fear to fall into their danger : for I trust my subjects, who have shown themselves all that I could have desired, and I hope will be the better for so clear an example of the wrath of God, which has fallen on the wicked.

I do not doubt that Randolph will have so amply given you all the news that I need not weary you with a longer letter, save to kiss your fair hands and pray God that He give you, Madame my good sister, most happy and long life, and the fortune wished you by

Your faithful and affectionate good sister and cousin forever,

MARIE R.

113. MARY AND PERSECUTION

Mary, like so many people who have tried to reconcile opposing parties, was to end in receiving the enmity of both. The Protestants from the start railed at her " tyranny," which consisted not in persecuting them, but in refusing to persecute their opponents. The Catholics were equally angry with her, because she refused to persecute Protestants. Their point of view is shown in this letter, written from Paris in March 1567. The writer was Vincenzo Laureo, Bishop of Mondovi, Papal Nuncio to Scotland and to Poland and later Cardinal Protector of Scottish Affairs at Rome. He had the best of reasons for knowing Mary's mind, for it was he who had tried to induce her to re-establish Catholicism by force. He is writing to the Cardinal Secretary of the Holy See.

. . . And if the Queen had done what was counselled and proposed to her by our party, with the promise of all the help necessary to that most just execution, she would find herself now mistress of her kingdom, with authority to restore it entirely to the Holy Catholic Faith : but she would not even hear of it, though the Bishop of Dunblane and Father Edward [1] were sent to her on purpose to persuade her to that most holy enter-

---

[1] Edward Hay, a Scots Jesuit of fine character and much charm.

prise. And please God that a forbearance so unjust may not
bring total ruin alike to Her Majesty and to that kingdom. . . .

114. WHAT WENT UP WITH DARNLEY

*This queer little end of red tape hangs from Darnley's coffin.
It is the list of royal furniture which went up in the explosion of
Kirk o' Field; and just a week after she had married Bothwell,
was presented for the Queen's counter-signature with other routine
domestic documents. The original is in French.*

Discharge of furniture which I had taken to the late King's
lodging, which furniture has been lost without any being recovered. And there was a bed-chamber, *salle*,[1] and dressing-
room, furnished as follows :

Firstly, a bed of violet velvet with double pends laced with
gold and silver, furnished with wood frame, palliasse, mattress,
bolster, and cover of blue quilted taffeta, and two other covers
and a pillow and case.

Also a small table with a green velvet cloth.

Also a high chair covered with violet velvet, seat and all.

Also sixteen pieces of tapestry, as well in his chamber as in
the *salle* and dressing-room, as well large as small.

Also in his *salle* a canopy of black velvet with double
pends.[2]

Also a high chair covered with leather.

Also a chaise percée covered with velvet, fitted with two
basins.

Also a little Turkey carpet and a chamber-pot.

Also a small bed of yellow and green damask, made crane-
fashion, with wood frame, palliasse, mattress, bolster, and its
cover quilted in green taffeta, with two other covers and a slip
and a tent of shot taffeta, in the dressing-room.

---

[1] *Salle* is not a " hall " in the modern sense, but any unspecified room : a
man writing in modern English would probably have written sitting-room.

[2] This was a specific mark of royalty.

N

Presumably there was other plenishing—there is no washing or eating tackle, for instance, no furniture for the servants, and nothing to cook with or to tend the fires : but these must have been either part of Darnley's luggage or bought for the occasion in the town.

115. MARY AND ELIZABETH

On the 1st May of 1568, the very eve of her unexpected escape, Mary wrote from Lochleven to the cousin who had promised to come to her help. The letter is a hurried scrawl, written furtively against time.

Madame my good sister, the slow passing of time in my weary prison, and the wrongs received from those to whom I have done so many benefits, is less weariful to me than to be unable to tell you the truth of my evil fortune, and of the hurts which have been done to me from many airts ; wherefore, having found the means, by a good servant here, to send you this word, I have delivered all my thought to the bearer, praying you to believe him as myself.

You remember that it has pleased you, divers times, to assure me that if you should see the ring which you sent me, you would help me in all my afflictions. You know how my brother Moray has all I own. Those who have anything agree to send me nothing : Robert Melvin at least says he dare not send it me, though I entrusted him with it secretly as my dearest jewel. For which cause I beg you, seeing these presents, to have pity on your good sister and cousin, and to be assured that you will never have a more near and loving kinswoman in this world. You can also consider the significance of the example practised against me, not only as a king or a queen, but as one of the meanest subjects.[1]

I beg you to have a care lest anyone should know that I have

[1] Mary means her imprisonment without trial : the phrase, in that context, has an appalling irony.

written to you, for that would cause me to be worse treated :
and they boast that they are warned by their friends of all you
say and do. Believe the bearer like myself. God keep you
from misfortune and give me patience and grace that I may one
day mourn to you my fortune, and say to you more than I dare
write, which may serve you no little.

From my prison this 1st May,

Your most obliged and affectionate good sister and cousin,

MARIE R.

*That letter was written on the 1st of May, this other before
that same month was over. Mary escaped from Lochleven on the
2nd. Her supporters' defeat at Langside on the 13th put an end
to her immediate hopes, and greatly strengthened her immediate
danger. Two days later she wrote a brief note to Elizabeth from
Dundrennan, and next day crossed the Solway and put herself in
the power of her professed friend and most deadly enemy. As
Scott puts it, " she judged of Elizabeth according to the manner
in which she would herself have treated the Queen of England in
the same situation."*

*Next day, rested, she wrote cheerfully from Workington. Two
days later, still as England's guest, and with royal honours, she
was taken to the stronghold of Carlisle. She waited nine days, and
then on the 28th—just under four weeks from her escape from Lochleven—Lord Scroop, the Governor, and Sir Francis Knollys brought
her Elizabeth's letters of condolence. She would not have known
yet that Elizabeth had ordered the sheriffs and justices of Cumber-
land to watch and guard her, while treating her as a guest : but
it was clear that Elizabeth had ignored her request for a meeting.
Anxious, but keeping her head and her self-control, she wrote that
day :*

Madame my good sister, I have received two of your letters,
to the first of which I hope to make answer with my own mouth :
and by Milord Scroop and your Vice-chamberlain [Knollys]
understand your natural good inclinations towards me ; which

in truth I have always promised myself, and I would that my affection towards you were as apparent as, without feigning, I truly bear it to you : and then you would think your good will better employed than I could persuade you by my own poor thanks.

Madame, I am grieved that the haste in which I wrote my last letter made me leave out, as I see by yours, the thing which chiefly moved me to write to you,[1] and which is the main cause of my coming into your kingdom : which is that having been this long time prisoner, and as I have written already, unjustly treated, I desired above all to come to you in person to make my complaint, as much for nearness of blood, likeness of rank, and profound friendship, as to clear myself in your sight of such slanderous words as they have dared to put forward against my honour, and also from the assurance I felt that beyond all these points, you would consider that, when they were banished for their crimes committed against me,[2] at your request I re-called these ungrateful subjects and restored them to their former condition, to the detriment and prejudice of my own, as then was manifest.   Thus since, in regard for you, I did what wrecked me, or came at least too near it, I may in justice turn to her who, meaning no ill, has caused the harm, so that she may repair the error which has ensued.

Now, I have sent Milord Herries, my faithful and well-loved subject, to inform you at length of all these things and of others, on which I have learned from Messieurs Scroop and Knollys that you are in doubt.   I beg you to believe him as myself, and forthwith to make me a resolved answer in writing whether it please you to find acceptable that diligently and without cere-mony I come to you, where more in detail I will tell you the

[1] She had not : but Elizabeth had ignored it.
[2] She means the Rizzio murder, which of course was obviously intended to cause her own death.   She probably still did not know that the English Govern-ment knew of it beforehand : but she did know that Elizabeth had sheltered the murderers and induced her to pardon them and receive them back in Scotland, to her own ruin.

truth of all that has happened to me, which I know you will be pleased to hear as you are pleased to write. Notwithstanding, as below you promise me by your letters to take my just cause into your own hands until you have returned me to the state to which it has pleased God to call me—I send for this purpose my cousin Milord Fleming, a faithful subject : so that, being by you assured of this, he may pass into France, and thank the King, Monsieur my good brother, for his offers and good offices, which I will reserve for another time, if I need them, as [I do those] of others in general, contenting myself with your aid and support, which I shall be no little bound, all my life, to recognise in all that is in my power.

If this is not the case (which I am certain will not be your doing, but that of some other whom I cannot judge, nor care to) at least I was certain that you would permit me, as freely as I came to throw myself into your arms as my chiefest friend, to seek aid, on your refusal, from the other princes and friends, my allies, according as it shall serve me without doing any prejudice to you, or to the old sworn friendship between us two. And whichever of these two you please shall be welcome to me—however much I prefer the one to the other—since, thank God, I do not lack good friends and neighbours in my just quarrel. Thus for me, all that matters is the delay, which (to speak to you frankly, as you do to me) I have already found somewhat harsh and strange, seeing that I have so frankly placed myself in your country, without conditions, and that, having stayed a fortnight in your castle, as almost a prisoner, I received no permission, when your councillors came, to go to you with my complaint, though I trusted you so much that I asked no more than to go to you and let you hear my true grievances.

Now, I beg you to think of what importance is my long delay ; and not to be cause of my ruin (of which, thank God, there is no other sign) make me know indeed the sincerity of your natural affection to your good sister and cousin and sworn friend. Remember, I have kept my promise ! I sent you my heart in a ring, and now I have brought you the real one, and my body with it, more surely to knit the knot that binds me to you.

Now, not to wrong the sufficiency of the bearer, in whom you may trust as in me, I will not weary you with longer discourse, save to present my affectionate remembrance to your good grace, and pray God to give you, Madame, in health, long and happy life.

From Carlisle, this xxviii of May.

Your very faithful and obliged, if it please you, good sister and cousin without change,

MARIE R.

She had news from Scotland before the letter went, and there is a postscript, very characteristic.

Since writing my letter I have had sure news that the gentlemen who call themselves Regents and Governors have proclaimed that they will seize and raze the houses of the honest party [*gens de bien*] and arrest their persons, by which you may judge how much the time I have lost is harmful to me ; for which I beg you—if at least, as I assure myself, you care for my welfare and that of this kingdom your neighbour—in all haste to inform these gentlemen that they must cease at once this persecution, for you will take a hand and maintain my just quarrel. The bearer will explain the need of this at length, and I will pray God to have you in his keeping.

I cannot forget also to thank you for the kind reception I have had in your country, chiefly from your Deputy Warden, Mr Lowther, who so far as a servant may without his master's express command, received me with all courtesy : which I beg you to show to have been pleasing to you, so that others may have no cause to do otherwise.

Mary did not, of course, get her interview with her cousin : and Fleming was refused a passport to France. The summer dragged through, and by September Mary had been tricked into

consenting to what was, in effect, her own trial in absentia—*a thing against not only international law, but English. It was first, however, put to her as a trial of her own rebels before an international commission. She did not like the idea, for the English claim to supremacy had been raised, and though the claim was not made officially it might be a* ballon d'essai : *but still the claim was not officially made, and the inquiry was her only chance of facing her accusers. She consented, and found that she was not to face them, nor was she even allowed to be so near the investigation that her Commissioners could refer to her : she was, in fact, rather farther away from them than she would be at the present in Hawaii . . . and without the telegraph.*

She did her best to counter the possible claim to supremacy : in the instructions to her Commissioners, she says, in the third article :

Or ye entir in onie conference, ye shall protest that albeit I be best contentit that the causis presentlie in difference betwix me and my disobedient subjectis be considerit and dressit be my deirest sister and cousin the Quenis Majestie of Ingland—or Hir Gracis Commissionaris auctorisit thairto, befoir al uthiris—that thairby I intend in na wayis to recognosce myself to be subject to onie judge on eird, in respect that I am ane frie Princess, having ane imperiall croun gevin to me by God, and acknawledgis na uthir superiour ; and thairfoir that I, nor my posteritie, be in na wayis prejudgit heirby.

That she took the trouble to state this so precisely, at a time when she was still not officially on her own trial, suggests that the hint at the claim to supremacy had reached her, whether officially or not. She could, of course, at any moment in the next nineteen years, have opened her door and returned, with Elizabeth's backing, to her kingdom if she would have played Johanna Baliol : but she would not even free herself by an abdication which would leave the realm to Moray and his friends. That was offered her, and she answered :

As for the resignation of my crown . . . I beg you not to weary me again, for I am resolved and deliberate rather to die than to do it : and the last word that I shall speak in my life shall be that of a Queen of Scots.

She held that resolution for nineteen years.

116. RIGHTEOUS INDIGNATION

In view of the refusal to allow Mary to confront her accusers and their evidence, there is a certain grim comedy in the anger of one of the foremost of them, Lethington, who writes to Norfolk in 1569 of the rumours which connect him (quite truthfully) with Darnley's murder :

I think thair is na natioun sa barbare whair it sall be refused ony man to be hard [*heard*] to defend himself.

117. MARY'S EMBROIDERIES

Few things bring home so well the long empty hours of frustration and inaction that, year after year, weighed down Mary's swift spirit, as this inventory of her needlework, made at Chartley in the last summer of her life. It is in French.

And first, Her Majesty's bed, containing
Six great pieces of needlework, raised with gold and silver, enriched with gold and silver sequins.

Three short hangings of the same work and fashion.

The trimmings of fringe of the said bed, in embroidery, made in tufts of bullion and sequins of gold and silver.

The seat and back of the chair for the same bed.

A table-cloth of carnation satin, worked with divers colours and purfled with silver cords and silver wire.

Three bands, and one ready to join, to edge the same table-cloth.

A cushion with yellow ground, scattered with red and white roses.

Another with white ground, with some compartments of irregular flowers.

Another, banded with work and green velvet, scattered with little silver stars.

Another, made of petit point, with a single device in the ground and several round it, of the arms of France, Scotland, Spain, and England in the four corners.

The history of Esther and Haman in a cushion.

Another cushion with a red ground, not yet raised, scattered with roses and thistles in compartments, matching the bed.[1]

Two pieces of canvas, worked with compartments of gros point in silk, for a little canopy, with its bands only traced in black paint.

Four terms [*classical heads on conventional pedestals*] in gros point.

The Seven Planets, in petit point, raised with gold and silver.

The device of the Star, in gros point, not yet finished.

The Tramontana, not yet finished.

A little cushion, made in braid stitch [*point tressé*] by the old Countess of Lennox, she being in the Tower.[2]

Fifty-two assorted flowers in petit point, drawn after nature, of which there are thirty-two not cut out, and the rest cut each in its square [i.e., ready to *appliquer*.]

124 birds of divers kinds, in petit point, also drawn from nature but not cut out.

116 others, begun to be cut out.

16 sorts of four-footed beasts, also in petit point, among which is a lion attacking a boar, which is only counted as one.

52 fishes of divers sorts.

A bed-hanging, begun, to have divers ovals put on to it.

---

[1] The rose, as an embroidery motif, was innocuous : but for Mary to hang her chief piece of furniture with roses and thistles together was a delicate reminder to her gaolers that even as prisoner she was their lawful queen.

[2] She had been imprisoned there again in 1565, on her son's marriage to Mary.

Seven figures in embroidery, representing certain ladies playing divers instruments of music.

Two ovals, to serve as border, of the same size as the said figures.

A cushion with dove-colour ground, with branches, trimmed with carnation satin and fringes.

Another cushion, in gros point, with long flaps [? *à queue de pan*] trimmed like the above-said.

Made at the manor of Chartley, the 18th July 1586, in presence of Her Majesty.

118. MARY'S SUPPORTERS

For several years, while the Queen wrote endless letters in her prison and turned from them to her endless embroideries, her supporters in Scotland were still holding out. On the 12th June 1571 the Marian lords holding the Castle of Edinburgh rode boldly into the town and even held a Parliament in the Tolbooth. They declared that the abdication the Queen had been forced to sign in Lochleven Castle had no value, having been extorted by force, and dealt vigorously with the excuses put forth by her enemies.

[The Quenis] bodie, spreit, nor sensis ar not so feblit and decayit that sche wer not abill to discharge hirself of the office God had callit her unto, as sufficientlie as onie quham thay desirit to be placit in the rowm : and ridiculus it had bein to lay upoun the schulderis of ane infant in the credill a burding quhilk hir bak culd nocht beir, [sche] beand knowen to be of sa greit pregnant wit and quik ingyne, brocht up in the maist frequentit theatir of the warld, continuallie exercisit in the tred of princelie affairis, indewit with sic wisdom and uthir natural giftis for ane prince, that hir maist malicius enemies cam nevir to that impudencie that they dirst argue hir insufficiencie to beir reul.   Quhither the Erl of Lennox [1] bak be abil to carie the

---

[1] Lennox, Darnley's father, had lately been appointed as Regent.   He was popularly known as the Sillie Regent.

heavie burdein quhilkis hir waik schulderis culd nocht beir, lat the warld juge, speciallie sic as ar acquentit with his naturalitie, and hes guid pruif how gravelie he can discours in mateiris of estait.

The followers of the Queen's Lords expressed their feelings with less of stately irony.   Here is a "rowstie rhyme" attributed to the garrison of the Castle.

Morton and all thair cumpanie,
Thoch England wald thaim fortifie,
  I cair thaim nocht ane leik.
For all thair greit munitioun,
I am in sure tuitioun
    This hald it sall me keip.
    My realm and princeis libertie
      Thairin I sall defend,
    Quhan traitouris sall hangit be
      Or maik sum schameful end.
        Assure thaim, I cure thaim
          Evin as thay do deserve.
        Thair tresoun, this sesoun,
          It sall nocht maik me swerve.

For I haif men and meit eneuch.
Thay knaw I am ane tuilzeour teuch,
  And wil be richt sune grevit.
Quhan thay haif tint als monie teith
As thay did at the siege of Leith,
  Thay wil be fain to leive it.
    Than quha, I pray ye, sal be boun
      Thair tinsal to advance,
    Or get sic compositioun
      As thay gat then of France ?

> Thus fylit, begylit,
>   Thay will bot get the glaiks.
> Cum thay heir, this twa yeir,
>   Thay sall not miss thair paiks.

cure, care for.   *tuilzeour*, etc., a bonny fechter and quick to take offence.
tinsal, loss.   *compositioun*, agreement.   *get the glaiks*, be " done."

119. THE RIGHTEOUS MAN

English cannon breached the Castle at last, and its wells were poisoned. Mary's last supporters died or surrendered, and she remained in prison.   For fifteen years her gaoler was the Earl of Shrewsbury, an honest gentleman who treated her with all the courtesy consisting with his obligation to hold her prisoner.   Her enemies disliked him : so long as she was under Shrewsbury's charge, there was no prospect of any success in plots for her—but also for none against her.   As early as 1576 Mary was writing to the Archbishop of Glasgow that Leicester was trying to get her out of Shrewsbury's hands.   In 1585 he succeeded ; she was put in the charge of Leicester's creature, Sir Amyas Paulett.

Paulett's reports on her draw his own portrait clearly.   He can complain vigorously enough on his own accord of the damp and cold of moated Tutbury, but when Mary, who had been laid up for five weeks with sciatica, makes the same complaint, he is extremely cross.

She importeth her lameness, and all her disease, to this house, although indeed she brought the same hither with her.   But I told her that her passionate and discontented mind did more increase her sickness than the coldness of this house, or any other thing whatsoever.

In the February of 1586, Sir Francis Walsingham, Elizabeth's Secretary of State—like Paulett, a devout Puritan—wrote to Paulett and his associate Sir Drew Drury :

After our hearty commendation, we find by speech lately uttered by Her Majesty that she doth note in you both a lack of that care and zeal in her service that she looketh for, in that you have not in all this time, of yourselves, without other provocation, found out some way to shorten the life of that Queen, considering the great peril she is subject to hourly, so long as the said Queen shall live. Wherein, besides a kind of lack of love towards her, she noteth greatly that you have not that care of your own particular safeties, or rather of the preservation of religion and the public good and prosperity of your country, that reason and policy commandeth, especially having so good a warrant and ground for the satisfaction of your consciences towards God and the discharge of your credit and reputation towards the world. . . .

We commit you to the protection of the Almighty.

Francis Walsingham.
William Davison.

Poor Paulett, knowing that his career was wrecked if he refused and that his neck would answer if he obliged, declined " to shed blood without law or warrant," and took his feelings out on his prisoner, by a careful campaign of petty insults and privation; and Walsingham had to try his second string.

He was head of the elaborate spy system that underlay all English public life : and one of his agents, under Walsingham's own constant supervision, had inveigled several young Catholic hotheads into a plot to free Mary and depose—and in the end to murder—Elizabeth. They were most carefully put in touch with Mary, in the hope that she would give scope for a capital charge. To Walsingham's fierce anger and disappointment, the conspirators would not make her privy to the murder part of the plot. She and they talked freely about her escape, and she certainly countenanced the kidnapping of Elizabeth : but nothing could be construed into knowledge of murder. At last came a copy of a letter of Mary's, on which Walsingham gleefully drew a little gallows. One sentence in it implies that she did know : but whether she wrote it in the original letter—as she swore she did not—or whether the desperate agent provocateur *inserted it in order to save his neck, has never been proved with any certainty.* One may observe, however, that the crucial sentence, on which all depends, contradicts the assumption made through the rest of the letter—that Elizabeth will still be alive after the plot has been carried out. Also, Mary, at this trial, was allowed to appear, although she was not permitted legal assistance or to confront the witnesses against her. She challenged Walsingham with forging this sentence. He denied it on oath : but the form that the oath took was not a denial that the sentence was forged, but denial that he had done anything "unworthy of his place." Walsingham was too sincerely religious a man to swear falsely in the name of God : but he had not considered it unworthy of his place deliberately to sacrifice the lives of several young Englishmen in order to lure Mary to her death. Mary, and most of the court, did not know that : but we do.

It was in August 1586 that the trap was sprung. The conspirators were arrested, and Mary was carried off from Chartley to Tixall, while her papers were ransacked and her secretaries Nau and Curle arrested. She returned to find Curle's wife, her bedchamber woman Barbara Mowbray, was in bed with a new-born baby, while her husband was on his way to the rack. Paulett describes what happened.

Sir,

This lady was removed hither the 25th of this present. . . . She visited Curle's wife, who was delivered of a child in her absence, before she went to her own chamber, willing her to be of good comfort, and that she would answer for her husband in all things that might be excepted against him. Curle's child remaining unchristened and the priest removed before the arrival of this lady, she desired that my minister might baptise the child, with such godfathers and godmothers as I would procure, so as the child would bear her name ;

which being refused, she came shortly after into Curle's wife's chamber, where laying the child on her knees she took water out of a basin, and casting it upon the face of the child, she said " I baptise thee in the name of the Father, the Son, and the Holy Ghost," calling the child by her own name Mary. This may not be found strange in her who maketh no conscience to break the laws of God and man. . . .

The Catholic Church of course, recognises lay baptism in emergencies : but Paulett was quite sincerely horrified, and it may have been for this reason that when he soon after cut down the Queen's entourage, Mrs Curle heads the list of the women who must go.

Nearly ten years later her brother had a hand in the rescue of Kinmont Willie from Carlisle. One feels that it must have given him satisfaction. Barbara, and her sister-in-law Elizabeth—one of the two women who attended the Queen on the scaffold—are buried in the same grave in St Andrew's, Antwerp, with a fine enamel portrait of their mistress set in their monument.

120. The Unrighteous Woman

On the 25th October 1586 Mary was sentenced to death. The sentence was not carried out till the first day of the following February, and meanwhile Mary greatly annoyed the good Paulett by her indifference to the imminent axe. He had taken down the canopy of her dais—the mark of her queenship, to which she had clung through all her imprisonment—on the grounds that now she was merely a dead woman. Mary hung in its place a picture of the Passion, and Paulett, furious, wrote to Walsingham :

This lady continueth in her former wilful and wicked disposition. No outward sign of repentance, no submission, no acknowledging of her fault, no craving of pardon, no mention of desire of life ; so as it may be feared lest as she hath lived, so she will die, and I pray God that this Popish ignorant priest be not admitted to her.

121. Comment s'en va une Reine

In those slow months, with the axe hanging over her head, Mary wrote on a leaf of her Hours of the Blessed Virgin :

O Domine Deus,
   Speravi in te :
O care mi Jesu,
   Nunc libera me.
In dura catena,
In misera poena,
   Desidero te.
Languendo, gemendo,
Et genu flectendo,
Adoro, imploro
   Ut liberes me.

But if her hopes were fixed on the next world, she did not forget the care of her friends in this.   Near midnight on her last night on earth, she wrote thus to Henri III, the King of France :

Monsieur my brother-in-law, having by God's permission—for my sins as I think—come to throw myself into the arms of this Queen my cousin, where I have had many weary troubles and passed near twenty years, I am at last, by her and her Estates, condemned to death : and having claimed my papers, by them removed, in order to make my will, I have not been able to recover anything which would serve, nor to win leave to make one freely, nor that after death my body should be borne, as I desire, into your kingdom, where I have had the honour to be Queen, your sister, and your ally from of old [*ancienne alliée*].

Today, after dinner, my sentence has been announced to me, of being executed tomorrow as a criminal, at eight in the morning.   I have not had leisure to give you a full account of all that has happened : but if you will please to believe my physician and these others my forlorn servants, you will hear the truth : as, thanks be to God, I despise death, and faithfully protest that I receive it innocent of all crime, even supposing I were in their jurisdiction. The Catholic religion, and the upholding of the right to this Crown which God has given me, are the two causes of my condemnation : none the less they will not let me say that it is for the Catholic religion I die, but for fear of a change in theirs : and for proof of this they have taken away my chaplain, whom, though he is in the house, I could not make them let me have to confess me, or to give me the Last Sacrament : but they have strongly urged me to receive the consolation and doctrine of a minister of theirs brought here on purpose. The bearer of this, and his companions, mostly your own subjects, will witness to you how I bear myself in this my last action.

It remains for me to beg you, as Most Christian King, my brother-in-law and old ally, who have always protested your affection for me, that you now make proof in all these points of your goodness, as much in Christian charity, easing my mind in the discharging of my conscience, which without you I cannot achieve : which is to reward my forlorn servants, leaving them their wages, and further to obtain prayers for a Queen who has once borne the title of Most Christian, and who dies a Catholic, stripped of all her goods. As for my son, I recommend him to you as he shall deserve, for I cannot answer for him. I have ventured to send you two rare stones, good for the health, desiring that for you with long and happy life. You will accept them as from your most affectionate good-sister, who dying bears witness of her good heart to you. Once more I recommend to you my servants. You will order, if you please, that for my soul's good I shall be paid a part of what you owe me, and that in honour of Jesus Christ, Whom tomorrow, at my death, I shall pray for you, you will leave me as much as will found an obit, and will make the needful alms.

This Wednesday, at two hours after midnight.

Your most affectionate and good sister,

MARIE R.

o

Then, with six hours to live, she wrote this very business-like memorandum, to enclose in the letter.

Memorandum of the last requests which I make to the King.

To have paid to me both what he owes me of my pensions, and the money advanced by the late Queen my mother, in Scotland, for the service of the King my father-in-law ; at the least so much that an obit should be founded for my soul, and that the alms and small foundations promised by me should be completed.

Further, that it will please him to leave me the use of my jointure for a year after my death, to reward my servants.

Further, if it please him, to leave them their pensions for their life-time, as was done to the officers of Queen Eleanor.[1]

Further, I beg him to receive my physician to his own service.

Further, that my chaplain be restored to his position, and for regard to me, provided with some small benefice, to pray God for my soul for the rest of his life.

Further, that Didier, an old officer of my kitchen, to whom I have given a clerkship as reward, may enjoy it while he lives, being already of great age.

Made the morning of my death, this Wednesday 8th February.

So signed,

Marie R.

Within six hours she had entered the great hall. This is the official eye-witness account of what happened, probably written for Burghley, since it is endorsed by him, " 8 Feb. 1586. The Manner of the Q. of Scots death at Fodringhay, wrn. by Ro. Wy."—probably Robert Wingfield. It is not so well known as some other descriptions more or less founded on it.

First, the said Scottish Queen, carried by [2] two of Sir Amyas Paulett's gentlemen, the Sheriff going before her, came most

---

[1] Henri's step-grandmother, widow of Francis I.   [2] Brought.

willingly out of her chamber into an entry next the hall, at which place the Earl of Shrewsbury and the Earl of Kent, Commissioners for the execution, with the two governors of her person and divers knights and gentlemen did meet her, where they found one of the Scottish Queen's servants, named Melvin, kneeling on his knees, who uttered these words with tears to the Queen of Scots his mistress : " Madam, it will be the sorrowfullest message that ever I carried, when I shall report that my Queen and dearest mistress is dead." Then the Queen of Scots, shedding tears, answered him, " You ought rather to rejoice than weep, for that the end of Mary Stewart's troubles is now come. Thou knowest, Melvin, that all this world is but vanity and full of troubles and sorrows : carry this message from me to my friends, that I die a true woman to my religion, and like a true Scottish woman and a true French woman. But God forgive them that have long desired my end ; and He that is the true judge of all secret thoughts knoweth my mind, how that ever it hath been my desire to have Scotland and England united together. Commend me to my son, and tell him that I have not done any thing that may prejudice his kingdom of Scotland : and so, good Melvin, farewell," and kissing him, she bade him pray for her.[1]

Then she turned her to the Lords, and told them that she had certain requests to make of them. One was for a sum of money which she said Sir Amyas Paulett knew of, to be paid to one Curle her servant ; next that all her poor servants might

[1] The Earl of Kent and Mr Beale, reporting to the English Privy Council, give this scene rather differently. " At the stairs foot she paused to speak to Melville in our hearing, which was to this effect. ' Melville, as thou hast been an honest servant unto me, so I pray thee to continue to my son, and commend me unto him. I have not impugned his religion nor the religion of others, but wish him well. And as I forgive all that have offended me in Scotland, so I would he should also, and beseech God that He would send him His Holy Spirit and illuminate him.' Melville's answer was that he would do so, and at that instant he would beseech God to illuminate him with His Spirit. Then she demanded to speak with her priest : which was denied her, the rather for that she came with a superstitious pair of beads and a crucifix." The two versions are not incompatible : this suggests that Kent and Beale came up to see what was stopping the procession, and heard only the last part of what she said.

enjoy that quietly which by her will and testament she had given unto them ; and lastly that they might be all well intreated, and sent home safely and honestly into their countries. " And this I conjure you, my lords, to do."

Answer was made by Sir Amyas Paulett, " I do well remember the money Your Grace speaketh of, and Your Grace need not to make any doubt of the not performance of your requests, for I do surely think they shall be granted."

" I have," said she, " one other request to make unto you, my lords, that you will suffer my poor servants to be present about me at my death, that they may report when they come into their countries that I died a true woman unto my religion."

Then the Earl of Kent, one of the Commissioners, answered, " Madam, it cannot well be granted, for that it is feared lest some of them would with speeches both trouble and grieve Your Grace, and disquiet the company, of which we have already had some experience, or seek to wipe their napkins in some of your blood, which were not convenient." " My lord," said the Queen of Scots, " I will give my word and promise for them that they should not do any such thing as your lordship hath named. Alas, poor souls, it would do them good to bid me farewell. And I hope your mistress, being a maiden Queen, in regard of womanhood will suffer me to have some of my own people about me at my death. And I know she hath not given you so strict a commission but that you may grant me more than this, if I were a far meaner woman than I am." And then (seeming to be grieved) with some tears uttered these words : " You know that I am cousin to your Queen, and descended from the blood of Henry VII, a married Queen of France, and the anointed Queen of Scotland."

Wherefore, after some consultation, they granted her that she might have some of her servants, according to Her Grace's request, and therefore desired her to make choice of half a dozen of her men and women. Who presently said that of her men she would have Melvin, her apothecary, her surgeon, and one other old man besides, and of her women, those two that did use to lie in her chamber.

After this, she being supported by Sir Amyas' two gentlemen aforesaid, and Melvin carrying up her train, and also accompanied with all the lords, knights, and gentlemen aforenamed, the Sheriff going before her, she passed out of the entry into the great hall, with her countenance careless, importing rather mirth than mournful cheer, so she willingly stepped up to the scaffold which was prepared for her in the hall, being two feet high and twelve feet broad, with rails round about, hanged and covered with black, with a low stool, long cushion, and block, covered with black also. Then, having the stool brought her, she sat her down; by her, on the right hand, sat the Earl of Shrewsbury and the Earl of Kent, and on the left hand stood the Sheriff, and before her the two executioners; round about the rails stood knights, gentlemen, and others.

Then silence being made, the Queen's Majesty's Commission for the execution of the Queen of Scots was openly read by Mr Beale, Clerk of the Council, and these words pronounced by the assembly, " God save the Queen." During the reading of which Commission the Queen of Scots was silent, listening unto it with as small regard as if it had not concerned her at all, and with as cheerful a countenance as if it had been a pardon from Her Majesty for her life; using as much strangeness [1] in word and deed as if she had never known any of the assembly, or had been ignorant of the English language.

Then one Dr Fletcher, Dean of Peterborough, standing directly before her, without the rail, bending his body with great reverence, began to utter this exhortation following, " Madame, the Queen's most excellent Majesty, etc.," and iterating these words three or four times, she told him, " Mr Dean, I am settled in the ancient Catholic Roman religion, and mind to spend my blood in defence of it." Then Mr Dean said, " Madame, change your opinion and repent you of your former

[1] Indifference.

wickedness, and settle your faith only in Jesus Christ, by Him
to be saved." Then she answered again and again, "Mr Dean,
trouble not yourself any more, for I am settled and resolved in
this my religion, and am purposed therein to die." Then the
Earl of Shrewsbury and the Earl of Kent, preceiving her so
obstinate, told her that since she would not hear the exhortation
begun by Mr Dean, "We will pray for Your Grace, that it
stand with God's will that you may have your heart lightened,
even at this last hour, with the true kingdom of God, and so
die therein." Then she answered, "If you will pray for me,
my lords, I will thank you : but to join in prayer with you I
will not, for that you and I are not of one religion."

Then the lords called for Mr Dean, who kneeling on the
scaffold stairs began this prayer, "O most gracious God and
merciful Father, etc.," all the assembly, saving the Queen of
Scots and her servants, saying after him. During the saying of
which prayer, the Queen of Scots sitting upon a stool, having
about her neck an Agnus Dei, in her hand a crucifix, at her
girdle a pair of beads with a golden cross at the end of them, a
Latin book in her hand, began with tears and with loud and fast
voice to pray in Latin ; and in the midst of her prayers she
slided off from her stool, and kneeling, said divers Latin prayers,
and after the end of Mr Dean's prayer, she, kneeling, prayed in
English to this effect, for Christ His afflicted Church, and for
an end of their troubles ; for her son, and for the Queen's
Majesty, that she might prosper and serve God aright. She
confessed that she hoped to be saved by and in the blood of
Christ, at the foot of Whose crucifix she would shed her blood.
Then said the Earl of Kent, "Madam, settle Christ Jesus in your
heart, and leave these trumperies." Then she, little regarding
or not at all, went forward with her prayers, desiring that God
would avert His wrath from this Island, and that he would give
her grief and forgiveness for her sins. These with other prayers
she made in English, saying she forgave her enemies with all
her heart that had long sought her blood, and desired God to

convert them to the truth ; and in the end of her prayer she desired all saints to make intercession for her to Jesus Christ, and so kissing the crucifix and crossing of her also, said these words, " Even as Thy arms, O Jesu, were spread here upon the Cross, so receive me into Thy arms of mercy, and forgive me all my sins."

Her prayer being ended, the executioners kneeling desired Her Grace to forgive them her death, who answered " I forgive you with all my heart, for now, I hope, you shall make an end of all my troubles." Then they, with her two women, helping of her up, began to disrobe her of her apparel ; then she laying the crucifix upon the stool, one of the executioners took from her neck the Agnus Dei, which she laying hands of, gave it to one of her women, and told the executioner he should be answered money for it. Then she suffered them, with her two women, to disrobe her of her chain of pomander beads and all other her apparel most willingly, and with joy rather than sorrow helped to make unready [1] herself, putting on a pair of sleeves with her own hands which they had pulled off, and that with some haste, as if she had longed to be gone.

All this time they were pulling off her apparel, she never changed her countenance, but with smiling cheer she uttered these words, that she never had such grooms to make her unready, and that she never put off her clothes before such a company.

Then she being stripped of all her apparel saving her petticoat and kirtle,[2] her two women beholding her made great lamentation, and crying and crossing themselves, prayed in

[1] Undress.
[2] Froude declares that when her black dress was removed she wore " Blood red from head to foot " and is very wroth about the melodramatic choice. Actually, we know that she wore a black satin bodice and a petticoat of " cramoisie brun " or dark red-brown velvet, banded with black. We know from Blackwood that she dressed for her death " as fittingly as she could and better than ordinary," and that she told her maids, " My dears, I would rather have left you this ' accoutrement ' than that of yesterday, if it had not been that I must go with some dignity to my death, and wear something more than my dress of everyday."

Latin. She turning herself to them, embracing them, said these words in French, " Ne criez vous, j'ai promis pour vous," and so crossing and kissing them, bade them pray for her and rejoice, and not weep, for that now they should see an end of all their mistress' troubles.

Then she, with a smiling countenance, turned to her men servants, as Melvin and the rest, standing upon a bench nigh to the scaffold, who sometimes weeping, sometimes crying out aloud, and continually crossing themselves, prayed in Latin, and crossing them with her hand bade them farewell, wishing them to pray for her even until the last hour.

This done, one of the women, having a Corpus Christi cloth lapped up three-corner-ways, kissing it, put it over the Queen of Scots' face, and pinned it fast to the caul of her head. Then the two women departed from her, she kneeling down upon the cushion most resolutely and without any token or fear of death, she spake aloud this psalm in Latin, " In te Domine confido, non confundar in aeternum, etc." [1]   Then groping for the block, she laid down her head, putting her chin over the block with both her hands, which holding there still, had been cut off had they not been spied. Then lying upon the block most quietly, and stretching out her arms, cried " In manus tuas, Domine," three or four times. Then she lying very still upon the block, one of the executioners holding of her slightly with one of his hands, she endured two strokes of the other executioner his axe, she making very small noise or none at all, and not stirring any part of her from the place where she lay ; and so the executioner cut off her head, saving one little gristle, which being cut in sunder, he lift up her head to the view of all the assembly, saying " God save the Queen."

Then her dressing of lawn falling off from her head, it appeared as grey as one of three score and ten years old, polled very short, her face in a moment by so much altered from the form she had when she was alive, as few could remember her

[1] Probably Psalm XXXI.   Her last words, *In manus tuas*, open the 6th verse.

by her dead face. Her lips stirred up and down for a quarter of an hour after her head was cut off.

Then Mr Dean said with a loud voice, " So perish all the Queen's enemies," and afterwards the Earl of Kent came to the dead body, and standing over it, said with a loud voice, " Such end of all the Queen's and the Gospel enemies."

Then one of the executioners, pulling off her garters, espied her little dog, which was crept under her clothes, which could not be got forth but by force, yet afterwards would not depart with the dead corpse, but came and lay between her head and her shoulders, which being imbrued with her blood was carried away and washed, as all things else were that had any blood was either burned or clean washed, and the executioners sent away with money for their fees, not having any one thing that belonged to her. And so, every man being commanded out of the hall, except the Sheriff and his men, she was carried by them up into a great chamber, lying ready for the surgeons to embalm her.

In a little collection of French and Latin elegies on Mary, published soon after, there is this epitaph :

> Marie, honneur du siècle, et son deuil larmoyable,
>   Qui d'un Roi des Français l'Épouse avait été,
>   Admirable en esprit, non pareille en beauté,
> Sans chef gît en ce lieu par un acte incroyable. . . .

> La majesté des rois, sa foi toujours entière,
>   Ses beautés qui pouvaient les tigres convertir,
>   Le droit des suppliants, ne l'ont su garantir
> Dans le propre pays dont elle est héritière.

122. THE POET AND THE KING

Mary's son and Darnley's—and George Buchanan's pupil— cuts an uninspiring figure beside his mother. But he was not the traditional Pantaloon. He had his oddities, and his own age laughed at them : but when Sully, that shrewd judge of a man, heard him described as a fool he dryly observed that James was the wisest fool in Christendom. He was, in fact, an able politician—the fact that he died in his bed is proof of that—and he had at least enough of the statesman's vision to care really and deeply for European peace and to risk his own popularity to seek it.

James was the patron of learned men at home, and the corre-spondent of others abroad. Here is a letter to the young scholar King of twenty-three from Du Bartas, the chief French writer on the Huguenot side. James had translated his long poem " Uranie," and he had replied by translating James's " Lepanto." The date of the letter is 1589.

Sire, I know not whether I should or should not write to you. If I write not, you will lay that to my scorn of your commands, and if I write, I can have no other theme than an Iliad of Mars. Yet better that the calamity of the time should excuse to you my disagreeable letter, than that silence should proclaim my disobedience. France falls from fever to plague. The King dare not, we cannot, our enemies will not cure her. The kingdom turns little by little into desert, Guyenne, Languedoc and Dauphiné by open warfare, and the other provinces by plague and famine. O thrice and four times happy your Scotland, which under a wise prince enjoys a peaceful repose ! But let us change quickly, so that my partner, whom I have by no means yet lost sight of, shall have settled his affairs. I go to caress the Muses in their dwelling of Le Bartas, meaning to pay my court to no prince in the world, save only to my Apollo of Scotland, to whom I shall speak by the blow-pipe of my pen.

Sire, adieu, from Nérac this 25th February.

The more I am in company with the Laird of Wemyss [1]

---

[1] Wemyss was the Scottish Ambassador to the future Henri IV, still King of Navarre, with a tiny court at Nérac . . . and cultivating Scotland at the moment, as he wished to marry his sister to King James, who declined the match, but was later to marry his son to Henri's daughter.

[*Oims*] the more I know him devoted to your service. It is why I beg you to remember the promise Your Majesty has made to me in his favour.   Your

                              DU BARTAS.

123. THE KING AND POETRY

James VI was not only a genuine classical scholar, but a patron and friend of the vernacular. When still in his teens he had written the pioneer critical treatise of British letters on the technique of vernacular poetry. (We are rather apt to forget that the great English outburst of the Elizabethan Age does not dawn till the Queen had been twenty years on her throne.) His " Reulis and Cautelis . . . in Scottis Poesie" is not inspired : but it is a piece of genuine analytic criticism, for which no pattern existed in Great Britain. His own versifying was mediocre, but in his youth he produced a good deal of it, even a verse masque for the Earl of Huntly's wedding.

This sonnet of his comes from a MS. collection apparently made by his son Charles as a boy. It was written for his young bride, Anne of Denmark and Norway, and if it lacks inspiration it has, when one recalls the writer's grim youth, a pathos that is genuine enough.

> As on the wings of your enchanting fame
> I was transported o'er the stormy seas,
> Who could not quench that restless burning flame
> Which only ye by sympathy did mease ; [1]
> So can I troubled be with no disease,
> But ye my only Mediciner remains,
> And easily whenever that ye please
> May salve my sores and mitigate my pains.
> Your smiling is an antidote agains
> The melancholy that oppresseth me,
> And when a raging wrath into me reigns,
> Your loving looks may make me calm to be.

[1] Allay.

How oft you see me have an heavy heart,
Remember then, sweet Doctor, on your art.

124. THE TRUE KING

*In the " Basilikon Doron," the treatise on kingship written for
his small son, James goes to the root of the conflict between types of
government with an aphorism good for our age to remember, even
if for king we must substitute committee.*

The true difference between a lawful good king and a usurping tyrant . . . The one acknowledgeth himself ordained for
his people, having received from God a burthen of government
whereof he must be accountable : the other thinketh his people
ordained for him.

125. KING AND PROPHETESS

*In 1592, when the Saints had just attained the height of their
power, a damsel of eighteen named Helen Guthrie, the daughter of
a saddler in Aberdeen, conceived herself called on to rebuke the
King. She waited for him as he went to see his hounds, and put
her remonstrance into the royal hands.*

In the name of the Father, the Sonne, and the Holie Ghost,
I lat you to wit that our mightie Father of Hevin hes bestowit
the gift and grace of trew repentance upoun me to lat you to
wit that ye abuis his godlie law and turnis nocht to amend ;
lang delay ye maik in turning. In the name of our Hevinlie
Father, Master, and Saviour Jesus, of quhome I haif this toward
us all, in the name of God luik that ye be diligent to set furth
that godlie law, and do ye be it, quhilk ye haif nocht done
heirintil. Repent : turn in tyme : spend na mair tyme in
vaine be mannis wisdome. . . . Taik tent in tyme, for ye be
far in the wrang. . . .

do ye be it, act according to it.

*And so on, to the length of nearly four octavo pages of print.
Had she presented the like to Andrew Melville, it is probable that
the lady would have fared ill.   James merely laughed till he could
hardly stand, swore cheerfully—for which she scolded him—and
sent her to the Queen, with instructions that she should be kindly
treated.   Her Majesty's remarks are not on record.*

126. PROPHET AND KING

*Everyone knows that Andrew Melville called King James
God's silly vassal :* [1] *but few know the circumstances in which the
epithet was used.*

*It was the core of the whole Scottish doctrine of kingship that the
Crown hooped together the various disparate elements in the nation,
by holding the balance equally between them, and preventing any
from dominating the rest to its own advantage.   It was the policy
that had ruined Mary, but it was to save France under Henri IV:
and had James's son been wiser, it might have saved Scotland.
James, on his reaching power, had attempted it, and had thereby
clashed with the religious Left, who claimed to be sole rulers of king
and kingdom . . . and were closely allied with the Auld Enemy.
They desired the forcible conversion or the extermination of all
Scots Catholics :   and James considered that he was King of Scots
of both faiths.*

Here is Melville's speech, as reported in his nephew's diary :

Mr Andro boir doun [the King] and utterit the commissioun
as from the michtie God, calling the King bot Goddis sillie
vassal, and taiking him be the sleive, sayis this in effect, throw
mekill hat resouning and monie interruptionis : Sir, we will
humblie reverence Your Majestie alwayis, namelie in publict :
but sen we haif this occasioun to be with Your Majestie in privat,

---

[1] The modern change in the meaning of the word makes Melville more
discourteous than he was. " Sillie " in those days meant feeble rather than
foolish.

and the truth is, ye ar brocht in extreim danger baith of your lyf and croun, and with yow the countrey and kirk of Christ is lyk to wrak, for nocht telling yow the treuth and giffing yow a faithfull counsel, we maun dischairge our dewtie thairin or els be traitoris, baith to Christ and yow.

And thairfoir, Sir, as divers tymis befoir, sa now again, I maun tell yow, thair is twa kingis and twa kingdomis in Scotland. Thair is Christ Jesus the King, and His kingdom the kirk, quhais subject King James the saxt is, and of quhais kingdom nocht a king, nor a lord, nor heid, bot a member. And thay quham Christ hes callit and commandit to watch over His kirk, and govern His spirituall kingdom, hes sufficient power of Him and auctoritie sa to do, baith togidder and severallie, the quhilk na Cristen king nor prince sould controll and dischairge, bot fortifie and assist, utherwayis nocht faithfull subjectis nor memberis of Christ.

And Sir, quhen ye war in your swadling cloutis, Christ Jesus rang frielie in this land, in spite of all his enemeis, and his officeris and ministeris convenit and assemblit for the ruling and weill of His Kirk, quhilk wes evir for your weilfair, defens, and preservatioun, quhen thir same enemeis wes seiking your destructioun and cutting off. And in sa doing, be thair Assembleis and meittingis sinsyne continuallie, hes bein terribil to thair enemeis, and maist stedabil for yow. And will ye now, quhen thair is mair nor extreim necessitie of the continual and faithfull dischairge of that deutie, drawen to your ain destructioun be a divilish and maist pernicius counsall, begin to hinder and dishart Christis servandis, and your best and maist faithfull subjectis, quarrelling thaim for thair convening and cair that thay haif of thair dewtie to Christ and yow, quhen ye sould rather commend and countenance thaim, as the godlie kingis and guid emperouris did ?

As to the wisdom of your counsall, quhilk I call devilische and pernitious, it is this : that ye maun be servit with all sortis of men to come to your purpois and grandeur, Jew and Gentill,

Papist and Protestant; and becaus the ministerie and Protestantis in Scotland is ower stark, and controllis the King, they maun be waiknit and brocht law, be steiring up a pairtie to thaim, and the King being aequall and indifferent, baith sall be fain to flie to him, sa sal he be weil servit. Bot, Sir, gif Goddis wisdom be the onlie trew wisdom, this will pruif meir and mad folie, for His curs can bot licht upoun it, so that in seiking of baith, ye sall lois baith : quhairas in cleving uprichtlie to God, His trew servandis sould be your sure friendis, and He sould compel the rest, counterfietlie and leinglie, to gif over thaim selffis, and serve yow, as he did to David.

James Melville adds :

Thir thingis and monie utheris wes spokin be occasioun in conference, with greit libertie and vehemence, till at last the King sattlit and dismissit us plesandlie.

James had reason for pleasantness, for Melville, by stating too plainly that to him the Kingdom of Christ meant Melville as ruler of King, Kirk, and Kingdom, rallied to James not only the Right or Episcopalian Wing of the Kirk, and the Catholics to whom the King was the sole hope of lives and goods, but the large body of Centre Protestants, who still hung uncertain between the Right and the Left. The four-year-old hegemony of Melville's party, apparently assured in 1592, crumbled abruptly, the balance swinging heavily to the Right, where it remained for the whole of the next thirty years.

severallie, individually.　　*dischairge*, fulfil.　　*rang*, reigned.　　*stedabil*, advantageous.　　*dishart*, dishearten.　　*a pairtie to thaim*, a party against them, an opposition.　　*leinglie*, lyingly.

127 NAMING THE BABY

The Ambassadors of the States General of the United Provinces (of the Netherlands) report, in 1594, that the Prince of Scotland is about to be christened.

His Majesty called the [Danish] Ambassadors and ourselves aside, saying that he wished to ask our opinion. His purpose was to consult, as the custom is, with the godfathers, concerning the name to be given to the young Prince. Whereon, after various things had been deliberated, we all agreed, considering kinship and other things beside, on Frederick Henry. Frederick in respect of the grandfather on the mother's side, the late King of Denmark, and Henry in respect of the Duke of Brunswick and of Mecklenburg, grandfather of the Queen on the mother's side : item, that the King of France is also named Henry, and so is the father of the Queen of England, although her ambassador was not yet present.[1] His Majesty said to baptise him with the name of Charles James,[2] but without wishing much weight to be given his words, he being of opinion, as are many others, that the name of James was unlucky, and he had for good reason given up Charles.

128. Christening the Baby

Frederick Henry the baby duly was : and here is an account of the christening, by an English eye-witness.

The Prince was baptised the 30th of August in the new Chapel Royal at Stirling Castle, made for the ———.[3] Thither went the King and sat at the upper end of the Chapel. Before him was set a well-garnished chair, and a board whereon was painted the arms of the King of France.[4] At his right hand was set the Earl of Sussex, Ambassador for England, with a large pall over his head of red taffeta ; next unto him was set

---

[1] Elizabeth was James's godmother and also to be godmother to the Prince. It is interesting to note that while one of the baby's grandfathers is mentioned, the other—also Henry—is pointedly not.

[2] His own, after his grandfather and his mother's brother-in-law and ally Charles IX. Charles was also the name of his father's brother, Charles Stewart, Earl of Lennox.

[3] This chapel had been built by James himself.

[4] The Ambassadors of Catholic powers, of course, could not attend in person at a Protestant ceremony ; but the Auld Alliance could not go unrepresented.

Sir Robert Bowes, ordinary Ambassador for Her Majesty.[1] Then the Ambassador for the Duke of Brunswick ; and last of all the two Ambassadors for the Estates of Holland and Zeeland ; these stood behind the Earl of Sussex, the Lord Wharton, and Sir Henry Bramley, knight, for no more Englishmen got access within the Chapel.

Upon the King's left hand sat the two Ambassadors of Denmark, next unto them the Ambassadors of Magdeburg. Betwixt the Chamber and the Chapel Royal, the Prince was carried by the Earl of Sussex, and then delivered to the Duke of Lennox,[2] and was received by the Countess of —— till the time of the baptism.

Then a sermon was made in the Scots tongue by Mr Patrick Galloway, one of the King's ordinary ministers, at the beginning ; when he had finished, the Bishop of Aberdeen discoursed in Latin upon the same text, to the end that the meaning thereof should be generally understood by the Ambassadors : and in the end they proceeded to the action of Baptism. My lord Ambassador of England arose and followed the King, the rest proceeded in order towards the place where the Bishop stood, the Duke of Lennox carrying the Prince in his arms, my Lord Sempill carrying a laver, my Lord Livingstone a towel, my Lord Seton the basin, and my Lord Hume a new crown of gold, with a pall carried over their heads by four barons, viz., Cessford, Buccleuch, Traquair, and the Constable of Dundee, came also to that same place. The Duke delivered the Prince to the Earl of Sussex, the Bishop asked the King if he did present that child to be baptized and to be ingraft in the mystical body of Christ ? He answered Yea ; then the Bishop recited *Credo* in Latin to the end, he asked the name of the child, the King answered Frederick Henry and Henry Frederick, the Bishop baptized him

---

[1] Sussex was the personal representative of Elizabeth, as the baby's godmother ; hence the royal canopy. Bowes was the resident Ambassador of England at the Scottish Court.

[2] Ludovic Stuart d'Aubigny, James's second cousin, son of the dazzling Esmé Stuart of his minority.

in the name of the Father, Son, and Holy Ghost, Frederick Henry
Henry Frederick by thrice repetitions ; then the heralds proclaimed with a loud voice those same names by their repetitions ;
the trumpets blew with great noise, there being many of them.

This done, the Lords that carried the materials aforesaid
retired out of the Chapel orderly under the Prince's pall, carried
as is afore said, to the Chamber, then all the guns were shot.

After their departure there came in two gentlemen of
England carrying a basin and a ewer and a towel, and came
before the Earl of Sussex, he arose immediately in the presence
of the King, as did all, to wash his hands, which was thought
strange by the multitude and nobility.

Then the Bishop ascended, and in Latin glorified God for
that action, and thanked all the Ambassadors orderly for their
assistance, beginning at the Ambassador for England, and
consequently to the rest (the copy which I think to obtain).
This done they went all forth in order to the Prince's Chamber,
where in their presence the Prince was crowned and created
Prince and Great Steward of Scotland, Duke of Rothesay,
Earl of Carrick, Lord of the Isles, Baron and Knight of Renfrew,[1]
then a number of knights were created, the names of whom
are superfluous to rehearse.

The gift that the Earl of Sussex, Ambassador of England,
gave is estimated to the value of 3000 pounds sterling.

The gift that was given by the Ambassador of Denmark is
two gold chains, one to the Queen and the other to the Prince,
either of them esteemed 500 crowns.

The gift given by the Ambassador of Brunswick is a chain
of gold, shapen to the fashion of a number of peascods, enamelled
green and every cod open, on the back wherein and in the stead
of the peas are contained in some of them fair and a great

---

[1] Old royal titles. Carrick was the Bruce earldom; Rothesay, Renfrew,
and the High Stewardship were hereditary in the House of Stewart. The Lordship of the Isles had been forfeited by the Estates in 1493, and had gone to the
Crown. It is still traditionally held by the heir to the throne, as are most of
these titles.

orient pearl, in others, hart, hind, buck, roe, dog, and at this chain hangs a fair tablet, on the one side whereof was the picture of the Duke of Brunswick, with his name all set about in fair diamonds and rubies : on the other side was the history of Actaeon and [the] fountain where Diana does stand, in a marvellous fair carbuncle, and the bloody streams coming from Actaeon by the biting of the dogs are made of fair polished rubies, the pap heads of Diana and her maids are of fair diamonds : briefly the curiosity of the setting of the stones is such that it is hard to tell whether the work of the history or the beauty of the stones be better, either of them doth so decore the other. This is given to the Prince, and to the Queen a small chain of gold made like a little shell-fish, which [they] do call in Scotland whelks.

The Ambassador of Magdeburg gave two gifts very fair and antique,[1] the one was a fair chain of gold made after this form, in the margin stiff divided, in the shape of a fair red rose, in the midst of either of them was placed a fair hyacinth, and the leaves of the rose striped with rubies and chrysolites, and at the mid hangs a very fair rose, the one side white and yellow, in the midst set with diamonds and hyacinths, the other with fair rubies : it is said by the giver thereof that it is made to represent the two roses of England. The chain is devised to be set on the forefront of a gown made after the French fashion, as the Queen now doth use.

The other is a fair tablet foursquare, on the one side is shapen curiously the Annunciation of Mary, and in one angle thereof the effigy of the Duke of Magdeburg, the wings of the angel are replenished with diamonds, there is a shape of a book lying on a desk before the Blessed Virgin, the two leaves whereof are made of two fair square plate diamonds. The other side hath the portrait of the Nativity of Christ, of the angel that told the tidings to the shepherds, and of the three Kings with their gifts, very finely wrought, garnished with a number of very fair

---

[1] Fanciful.

diamonds, rubies, chrysolites, and hyacinths. The work had the shape of a little book in all respects, with clasps and marvellous fair oriental pearl hanging at it. It is esteemed worth 2000 crowns of gold that weigheth 8 oz in weight. This for the Prince.

The Ambassadors of Holland and Zeeland have given two fair and large cups of gold, either of them weighs ten pound weight. They have given a golden coffer in which is contained a letter of obligation, superscribed by them two and divers other chief governors thereto, to pay to the Prince yearly during his life-time 5000 guelderlings, which is esteemed to be 500 pound sterling . . .

—*about £10,000 in modern money, which would give their godson plenty of pocket-money.*

129. WRINGING ROYALTY

Here is James on a less dignified occasion : it is from a letter by the scholarly English gossip, Joseph Meade, in January 1622.

The same day His Majesty rode by coach to Theobald's to dinner, not intending, as the speech is, to return till towards Easter. After dining, riding on horseback abroad, his horse stumbled and cast His Majesty into the New River, where the ice broke : he fell in, so that nothing but his boots were seen. Sir Richard Young was next, who alighted, went into the water, and lifted him out. There came much water out of his mouth and body. His Majesty rid back to Theobalds, and went into a warm bed, and as we hear is well, which God continue.

130. FAMILY LETTERS

Here is a letter to James from his son Henry, Prince of Scotland, written in 1601. It is in Latin, in a large careful print hand : the " Deo juvante " is a marginal afterthought.

Most Serene King and most loving Father, since I have now fulfilled my seventh year, and from increasing age some increase of studies is looked for, I have thought it my duty to give some proof to Your Majesty how much I have until now advanced in letters. I wish also to perform in deed what my tutor in my name has promised in word. If you will graciously accept this, you will enhearten me to pursue my studies more cheerfully, with God's help, Whom I pray very long to preserve Your Majesty to me in safety.

Your Majesty's most obedient son,
HENRY STEWART.

To the most Serene King,
His most Honoured Father.

This, also to James, is from his younger son Charles, Duke of Albany and York. It is evidently composed some time after the Union of Crowns, which took place when the Prince was three.

SWEETE

Sweete Father/i learne to decline substantiues and adiectiues/giue me your blessing/i thank you for my best man

Your louing sone
YORK.

This is from Queen Anne to James. There is no date, but the language is English rather than Scots, which suggests some time considerably after the Union, at which event they had been married for fourteen years. It is in her own hurried vigorous writing, with the signature thriftily turned into the margin.

SIR,

Your Majesty's letter was welcome to me. I have been as glad of the fair weather as yourself, the last part of your letter you have guessed right that I would laugh, who would not laugh both at the persons and the subject, but more so at so well chosen a Mercury between Mars and Venus. You know that women hardly can keep counsel. I honestly desire Your

Majesty to tell me how it is possible that I should keep this secret that have already told it and shall tell it to as many as I speak with ; if I were a poet I would make a song of it, and sing it to the tune of, Three fools well met.

So kissing your hands,

I rest your

ANNA R.

Finally, here is one from Charles to his mother—an older Charles, but not yet out of his teens, as the Queen died in 1619. It is in a clear and decorative hand.

Most worthy mistress, seeing I can not have the happiness to see Your Majesty, give me leave to declare by these lines the duty and love I owe to you, which makes me long to see you. I wish from my heart that I might help to find a remedy for your disease, the which I must bear more patiently because it is the sign of a long life : but I must for many causes be sorry, and specially because it is troublesome to you, and has deprived me of your most comfortable sight, and of many good dinners, the which both I hope by God's grace shortly to enjoy : and when it shall please you to give me leave to see you, it may be I shall give you some good recipe which either shall heal you or shall make you laugh. The which wishing I may obtain by Your Majesty's most gracious favour, kissing in all humility your most sacred hands and praying for your health and long prosperity, I end,

Most worthy mistress

Your Majesty's most obedient and humble servant,

CHARLES.

XI

DEFENCE OF THE REALM

You will not have any means of abridging this war, indeed of emerging from it safely, unless risks are run.
MR WINSTON CHURCHILL, in 1940

131. THE ENTHUSIAST

We have lived of late years under the shadow of war—actual war, war of nerves, diplomatic attack, or any combination of these three. For three full centuries all that went on in Scotland, from constitutional developments to lyric verse, had all these for a steady background : and the assailant had five times Scotland's man-power, a good deal more wealth, and a barren frontier zone, while Scotland's richest land lay on the March.

Here is a letter written to Henry VIII soon after Flodden by Lord Dacre, Warden of the English Marches. His opening sentence echoes, rather grimly, the Border owerword, " We shall have moonlight again."

Please it Your Grace, as for the raid to be made upon your West March, I cannot see how it can be done conveniently unto the next light. . . . In the next light, I shall, God willing, perform the said raid, and in the meantime shall cause small raids to be made, which shall be as great annoyance to the Scots as a great raid should be, and thus shall your money be employed to the best I can and to the greatest hurt and destruc-tion of the Scots : for I shall be as good a husband thereof as I would be of mine own.

A little later, when the Queen-mother's plot to kidnap the little King and take him to England had just come out, and she had fled there with her husband Angus, Dacre writes to Wolsey, to tell him that the Regent, Duke of Albany, would send the Queen's rents, plate, and jewels to her, and says also :

I labour and study all that I can to make division and debate [in Scotland], to the end that if the Duke will not apply himself, that then that debate may grow that it shall be impossible to him to do justice.

132. Reply to an Ultimatum

We are used today to seeing a small power being ordered by a larger and well-armed neighbour to change its government at once, or else . . . The Scots Estates confronted that situation in the beginning of 1522, with a child King, a treacherous Queen-mother heading a powerful Fifth Column, and a fighting force that was still depleted by Flodden.

The points of the ultimatum they received are embedded in this, which was their answer to it. The reader should know that the Duke of Albany, though Admiral of France, was James IV's cousin and heir to the crown after the nine-year-old King. The Estates had appointed him Regent and the King's Guardian. Henry was the King's uncle.

To the Richt Excellent Richt Hie and Michty Prince, the King of England.

Right Excellent Richt Hie and Michty Prince,

The thrid day of Februar instant, we resavit your Patent Letteris undir your Privie Seil, datit at Greinwiche the xiv day of Januar last passit, beiring in effect that

Howbeit, in consideration alsweill of the proximitie of bluid betuix the King our Soverain Lord your nevoy, and Your Grace, as of his minoritie and tendir age, ye haif hitherto bein agreabil to live in tranquillitie and peace with him, his realm, and us,

Nocht the les, ye now undirstand that the Duke of Albany is heir arrivit, furnischit in maneir sowning to hostilitie and weir, taiking upoun him as Governour the custodie of our said Soverain, and as ye ar informit, hes committit the keiping and governance of him to ane strangear of small reputatioun, procuring dampnabil divorce of the Quene your Sister and hir husband, intending thairthrow to contract mariage with hir, quhairby our said Soverain Lord, as to Your Grace appeiris, is in danger to be distroyit, and your sister in point of perditioun ; quhilk inconvenientis til eschew, ye by your greit labouris causit lang or now the King of France faithfullie [to] promitt to keip the said Duke in France, and think that he is cuming heir for accomplishing of his dampnabil interprise in covert maneir, and without knalege of the said King, like as he hes expreslie declairit to your Ambaxiatour resident in his court ;

And that, howbeit the said Duke laitlie desirit at Your Grace Prorogatioun of Trewis,[1] yit regarding the dangeris abuve writen, and that gif he wer establishit at rest in this realm, he suld abuse us, and sa aspire to the Croun of the samyn, ye haif refusit to grant onie Trewis or Peace at his request during his residence heir ; howbeit, he being excludit fra us, ye culd haif bein agreabil thairto, gif the samyn had bein demandit be us, desiring us heirfoir that we nouther aid, favour, nor assist the said Duke in his pervert purpois, nor suffer him to remain in this realm, assuring us that, gif we utherwayis do, suffering his remaining, ye will thairthrow taik provocatiounis with your confederatis,[2] to do us all displesour and dampnage at your power, as farder in the saidis letteris mair at lenth is conteinit.[3]

Richt Excellent, Richt Hie and Michty Prince,

In our maist humbil maneir, we thank Your Grace of the favour ye beir to the King our Soverain Lord your Nevoy, and the guid mind that, quhill now, Your Grace hes had to lif in peace and tranquillitie with His Hienes, his realm, and us : in quhilk we beleif fermlie ye will yit continew, ye being als

---

[1] A formal declaration that hostilities were suspended, indefinitely or for a given time.

[2] Allies. They included Scotland's major ally, Francis I, who as the earlier passage of Henry's letter had hinted, might possibly think the English the better bargain.

[3] Henry's diplomatic style resembled the public one of the late Herr Hitler.

largelie informit in al behalfis of the treuth as ye haif bein of the contrair, be sic persounis [as] we weill persaif nouther luvis Your Gracis honour nor the weil of this realm. Howbeit, we marvel greitlie that Your Hienes, being sa verteous ane Prince,[1] sould gif onie faith or credence to thaim, speciallie in the pointis conteinit in your said letteris, upoun quhilk the informatioun maid to Your Grace hes sa litill appeirance of liklihood to be trew :

For, in the First,

Quhair it hes bein reportit to Your Grace [that] the Richt Illustre Prince, Duke of Albany, Tutor of Law [2] to our said Soverain Lord, chosin and oft-tymis callit be us to the Governance of this Realm, sould now be cuming heir in maneir of hostilitie, taikand into his handis the custodie of our said Soverain Lord, and deput the governance of him to ane strangear of small reputatioun ;

Pleis Your Grace undirstand, that we perfytlie knaw thair informatioun is maid to Your Grace contrair to the veritie ; for it is weill knawin how desirous he hes at all tymis bein, and is, to the procuring and keiping of guid peace ; and that he wald nevir intromit in onie maneir with the custodie of the King our Soverain Lordis persoun, nor constitut onie servand or officiar in his hous, bot alwayis hes referrit and referris all sic thingis to be orderit be us. And we, with avise of the Quenis Grace his Moder, baith afore the first cuming of our said Governour and sinsyne, haif sa substantiallie providit for the sure custodie of his persoun, deputing thairto certain of the maist aigit, famous, and honorabil lordis of this realm, quhilk yit continuallie perseveiris awaiting on the samyn, and all uthirwayis in maneir as we will ansuer to God and to the Warld, quhatevir be colourit or allegit in the contrair, marvelling not litell that Your Grace sould reput us of sa small honour, conscience, and provisioun that we, for onie plesour or profit in this erd, wald overluik the

---

[1] Henry invariably gave himself credit for the highest motives.
[2] Guardian by law—as adult male next-of-kin.

suretie of our naturall Prince and Soverain Lord, or that onie utheris sould be mair attentif to his conservatioun than his propir Moder and we as trew subjectis.

Forthir, Richt Excellent, Richt Hie and Michty Prince,

We sie nane appeirance quhy Your Grace [sould] belieff or gif credence that our said Lord Governour, quha hes bein nourist with sa grait honour and had sa tendir familiaritie with Papis [1] and greitest princeis in Christendome, wald sa far neglect his fame and conscience as imagine or think onie harm and dis-plesour to our Soverain Lordis persoun, nor to induce onie Princes to leif hir lauchful husband for his caus, nor he to separat himself fra his ain spousit wyf, being ane ladie sa vertuous and be quham he hes sa greit lordschippis and possessiounis. In guid faith, we fermlie beleif that the Quenis Grace your sister, nor he nouther, ar nor hes bein mindit thairto in onie maneir.

Richt Excellent, Richt Hie and Michty Prince,

Quhairas Your Grace, for avoiding of the dangeris abuve expressit, be your letteris ye with your labouris and instance persuadit the King of France faithfullie to promitt that he sould nocht suffer our said Lord Governour return in this realm ;

Quhat promissis or conventiounis ar passit betuix yow thair-upoun we knaw nocht. Howbeit, we weill undirstand quhat is betuix our Soverain Lord and us. Bot of ane thing, pleis it Your Grace be informit that, considdering how vertuouslie our said Lord Governour had himself, durand all the tyme of his residence heir, trewlie servit the King our Soverain Lord ; how weil mindit he evir stude to the augmentatioun of peace betuix thair [? thir] realmis ; how diligent he wes in repressing the dampnabil interprise of our Soverain Lordis untrew liegis, quhilk tresounabil attempt to haif put handis on his maist nobil persoun and transportit the samyn furth of this his realm—quhairof monie wer convict in Parliament [2]—we doubt nocht bot

---

[1] Albany was closely connected by marriage with the Pope.
[2] Henry had been a party to this enterprise : it is uncertain how much the Estates knew about this, but they probably guessed something.

it will cleirlie appeir to all Cristen Princis that Your Grace
sould haif schawin mair evident taikinnis of luve and amitie
towart our Soverain Lord [by] procuring and solisiting at the
King of France the hastie returning of the said Governour to
the keiping and interteining of this realm in policie and justice,
than to haif gevin impediment to the samyn, suffering, as is
plainlie allegit, be your command your Wardennis and officiaris
on your Bordouris continuallie to aid, favour, and reset the
traitouris, rebellis, and brokin men of this realm, incitand thaim
to the contemptioun of thair and our Soverain Lordis auctoritie,
ryding with convocatioun of theifis, traitouris, and misdoaris
thair complicis, sa monie as thay micht be, and als far within the
land as thay durst, robbing, spulzeing, and overthrowing the
trew liegis of this realm at thair power.

And mairattour, be Your Gracis lettir foirsaid, it appeiris
that quhatsumevir guid service be done be our Lord Governour
and us to the King our Soverain Lord your nevoy, and comoun
weill of this realm, is litel regardit, bot rathir takin in evill pairt
be Your Grace ; and quhatsumevir licht report is sinisterlie
maid be onie Scottis traitour or fugitive for his demeritis fra
our lawis, hes ferm credence be the Principallis of Your Gracis
Counsall : quhairupoun, gif swa sic continew, we sie nocht
how amitie and guid luve may increas betuix our said Soverain
Lord your nevoy and yow.

Nocht the les, may it pleis Your Grace withdraw your
credence fra sic fals reportis, nocht suffering the Bischop of
Dunkeld [1] nor uthiris our Soverain Lordis rebellis [to] be resett
within your realm, and be contentit that with our said Lord
Governouris presens we may haif ane abstinence of weir for
ane, tyme quhill ane ambaxat [2] may be maid reddie, the King
our Soverain Lord sal in the mein tyme, with avise of his Tutor

---

[1] Gavin Douglas, alas ! He had thought it wiser to flee to Henry's court.
But his guilt seems to have been less than that of his brother Angus, the Queen's
husband, and a great deal less than that of the third brother, Sir George, who was
the political brains of that evil house.

[2] Embassy.

our Governour, send unto Your Grace his ambassadouris for establishing of farder peace. Be the contrair, Your Grace standing sa mindit that ye can nocht be agreabil to haif peace nor trewis with the King our Soverain Lord nor us, without we avoid and caus depairt the said our Lord Governour furth of this realm, we maun, as enforsit thairto, and til our greit displesour, maik knawen til all Cristen Princis, and speciallie to our Soverain Lordis confederatis and freindis,[1] quhat necessarilie is ensewit upoun theis your deliberatiounis. That is to say, outhir ye will that we, without onie relevant caus, taik fra our said Lord Governour, he nevir offending, the tutele of our Soverain Lord perteining to him of law, and deprive him of the office of Governour, to the quhilk he is chosin be us all, and sa louabillie [2] hes exertit the samyn durand al the tyme of his being in this realm, that na creatour may of resoun lay reproche nor dishonour to his chairge—the quhilk thing, an we sa did, wer expres againis all equitie, justice, and commoun weill of this realm : or, be the contrair, we assisting [3] to him, ye will move weir, and do unto us al the dampnage and displesour that may lie in your power. And gif this your querel be just or resounabil, God be the juge, sen it may be na bettir, for we haif alwayis desirit, and desiris, to live with Your Grace in guid amitie and peace, gif we may haif it without extreim inconvenientis.

Howbeit, we ar resolut that, or we sould consent to do sa greit hurt to the King our Soverain Lord and Commoun Weil of this realm, sa greit dishonour to our selffis, and sa greit wrang to our said Lord Governour, as to amove him furth of this realm and lif in divisiounis and daylie trubil amangis ourselffis, as this lang tyme by-passit we haif dune, he being in France : we wil with his presens taik our aventure of peace and weir as sal pleis God to send it, assurand Your Grace that for the caus abuve specifyit, and utheris enow quhilk we sall schaw in tyme and

[1] A gentle reminder that France, whom Henry was anxiously courting, was Scotland's ally, and that the Empire was feeling for an alliance.
[2] In such a praiseworthy manner.
[3] Standing by or adhering to.

place, we nouthir may nor will, at request of Your Grace or onie uthir prince, consent or suffer in onie maneir that our said Lord Governour depairt furth of this realm durand the King our Soverain Lordis minoritie and less aige.

And gif, for this caus, we happin to be invadit, quhat may we do bot taik God to our guid querel in defens, and do as our progenitouris and foirbeiris hes bein constreinit to do, for the conservatioun of this realm heirtofoir.

Gevin undir our Soverain Lordis Privie Seil at Edinburgh, the xi day of Februar, the yeir of God one thousand five hundred and twenty-one yeiris.[1]

Your humbil oratouris and servandis with all lauchfulnes,
　　　The Chancellour and Thrie Estaitis
　　　　　　　　　of the Realm of Scotland.

133. The Devil at Jeddart

In the September of the following year the Earl of Surrey—not the English commander at Flodden, but his son—wrote the following despatch to Cardinal Wolsey, and probably gave some thought to its composition.

Pleaseth it Your Grace to be advertised that upon Friday at x a clock at night I returned to this town, and all the garrison to this place assigned, the Bishopric men, my Lord of Westmorland and my Lord Dacre in like wise, every man home with their companies, without loss of any men, thanked be God, saving eight or ten slain and divers hurt at skirmishes and saults of the town of Gedworth[2] and the fortresses; which town is so surely burnt that no garrison or none other shall be lodged there until the time it be new builded : the burning whereof I committed to two sure men, Sir William Bulmer and Thomas Tempest.

The town was much better than I weened it had been, for there was two time more houses therein than in Berwick, and

---

[1]　1522 by our reckoning.　　　　　　[2]　Jedburgh.

well builded with many honest and fair houses therein, sufficient to have lodged a thousand horsemen in garrison, and six good towers therein, which town and towers be cleanly destroyed, burnt, and thrown down. Undoubtedly there was no journey made into Scotland in no man's day, leaving with so few a number, that is recounted to be so high an enterprise as this, both with this country men and Scots, nor of truth so much hurt done ; but in the end a great misfortune did befall, only by folly, that such order as was commanded by me to be kept was not observed, the manner whereof hereafter shall ensue.

Before mine entry into Scotland, I appointed Sir William Bulmer and Sir William Overs to be marshals of the army. . . . In the vanguard I appointed my Lord of Westmorland as chief, with all the Bishopric,[1] Sir William Bulmer, Sir William Overs, my Lord Dacre with his company, and with me remained all the rest of the garrison and the Northumberland men. I was of counsel with the Marshals at the ordering of our lodging, and our camp was so well environed with ordnance, carts, and dikes that hard it was to enter or issue but at certain places appointed for the purpose ; and assigned the most commodious place of the said camp for my Lord Dacre's company, next the water and next my Lord of Westmorland. And at such time as my Lord Dacre came into the field, I being at the assault of the Abbey, which continued unto two hours within night, my said Lord Dacre would in no wise be content to lie within the camp, which was made right sure, but lodged himself without, where-with at my return I was not content, but then it was too late to remove.

The next day I sent my said Lord Dacre to a strong hold called Ferniehurst, the lord whereof was his mortal enemy, and with him Sir Arthur Davy, Sir Marmaduke Constable, with 700 of their men, one *cortoute* and divers other good pieces of ordnance for the field. The said Ferniehurst stood marvellous strong, within a great wood. The said two knights with the

[1] County Durham.

most part of their men and Strickland, Your Grace's servant, with 300 Kendal men, went into the wood on foot with the ordnance, where the said Kendal men were so handled that they found hardy men that went no foot back for them. The other two knights were also so sharply assailed that they were enforced to call for more of their men, and yet could not bring ordnance to the fortress unto the time when my Lord Dacre with part of his horsemen lighted upon foot, and marvellously hardily handled himself; and finally with long stikmishing and much difficulty got forth the ordnance, won the house, and threw down the same.

At which skirmish my said Lord Dacre and his brother Sir Christopher and Sir Arthur and Sir Marmaduke and many other gentlemen did marvellous hardily, and found the best resistance that hath been seen since my coming to these parts, and above 30 Scots slain and not passing four Englishmen, but above sixty hurt. After that, my said Lord returning to the camp, would in no wise be lodged in the same, but where he lay the first night, and he being with me at supper about eight o'clock, the horses of his company brake loose, and suddenly ran out of the field in such number that it caused a marvellous alarm in our field; and our standing watch being set, the horses came running along the camp, at whom were shot above one hundred sheaf of arrows and divers guns, thinking they had been Scots that would have saulted the camp. Finally the horses were so mad that they ran like wild deer into the field, over 1500 at the least in divers companies, and in one place above fifty fell down a great rock and slew themselves; and above 250 ran into the town, being on fire, and by the women taken and carried away, right evil burnt; and many were taken again; but finally by that I can esteem by the number of them that I saw go on foot the next day, I think there is lost above 800 horses, and all with folly for lack of not lying within the camp.

I dare not write the wonders that my Lord Dacre and all his company do say they saw that night, six times, of spirits and fearful sights. And universally, all their company say plainly, the Devil that night was in among them six times, which misfortune hath blemished the best journey that was made in Scotland many years. I assure Your Grace that I found the Scots at this time the boldest men and the hottest that ever I saw any nation : and all the journey upon all parts of the army kept us with so continual skirmishes that I never saw the like. If they might assemble 40,000 as good men as I now saw 1500 or 2000, it would be a hard encounter to meet them. Pity it is of my Lord Dacre's loss of the horses of his company. He brought with him above 4000 men, and lodged one night in Scotland in his most mortal enemy's country. There is no hardier nor better knight, but oftentime he doth not use the most sure order ; which he hath now paid dearly for.

Written at Berwick, the 27 of September,

Yours most bounden,
T. SURREY.

To my Lord Legate's good Grace.

134. FIFTH COLUMN LADIES

Even in the days of its worst, and very serious, corruption, disloyalty to Scotland was very rare among the clergy of the Old Church. The lady here was probably a creature of Queen Margaret, who, loyal in the life of her husband James IV, after his death was involved in constant plots against the kingdom of her little son.

The letter is from the Marquis of Dorset, Warden of the English East and Middle Marches, to Henry VIII, and was written in April 1524.

Please it your most noble Grace to be advertised that of late the Queen's Grace of Scotland your sister wrote her especial letters of request as well unto my lord your Lieutenant as to me, to forbear and save from burning a poor religious house of nuns called Coldstream, the Prioress whereof Her Grace reporteth to be very good and kind unto her. Whereupon both my Lord Lieutenant and I have granted her request, and have so written unto Her Grace accordingly. Another cause which moved us the sooner to assure the said house, was by cause the Prioress thereof is one of the best and assured spies we have in Scotland, for which cause we may not spare her.

Coldstream, of course, was in an admirable strategic position for her work, and there are many reports from her in the official correspondence of the time. The Prioress of Eccles, a " cell " or dependent house of Coldstream, was also a spy. It seems to be she who wrecked Albany's plans in 1524, *and caused the failure of his expedition.*

135. THE TOURIST

Our generation has seen many foreign tourists arrive in countries due for annexation. Here is a letter from one in the reign of James V. It is not dated, but since it was written to Thomas Cromwell as Secretary to Henry VIII of England, it must come between 1534 *and* 1540. *The writer was an English ex-monk, who had found the Carthusian Order too austere, so left it and turned medical student instead, wandering through many universities and writing accounts of his travels. He is, by the way, the original Merry Andrew.*

After humbly salutation with due reverence, I certify your Mastership that I am now in Scotland, in a little university or study, named Glasgow, where I study and practise physic, as I have done in divers regions and provinces for the sustentation of my living ; assuring you that in the parties that I am in, the King's Grace hath many, aye and in manner all manner of persons (except some scholastic men) that be his adversaries and speaketh perilous words. I resort to the Scottish King's house and to the Earl of Arran, named Hamilton,[1] and to the

[1] James's second cousin, and, until the birth of his son in May 1538, his heir presumptive.

Lord Evandale, named Stewart, and to many lords and lairds, as well spiritual as temporal : and truly I know their minds, for they take me for a Scottish man's son, for I name myself Ker, and so the Kers calleth me cousin, through the which I am in more favour. . . .

Would to Jesu also that you had never an alien in your realm, specially Scots, for I never knew alien good to England, except they knew profit and lucres should abide them, etc. [*sic*] In all the parts of Christendom that I have travelled in, I knew not five English inhabitors, except they be scholars for learning.

He then makes lavish professions of gratitude and affection, and hopes that his old connection with the Carthusians, whom Henry had just been disembowelling alive for refusing to recognise him as head of the Church, will not be held against him, and concludes :

New[s ?] I have to write to you, but I pretend to be with you shortly, for I am half weary of this barren country, as Jesus Christ knoweth, Who ever keep you in health and honour. From Leith, a mile from Edinburgh, the 1st day of April, by the hand of your poor scholar and servant,

ANDREW BOORDE, priest.

136. PROVISION OF SHELTERS

In 1535, about the time the above letter was written, the Estates enacted :

Item, it is statut and ordainit for saiffing of men, thair guidis and geir upoun the Bordouris in tyme of weir and all uthir troublous tymis, That everie landit man, dwelland in the Island or upon the Bourdouris, havand thair ane hundreth pund land in extent, sall big ane sufficient barmkin upoun his heritage and landis, in place maist convenient, of stane and lyme, contenand thrie scoir futis of the squair, ane elne thik and vi elnis heicht, for the resett and defens of him, his tenentis, and thair gudis in troublous tyme, with ane tour in the samyn for him self gif he thinkis it expedient ; and that all uthir landit men of smaller rent and revenew big pelis and greit strenthis for saifing of thair selffis, men, tenentis, and gudis. And that all the saidis strenthis, barmkinnis, and pelis be biggit and completit within twa yeiris.

A barmkin is a large fortified enclosure ; a pele the same thing on, apparently, a smaller scale. Our familiar peel-tower is a tower with a wall round it.

137. HOME GUARD

In 1540, just four hundred years before the recruitment of the Home Guard we knew, the Estates were making arrangements for another, which was soon, and very bitterly, to be needed.

Item, that exercitatioun may be had throwout all the realm amangis all our Soverain Lordis liegis, for exercing of thair persounis in ordour, swa that be leirning of ordouris and beiring of thair wapnis in tyme of peace, thay may be mair expert to put thaim selffis in ordour hastilie and keip the samyn in tyme of neid ; it is thocht that this artikil is verie necessar to be providit : And thairfoir statutis and ordainis that everie scheriff, stewart, bailie, provost, aldermen and baileis of burrowis, lords and baileis of regaliteis, at everie wapinschawing concur and sit doun with the Kingis Gracis Commissiounaris that sall happin to be deput to thaim, and thay togidder to consult with the maist abil persounis of the schire, and eftir that thay haif rollit the namis of everie man, with thair harness and wapnis, chese ane abill man for everie parochine or ma, as it is of greitnes, and for smaller parochinis ane, quha sall be capitan or capitanis to the cumpaneis of the saidis parochinis, and sall leir thaim to gang in ordour and beir thair wapnis, and sall convene the saidis cumpaneis of the saidis parochinis twice at the leist in everie moneth of the monethis of Maii, Junii, and Julii, at quhat dayis thay sall think maist expedient upoun halidayis befoir nune, and als in all utheris monethis gif thay may guidlie, and thair exerce thaim in maneir foirsaid ; and that na man disobey the saidis persounis, capitanis, to be deput and chosin as said is ; undir the pain to be punischit at the Kingis Gracis will.

exercitatioun, drill.   *wapinschawing*, local kit-inspection.   *concur*, meet.
rollit, enrolled.

138. NEIGHBOURS WILL BE NEIGHBOURS

In a confidential despatch of the 15th October 1541, Henry VIII's Commissioners of the Marches apologise to the King for their slowness in stirring up the English Borderers to raid Scotland. One John Heron has reported to them that he has been trying to induce the men of Tynedale and Redesdale to do so.

Nevertheless, as he said, for anything that he could therein devise, unless he were in their company personally himself, he could not bring to pass that the Tynedale and Redesdale men would commit slaughter of any of the notable surnames of Liddesdale, for fear of a deadly feud ; and proving him further, what the said Tynedale or Redesdale men might be induced to do in the head of Teviotdale, upon the Water of Rule, or Jedworth Forest, and thinking as he said that that might be brought to pass, finally we persuaded him as earnestly as we could to go about the executing thereof with effect ; and if he could not compass the doing thereof without his own personal presence, then he, being no officer of the Marches, and dissembling a grief or cause of deadly feud of his own, should rather than such slaughter should be undone, be present at the doing of it himself, so that always it should be done in Liddesdale. And so being resolved to do, the said John Heron in manner undertook the next time to compass the same. And because the Liddesdale men stood in dread of such company as came into this country with us [and] Sir Ralph Ellerker and Sir Robert Bowes, thinking that we intended to make some incourse upon them, we thought best to draw ourselves to Berwick . . . thinking the far distance of us from them should rather put them out of dread, and cause them more quietly to keep their own houses. . . .

And yesterday, the 14th of this instant October, the said John Heron came unto the Castle of Etal, where he gave information to us of some new attemptats done by them of Tynedale and Redesdale in Scotland, and other affairs in those parts, the which we have caused him to put in writing, as Your Grace shall perceive in a schedule here enclosed.

Finally, as well by all the means we can travail in this matter, by the information of John Heron or otherwise, we cannot perceive that it will in any wise be brought to pass to have the Tynedales or Redesdales to commit any slaughter or be brought into deadly feud with the Liddesdale men or any other the thieves of the Borders of Scotland, so that John Heron himself as it seemeth rather feareth that they will assent to betray him, than to be in deadly feud with the said Liddesdale men or other Scots thieves their old accomplices and company ; so that we be almost desperate of any good success in these matters to be accomplished by the Tynedale and Redesdale men.

Nearly fifty years later, a gentleman named James Rither— a man from Kent, at the other end of England—is again annoyed at the Borderers' neighbourly habits. His letter is of August 1590 . . . *when the countries had for five years been formal allies.*

By long observance I have ever noted (Right Honourable) the people of this isle, though always divided by the ancient enmities of England and Scotland, yet the nearer any part of our pale is to Scotland, the less enmity, the more accordance in manners ; not that the Scots take of us, but we of them, as the evil is ever more infective than the good. . . .

Also out of these parts I perceive divers that have horses to sell, and were wont to carry them to the great horse-fair at Malton in the east part of this shire, are now purposed to go

to Carlisle with them.   They found means to convey them into
Scotland from inward fairs, but why should that needy nation
esteem our horses at a greater price than our own country
people do, for it is the hope of Scots money that draws these
horses to Carlisle, and so do the sellers confess.

dissembling, pretending.   *travail*, labour.

139. Total War

*On the 2nd September of 1543 the Duke of Suffolk wrote to the
English Privy Council :*

We shall give them such a buffet upon their Borders as shall
make them to repent it, seeing that the corn is now in the houses
and stacks the which they should live by, by the whole year,
shall be so destroyed that they shall be the more easier to meddle
with hereafter.

*Five months later, however, he was less certain than he had
been in autumn over the Scottish reaction to total war, and wrote
very sensibly—and in the circumstances very bravely—to Henry
VIII :*

Most humbly beseeching Your Highness of pardon for that
I shall declare my poor opinion what I think as far as my poor
wit will extend, unto what annoyance the army by sea can do
to Your Highness' enemies, which is but only the burning of
Edinburgh if the Castle will not yield, which I fear me will not,
but that I think it must be won by force, which I fear the army
that shall go by sea shall not do ; and also the said army may
destroy on both sides the Firth such places near their ships as
foot men may do . . . which when it is done, Your Majesty
not offended, shall be never the nearer of Your Highness' godly
and noble purpose, nor those that counteth themselves Your
Majesty's friends, if ye have any there, to be either holpen or
relieved thereby, but rather to be in the worse case.   For as I

think, all Scotland will say "What false traitors are those, or unhappy men are they, that would take the King of England's part, or think that the King of England intendeth any goodness to the young Queen his niece or to the realm of Scotland, but only to the destruction of the same." By reason whereof, after Edinburgh so burnt, Your Highness shall have nothing in Scotland but by the sword and conquest. . . .

And he goes on to commend Fifth Column and diplomatic tactics rather than brute force. The despatch lost him his command, which was given to Henry's brother-in-law Hertford : and, on the 10th April, Henry's Privy Council sent Hertford his orders. Suffolk had evidently learnt his lesson, as he signs with the rest, who include the famous Bishop Gardiner.

His Majesty's pleasure is that you shall . . . put all to fire and sword, burn Edinburgh town, so razed and defaced when you have sacked and gotten what ye can of it as there may remain forever a perpetual memory of the vengeance of God lighted upon them for their falsehood and disloyalty. Do what ye can out of hand and without long tarrying to beat down and overthrow the Castle, sack Holyrood House and burn and subvert it and all the rest, putting man, woman, and child to fire and sword without exception, where any resistance shall be made against you ; and this done, pass over to the Fifeland, and extend like extremity and destruction in all towns and villages whereunto ye may reach conveniently, not forgetting among all the rest so to spoil and turn upside down the Cardinal's [1] town of St Andrews as the upper stone may be the nether, and not one stick stand by another, sparing no creature alive within the same. . . . And after this sort spending one month there, spoiling and burning as afore is said, with wise foresight, which His Highness doubteth not ye will use. . . . His Majesty thinketh verily, and so do we, and be sure ye shall find the same,

[1] Cardinal Beaton, Archbishop of St Andrews, one of the Council of Regency for the young Queen, and the chief leader of resistance to Henry.

this journey shall succeed most this ways to His Majesty's honour. . . .

Furthermore, His Majesty's pleasure is you shall take order with the Wardens that the Borderers in Scotland may be still tormented and occupied as much as can be conveniently, now specially that it is seed-time, from the which if they be kept and not suffered to sow their grounds, they shall by the next year be brought to such a penury that they shall not be able to live nor abide the country. And thus fare your lordship most heartily well. From Westminster the 10th day of April 1544.

140. THREE TOWNS

The orders were duly put into execution. This is an eye-witness account of the expedition, written soon after for Lord Russell, Henry VIII's Lord Privy Seal, and printed in London before the end of the year.

An English force landed at Leith, and took it by surprise. Edinburgh was under the command of Bothwell (the father of Queen Mary's husband) and the rather dubious Lord Hume. They offered to surrender on conditions. The English refused the conditions, and set about a bombardment of the city, beating in the Canongate Port. Bothwell and Hume withdrew the garrison to the Castle.

And finally it was determined by the said Lord Lieutenant utterly to ruinate and destroy the said town with fire ; which, for the night drew fast on, we omitted thoroughly to execute on that day, but setting fire in three or four parts of the town, we repaired for the night into our camp. And the next morning very early we began where we left, and continued burning all that day and the two days next ensuing, continually, so that neither within the walls nor in the suburbs was left any one house unbrent, besides the innumerable booties, spoils, and pillages that our soldiers brought from thence, notwithstanding abundance which was consumed with fire. Also we burnt the abbey called Holyroodhouse, and the Palace adjoining the same.

They then moved toward the Border, devastating the country, including Haddington and its " great nunnery."

That night they looked for us to have burnt the town of Dunbar, which we deferred to the morning at the dislodging of our camp, which we executed by 500 of our hagbutters, being backed with 500 horsemen. And by reason we took them in the morning, who having watched all night for our coming, and perceiving our army to dislodge and depart, thought themselves safe of us, were newly gone to their beds, and in their first sleep closed in with fire, men, women, and children were suffocated and burnt.

After further calm description of such matters, the whole narrative ends with the pious sentiment :

In these victories, who is to be most highest lauded but God, by Whose goodness the Englishmen hath had, of a great season, notable victories and matters worthy triumph.

Meanwhile other expeditions were at work. A despatch of Hertford, a little after the sack of Edinburgh, tells how Lord Eure gave the Provost and townspeople of Jedburgh

a summons to deliver the town and abbey to Your Majesty's use and behoof, with promise and assurance that if they would so do, and become Your Majesty's true subjects, they should not only sustain no damage ne hurt in their bodies ne goods, but also that garrison should be left and laid with them to keep the town and defend them from all enemies, and that if they refused the same, to stand to their adventure ; in which case they might be assured to have all rigour and extremity ministered unto them, and neither man, woman, nor child be left alive, without mercy or pity to be extended to them in that behalf.

The Provost, who could doubtless remember the burning of the town twenty years before, and who would have heard the news of the sack and destruction of the capital and of the Lothian burghs, asked for twelve hours to consider. It was refused, and, as he declined to surrender out of hand, the town was at once sacked, leaving, as Hertford says proudly, " not two houses unburnt." " The abbey likewise they burnt, as much as they might for the stone-work." Our ancestors did not buy their freedom cheaply.

141. BORDER BOOK-KEEPING

There is a carefully kept register of the loot taken from the Scottish Borders between early July and mid-November of that same year of 1544. Here is a specimen entry :

Sir Ralph Eure's Letters, 27th Octobris.

Mr Norton, Mr Nesfield, etc., rode to the town of the Lord of Bonjedward and burnt it, and brought away 10 prisoners, 100 nolt, 200 sheep. . . .

The Lord Eure's Letters of 4th Novembris.

The garrison of Cornhill and Thomas Foster's company, etc., rode into the Merse to a town called Gordon, and there took up the same, and brought away 85 nolts, 18 nags, 40 sheep, 10 prisoners, and inside gear

. . . and so on for page after page. The totals for the period— just over four months, with winter setting in—are summed up neatly :

> Towns, towers, steads, barmkins, parish churches, bastel houses, 192.
> Scots slain, 403.
> Prisoners taken, 816.
> Nolt, 10,386.
> Sheep, 12,492.
> Nags and geldings, 1,296.

Goats, 200.

Bolls of corn, 850.   [*It was generally burnt* in situ.]

Inside gear, etc.

142. War of Nerves

There was, of course, no radio in those days : but Scots " will to resist " was attacked by many pamphlets. One by a certain Nicholas Bodrugan expounds the advantages of coming under the English code of law. He is an expert, who is familiar with the laws of both kingdoms and

I dare affirm that the most wicked law that ever was given in this realm containeth not half so much iniquity as the best of [the Scots laws] do.

This is from an " Epistle Exhortatorie " in the name of the Protector Somerset, uncle of Edward VI—the Hertford of § 137 and § 138.

It maketh us to marvel what evil and fatal chance doth so dissever your hearts and maketh them so blind and unmindful of your profit and to still conciliate and heap to yourself [*sic*] most extreme mischief : the which we (whom you will needs have your enemies) go about to take away from you, and perpetually to ease you thereof.   And although by all reason and order of necessity, it should be rather more convenient for you to seek and require moderate agreements of us (whom God hath hitherto according to our most just, true, and godly meanings and intents, prospered and set forward with your affliction and misery) than that we, being superiors in the field, masters of a great part of your realm, should seek upon you.   Yet to the intent that our charitable mind and brotherly love should not cease by all means possible to provoke and call you to your own commodity and profit, even as the father to the son or the elder brother would do to the younger brother, and as the loving physician would do to the mistrustful and ignorant patient, we are constant to call and cry upon you to look on your state, to avoid the great calamity the country is in : to have us rather brothers than enemies, rather countrymen than conquerors. . . .

It then goes on with an attempt to discredit the Scots Government, and extols Henry's wisdom in attempting to marry his son to the young Queen. Nothing is said of his efforts to kidnap her and her father before her, or of his financing of the Regent's murder.

But the Scots remained, as the Englishman Hall puts it in his Chronicle,

ready to defend their country like brute beasts.

143. The Germans in Scotland

On the 25th November 1546, Scotland having still held firm, the French Ambassador to England, Odet de Selve, writes to the Admiral of France :

Monseigneur, it is said in some quarters that the preparation which the King of England claims to be about to make for the Scots War, at this present time, and on which he can already count, are 12,000 landsknechts,[1] 200 horse from Cleves, 1500 Albanians, besides what he will raise from his own country, where the count is made by parishes which they say are of the number of 40,000 or thereby, which can yield at the least a man apiece, and that he has, through merchants, caused much corn to be bought in Denmark, to take to the frontier of the Scottish Marches, where he has also made great provision of biscuit and of salt meat. And several say that on the sea the Flemings will join the English against the said country of Scotland. . . .

The Editor does not know if De Selve's figures are correct : but German and Albanian troops were in fact used, and Spanish also. How many burgesses of Haddington know that Albanians once fought in their lovely High Street ?

[1] German heavy infantry.

144. ENGLAND IS SURE

Just over a year later—in the December of 1547, *with Pinkie over—De Selve writes again to the Constable of France that Somerset has warned him that France cannot count upon the Scots Alliance,*

for he could say that he had the said kingdom of Scotland in his hand, and it was no use putting forward the examples of King Robert nor of old times, when war was not made as it is at present, for the conquests and losses of kingdoms depended on the chance of a battle, and there were no fortifications, so that one could never be sure of keeping what one had conquered : but that he is doing and hopes to do the reverse.

The worthy Protector, however, was unduly sanguine. The war cost Scotland hideous loss and suffering ; but his successor Northumberland had to make peace in 1550 *without conquering Scotland, and even without inducing her to break the French Alliance or to marry her Queen to the young King of England— the avowed aims for which the war had begun.*

145. ALLIED IMPRESSIONS

Now that so many young Scots officers have served in France, there is a special interest in the memoirs of a young French one who served in Scotland. The " Histoire de la guerre d'Escosse " of Jean de Beaugué, gentilhomme françois, was published in Paris in 1556. *It describes the author's experience as a member of the French Expeditionary Force in Scotland in the terrible year* 1548. *He was a keen young professional soldier, apparently an engineer, very modest and likeable, a good friend to Scotland, and devoted to his commanding officer and to the French Queen Dowager, who was so gallant a leader of the resistance.*

Here are his professional impressions of various Scots towns. Incidentally, how many Dundonians know that German troops, four hundred years ago, were fighting through the streets of their native city?

[The English command] sent sixteen to seventeen hundred landsknechts and some English horse and foot who went with them to Dondy, one of the finest and most populous cities in all the kingdom, into which they entered without any difficulty. For although Dondy is one of the richest and best-built places in all the kingdom, and the easiest to make impregnable, since the Scots have always been careless to fortify it the inhabitants had no other enclosure nor fort to retire to but their houses. And through this lack the English did not find there much resistance.

It was a couple of centuries since invasion had seriously menaced the North-east towns, and this lack of defence was found in all of them. " Montrosts " appeared to Beaugué a " beau bourg," but its fort was only of earthworks and badly sited.

Aberdim is a fair and rich city, inhabited by a goodly people, set in the province of Marach, on the edge of the sea. It has not a good roadstead, but the port is very safe and easy, save for the entrance, which is narrow. It is easy to fortify, being closed on both sides by the Dom and Dé, two rivers not easily fordable. And in other places having the plain open and spacious, to set up there boulevards and defences, to prevent a mount, which is on the bridge side, from bringing a battery to bear on it. One could at very small cost make a citadel there, which could command the port and the whole city, in which is an episcopal see and a university well ordered and accomplished.

As for Saint Ian d'Eston [*St Johnstoun—Perth*] it is a very pretty place, pleasant and well fitted to make a strong town,[1] which could be made safe for the inhabitants by building a citadel where stands the Church of the Holy Rood.

---

[1] *Bonne ville.* The phrase has a technical military sense, of a town adequately fortified.

146. The Co-Prosperity Sphere

Somerset could not use films of the invasion to impress, or depress, foreign diplomats : but in 1548 a detailed account of the exploits of Dacre's recent expedition was published in London.   It seems to be meant for distribution in Scotland, as its preface directly addresses Scottish readers, telling them how kind it was of England to wish to join their country to herself, and how lucky they might think themselves if she did.

What can be more for your universal commodity, profit, and weal ?   Whereby, even at once, of foreign foes ye shall be accepted as familiar friends, of weak you shall be made strong, of poor, rich, of bond, free.   And whether this now be rather offered of us, or sued for by you, I make yourselves judges.   Yet seek we not the mastership of you but the fellowship, for if we did, we have, ye wot, a way of persuasion of the rigorous rhetoric so vengeable vehement (as I think ye have felt by a nation [*action ?*] or two) that if we were to use the extremity of argument, we were able to beat reason into your heads, or about your heads, that I doubt not ye would quickly find what suddenness it were to stand in strife for the mastery with more than your match.   We covet not to keep you bound that would fain have you free.[1]

After the preface, of which this is an excerpt, there follows a very detailed account, with much classical and biblical ornament, of events by sea and land, from the battle of Pinkie to a cheerful description of a hideous outrage on a woman in childbed, all which, of course, will be repeated until the Scots give in, and accept the benefits of annexation.

---

[1] *Bound* in English diplomatic language of the time means continuing independent and in alliance with France : *free* means submitting quietly to annexation by England.   Many modern historians retain this use.

147. Scotland in Extremis

A counterblast to the English propaganda survives in the " Compleynt of Scotland," written early in 1549, with the war nearly seven years old and at its grimmest. The author appears to have been one Wedderburn, probably a Border man, almost certainly a priest, and quite certainly a scholar and a patriot.

He begins by a long dedication to Queen Marie as the leader of the resistance, saying that he ventures to speak from

ane affective ardent favour that I haif evir borne towart this affligit realm quhilk is my native countrey.

His address is more than mere courtly compliment : he clearly valued the loyalty she had shown to the kingdom of her husband and her daughter—she who might have gone back to live happily in her own country ; and he shows a warm and human sympathy to the mother who has been parted from her children, the woman struggling to defend his country against

thre vehement plagis, quhilk hes almaist succumbit our countrey in final evertioun.   That is to say, the cruel invasiounis of auld enemies, the universal pestilens and mortalitie that hes occurrit merciles amang the pepil, and the contentioun of divers of the Thre Estaitis of Scotland.

He sees his countrymen under the wrath of God, and draws parallels with the troubles of Israel, quoting Moses and Isaiah. Then, turning aside in the long Monolog Recreatif, he pictures the happy Scotland of the past, before the war : and then comes a vision of Scotland as she is—borrowed, no doubt, in part from Alain Chartier's earlier vision of a France in the same condition for the same cause, but full of a passion that is not second-hand.

I thocht that thair appeirit to me ane ladie of excellent extractioun and of anciant genologie, maikand ane melancolious cheir for the greit violens that sche had susteinit and endurit.   It appeirit be hir woful countenaunce that sche wes

in greit dout and dreddour for ane mair dolourous future ruin
that wes appeirand to succomb hir hastilie in the maist extreim
exterminatioun.   Hir hair, of the colour of fyne gold, wes
feltrit and trauchlit out of ordir, hingand ovir hir schulderis.
Sche had ane croun of gold, hingand and brangland that it wes
lyke to fall doun fra hir heid to the cauld erd.   Sche buir ane
scheild, in the quhilk wes gravit ane reid rampand lyoun in ane
feild of gold, borderit about with doubil flour delicis.   This
reid lyoun wes hurt in monie placis of his bodie.   The accoutre-
mentis and cleithing of this dolorous ladie wes ane syde mantil
that coverit all hir bodie, of ane mervellous ingenius fassioun,
the quhilk hed bein tissu and wrocht be thre sindrie fassiounis
of werkmanschip.   [On] the first pairt, quhilk wes the bordour
of hir mantil, thair wes monie precius stanis, quhairin thair wes
gravin scheildis, speiris, swerdis, bairdit hors harnes, and all
uthir sortis of wapnis and munitiounis of weir.   In the middis of
the mantil, thair wes gravin in characteiris, beukis and figuris,
divers sciencis divine and human, with monie cheritabil actis
and supernatural miraclis.   On the thrid pairt of that mantil I
beheld, broderit about at hir tail, al sortis of cattel and profitabil
beistis, all sortis of cornis, herbis, plantis, grein treis, schippis,
marchantreis, and monie politic werkmanlumis for mechanic
craftis.

This mantil, quhilk had bein maid and wrocht in auld tymis
be the prudent predecessouris of this foirsaid ladie, wes revin
and raggit in monie placis, that scantlie micht I persave the
storeis and figuris that had bein gravin, wrocht, and broderit in
auld tymis in the thre pairtis of it.   For the first pairt of it
wantit monie of the scheildis and harnes that wes first wrocht in
it, and ane uthir pairt of the scheildis and harnes wes brokin
and rustit, and redie to fall and tyne furth of the bordis of
that mantil.   Siclyke the pleasand werkmanschip that wes in
the middis of hir mantil wes separat fra utheris, and altrit fra the
first fassioun, that na man could extract onie profitabil sentens
nor guid exempil furth of onie pairt of it.   Now to speik of the

thrid pairt of hir mantil, it wes werst graithit and spilt be ane
greit differens nor wes the tothir two pairtis of that mantil : for
it appeirit that all the grein treis, cornis, bestialitie, mechanic
craftis, and schippis and marchandreis, that had bein curiouslie
wrocht in auld tymis in the bordour of the tail of that mantil,
wes spilt and destroyit, and the erd wes becum barran and
sterile, and [sa] that na ordinaunce of policie could be persaivit
in it, nor esperance of relief.   Now to conclude of the fassioun
of this ladeis mantil, it wes baith alterit in colour and in beautie,
and revin in monie placis, hingand doun raggit in peicis in sic
ane sort, that gif thay had bein present that wrocht and maid it
in the beginning, thay wald haif cleir miskennit it, be resoun
that it wes sa alterit fra the first fassioun.

*The ragged but still royal lady addresses her three sons, the
Three Estates, and bids them rise from their sickness and come to
her succour.   Nor is all that she says to them yet out of date.   The
essence of the whole is in one brief passage.*

The natural love of your native countrey sould be insepar-
ablie rutit in your hairtis, considerand that your lyvis, your
bodeis, your habitatioun, your frendis, your livingis and
susteinar, your heil, your peace, your refuge, the rest of your
eild, and your sepulture is in it. . . . All pepil ar disnaturalit
fra thair guid nature quhilkis in necessitie enforsis thaim nocht,
at thair power, to purchas and til avaunce the public weil of
thair native countrey.

Cheir, bearing, manner.   *dreddour*, fear.   *brangland*, shaking.   *syde*,
wide.   *tissu*, woven.   *bairdit* (of a horse), wearing armour.   *politic
werkmanlumis*, skilfully contrived tools and machinery.   *graithit*, the normal
sense is to be prepared or fit.   *cleir miskennit*, completely failed to recognise.

148. COMMANDOS

*After Pinkie in 1547, Hume Castle, the key of the East March,
had been lost.   It was held by Lady Hume with a small force, and
was taken by the effective stratagem of threatening to hang her son*

before her eyes. She tried to call the English commander's bluff, but the sight of the young man with the rope round his neck was too much for the poor soul, and she gave in. Beaugué, who tells how the castle was recovered when he was in Scotland a couple of years later, is very careful to say that he does not blame her.

As soon as Milord Grey [of Wilton] had withdrawn to England, Milord Hume [le Milhord de Hume] having withdrawn his command to the cover of the mountains about a league from Hume, sent seven or eight of his men towards the castle—those same that for that very purpose had, by the order of the Queen Dowager and of the Lady Hume their mistress long favoured the English and helped to set up boulevards,[1] couillons, and casemates that were made there, and by this means had noted sufficiently the manner of their watches and sentinels. These, then, dressed as countryfolk and without arms, being taken, with some victuals, by the English, and brought to Hume, were questioned separately as to the whereabouts of the French Army and of him whom they called Milord Hume.

As they had been instructed by the Queen, they were all found to agree in their answers, and said they all belonged to Edinburgh. The English, believing them, counted out payment for their victual, and asked them to come again often. Which same the seven, by their master's orders, did the next day, arriving one after another at the castle, where, being surprised by the night before they were dismissed by the English, and—as if Heaven had decided to favour their ploy— chancing on a time of heavy rain, with a storm as violent as might be coming on, they did not have to be begged to stay, but agreeing at the first invitation, as soon as they had their cue, were able, as night fell, to make an opportunity of sleeping where they would be able to help their friends.

These, being guided by the eighth man, who knew all the best approaches to the castle, came pretty close, where they

---

[1] Originally ramparts—the word became our *bulwark*.

halted waiting until the commanding officer—who was an English captain, personally brave but with small practical experience of war—had made his round, sure that, as was his habit, he would go to bed immediately afterwards. Now, they had recognised him by the lantern which he commonly had carried before him, for which reason they approached little by little, more assuredly, until a gentleman of the name of Hume, aged more than sixty, who led all the party, climbed up a turf wall, which being built *en talus* [1] and freshened with the heavy rain, was reasonably easy to climb.

When this gentleman was about his own height from the edge of the wall, he was going on, but as he raised himself, an Englishman placed as sentry in that same place, having glimpsed him, gave a vigorous alert, not only to the guard but to the whole garrison. At the noise, the English captain, who was between sheets, turned out in a hurry, armed with a cutlass and a steel buckler and for the rest in his nightshirt, and ran to the place where the alarm had been given ; where seeing, as he judged, no likelihood that anyone was there, the weather being so wet and so cold, he lost his temper and cursed the sentry for raising a false alarm. " The French," said this Captain of Hume, " are too far away to come and do themselves in [2] by reconnoitring our walls, and the Scots too poor fighters to spend nights like this in risking their precious lives." With which words the worthy Captain retired to his quarters.

But the Scots whom he had insulted, and who had very well heard what he had said, as soon as they thought he had got to bed again and the rest had quieted, sent up once more the old gentleman, who as we have said was over sixty, to guide them in carrying out their attempt. He, hearing the sentry whistling on his beat, climbed again, as quietly as he could, to the parapet, and seeing from there that his whistler had turned his back, fell on him dagger in hand, and gave him such strokes in the throat

---

[1] Military term for the sloping face of an earthwork.
[2] " Se venir achever de perdre."

and in the belly that his soul found room enough to leave his body. And he found himself so well followed by his men, and helped by those who had entered the day before, that those who met any English put them to the sword. Nor was Milord de Hume less to be praised for having beaten his enemy and recovered his place by this stratagem than if he had carried it by assault after a furious bombardment and a long and costly siege. For it is an incomparable glory to a leader to use arms to such advantage that, saving his own men from danger, he overcomes his enemy and gives the full effect to his own intentions.

149. Nemesis

Beaugué was probably not at the capture of Hume, since he does not use the first person plural in writing of it. He does use it of the capture of Ferniehurst by the French, so, though as usual he does not say so, he was no doubt there.

The English captain of the place was a sadistic brute, who had made himself loathed by the whole countryside. He offered to surrender on terms, but was told he would get none : so the fight continued.

Meanwhile, a great number of Scots who had followed M. d'Essé, dismounting and turning loose their horses, as is their custom, had done so much that they had forced the gate of the courtyard where we were. The English captain, seeing this, and thinking to himself that if he were to fall into the hands of the Scots, against whom he had committed so many crimes, he would be killed, promptly came out through the breach, and seeking to save himself, surrendered to the Seigneur de Dussac and La Motte Rouge. They, intending to treat him by the conventions of war, were trying to get him away out of the crowd, when they came on a Scot who recognised him for the cruel tyrant who had raped his wife and daughters. And remembering such outrage, before anyone could grasp what he would do, he cut off his head so neatly with one blow that it leapt four paces from his body. Which was at once greeted with wild yells by more than a hundred Scots, and raised on high to show the vengeance they had taken upon his foul and filthy cruelties. Then, after many of them had steeped their hands in the carrion's blood, with as much joy as if they had stormed the city of London, they took the head and hung it on a stone where three roads met, where they left it for all passers-by to see.

Cruelty had bred cruelty in that war. Beaugué's own prisoner was put to a grim death. Beaugué was startled, and says so plainly : but he adds that after what the Scots had suffered he could not blame them for vindictiveness.

150. The Fate of Aggressors

In the " Compleynt of Scotland" the writer looks back at history in a passage that comes home to our minds today . . . though it does not always so happen in history.

The famous historiographouris and croniklis of al countreis maikis manifest of the miserabil ruinis that God sendis on wrangeous conquestouris, quhilkis be ambitioun and outrageous pride hes be thair tyrannie invadit uthir countreis, and eftirwart hes tint thair ain countrey and thairself hes maid ane evil end.

151. The Onlooker

Another Frenchman, Michel de Castelnau, Seigneur de Mauvissière et de Concressault, has a word to say in his memoirs of that war. He had been Ambassador to both Scotland and England.

The Scots are a fierce, stubborn, and warlike nation, who cannot be dominated by force, unless one should completely wipe them out, which would be too difficult, considering the nature of the country : and one cannot tame their wild spirit with the rod, but by treating them gently and with courtesy.

152. WAR AND PEACE

Nothing caused James VI more trouble with his English sub-jects than that, while they were still in a highly, if economically, chauvinistic mood, his passion was for European peace, which he tried to secure by counterbalancing the Germanies with a Western Union of Britain, France, and Spain.

He had early thought a good deal on the subject. This is how he states, in the " Basilikon Doron," the duties of a king in regard to war.

After recommending that neighbouring states should be treated by the rule " Do as you would be done by,"

If any of them will not abstain, notwithstanding whatever your good deserts, to wrong you or your subjects, crave redress at leisure, hear and do all reason ; and if no offer that is lawful or honourable can make him abstain nor repair his wrong-doing, then for last refuge, commit the justice of your cause to God ; giving first honestly up with him,[1] and in a public and honour-able form. . . .

Before ye take on war, play the wise King's part described by Christ, foreseeing how ye may bear it out with all necessary provision : especially remember that money is *Nervus belli.* . . .

There follows some very sound practical advice on discipline in war, and on the King's part in securing it.

And as I have counselled you to be slow in taking on a war, so advise I you to be slow in peace-making. Before you agree, look that the ground of your war be satisfied in your peace, and that ye see a good surety for you and your people : other ways an honourable and just war is more tolerable than a dishonour-able and disadvantageous peace.

[1] Breaking off relations with him.

153. RAW MATERIAL

After 1550 there was no official war between Scotland and England : but there was plenty of unofficial and semi-official fighting, much armed intervention in Scots civil contests, and a constant underground activity. Here are some extracts from an English agent's report of 1585. He gives a long and carefully annotated list of Scots lords, neatly tabulated in geographical order.

Montrose : John Graham, a man above thirty years of age ; born of the same mother with the Earl of Athol. His wife the Lord Drummond's daughter. His power not great ; in affection French ; and in religion doubted. He seems to depend on the Earl of Argyle, the rather to fortify himself against the Earl of Angus and his friends, whose wife he is charged to have dishonoured. The man is for courage and spirit a principal among the nobility of Scotland.

Argyle : Colin Campbell, a man of forty years and above, of a great house, living, and power, chiefly of Highlandmen. He is now Chancellor and by inheritance Chief Justice. Religious and of good nature, but weak in judgment and overmuch led by his wife ; a man very sickly and not like to live long.

Hume : Alexander Hume, a young man of seventeen years of age ; of a great living and many friends, though they all follow him not. Himself of no very good government or hope. His mother is daughter to the Lord Gray, and now wife of the Master of Glamis. His surname and power upon the Border is very great.

Boyd : Robert Lord Boyd, a man past sixty years ; he is accounted wise and of good wealth and power. His ancestors were great in the days of King James the Second.[1] Himself hath put off many storms. He is a favourer of the Douglases, and always hated of the House of Lennox.

[1] The agent's history is not as accurate as his comments are shrewd. The Boyds rose to power in the minority of James III.

154. Frontier Incident

Here is the raw prose of one of the greatest of the Riding Ballads, as recorded in the contemporary " diarey " of Robert Birrel, burgess of Edinburgh.

The same 6 of Aprile 1596, the Laird of Buccleugh passit to the castell of Carleill with 70 men, and tuik out Will: Kynmonth out of the said castell, the said Will: lyand in ironis within the iron yett.   This he did with shouting and crying and sound of trumpet, puttand the said toun and country in sic ane fray, that the lyke of sic ane wassaledge wes nevir done since the memorie of man, no in Wallace dayis.

fray, alarm.   *wassaledge*, vassalage, service—feat of arms.

Here is a fuller, though a later, account, written, one guesses, by an eye-witness.   It is at least after 1603, since it refers to the late Queen Elizabeth : and the language is a very early form of Scoto-English rather than actual Scots.   It comes from the collection known as the Warrender Papers, a mass of manuscript material apparently got together for Archbishop Spottiswoode's " History of the Church and State of Scotland." [1]

There was for the time Warden of the West Marches of England for the Queen, the Lord Scroop ; and for the King the Lord of Buccleuch.   The Deputies of these two officers having met at a Day of Trews [2] . . . the place of their meeting was at the Dayholm of Kershope, where a burn divides England from Scotland and Liddesdale from Bewcastle.   There met for the Lord of Buccleuch Robert Scott of Hayning, and for the Lord

---

[1] Spottiswoode himself was about thirty when the affair took place.   He died in 1639, so an eye-witness might have written this when no more than in his early sixties, yet at a time when Border Law was something that needed explaining.

[2] The Days of Trews or Truce were regular meetings between the opposite Wardens, for the settlement of differences involving nationals of both kingdoms. The text explains the regulations in force.

This particular meeting was held just at the place where the L.M.S. railway crosses the Kershope Burn into England, at the small country station of Kershope-foot.   The actual spot would be between the railway line and the Liddel.

Scroop Mr Salkeld . . . that was his depute for the time. There was mutual truce taken, and intimate by sound of trumpets and proclamation in Their Majesties' names to the troops on both sides before their meeting, as the custom was. Wherefore the meetings were called Days of Trews, seeing therethrough parties on both sides, that otherwise were under deadly feud and in quarrel, did usually in peace and assurance meet and do their business one beside another, and converse mutually and in assurance with such as they had occasion withall.

Upon the truce taken, the officers or deputies kept their meeting, made mutual redress of such wrongs as had occurred before that time, and sundered in very good terms, either party returning homeward. By the way, it is to be remembered that the tenor of such truces as usually were taken betwixt the Wardens or their Deputes in the Princes' names bare that upon pain of death, presently to be executed, all persons whatsomever that came to these meetings should be safe for any proceeding at present occasion, from the time of the meeting of the Wardens or their Deputes till the next day at the sun rising, within which space it was presupposed that every person that came there might be returned to their own house, for otherwise many parties that were under feud and quarrel with one another, the strongest side might have taken advantage of the weakness of the other, if the grudge had been between the Wardens : or the strongest particular parties of either side might, seeing the weakness of the other there, in his return homeward towards his house, from the great troops had sundered, upon any intelligence might have taken the occasion of revenge by putting himself in his way.

Now this truce being thusways aretted,[1] and the business done by the Deputes that they met for, there was one called William Armstrong of Kinmont, Scotsman and a Borderer, in company with the Scottish Depute, whom against some of the English had quarrel, as was alleged : who being sundered from

---

[1] *Arrêté*, officially established.

the Depute and riding homeward, his way lying down Liddes-dale, the which is at that part divided from England but by a river, easily passable, called Liddel, and the English Depute holding his way down the English side, in sight and within a mile of the other's way, those who had the quarrel against him, as afterwards for a weak excuse the Deputy of England did pretend, seeing him riding on his way with but three or four in company, and lippening for no harm as that day fell, they made a chase of more than 200 men out of the English troop, chases the said Will of Kinmont more than three or four mile, comes to him and takes him prisoner, brings him back to the Deputy of England, who carried him away with him prisoner to the Castle of Carlisle. But the very truth was that the English Deputy, thinking to do good service by the seizing of such a notorious offender, caused break the truce himself. Where, and seeing the same was done by plain breach of the truces, the Lord of Buccleuch, as the King's officer, did write unto Mr Salkeld the Deputy of England immediately and in absence of the Lord Scroop for redress thereof.

Mr Salkeld by his answer did excuse himself, and refer the matter unto the Lord Scroop, Warden,[1] who for the time was at a house of his own in the country. The Lord Scroop, therefore, was written to in the same sense by the Lord of Buccleuch, to wit for the setting of the prisoner at liberty without condition or band, seeing he was unlawfully taken and con-sequently to the touch of the King.[2] It was answered that he could do nothing thereanent, seeing that the prisoner had been such a malefactor, without the privity of the Queen and Council of England. So as his answer tending to delay, the Lord of Buccleuch, being loth to inform the King of the matter, lest the same should have bred some mistaking between the Princes, he made trial by one Robert Bowes, then Resident Ambassador for the Queen in Scotland, who upon his desire and information

---

[1] " Passed to you, please."
[2] The dignity of the Crown was involved.

did write very seriously unto the Lord Scroop for redress of the matter, and that the matter should come to no further hearing.

Nothing was done or answered to a purpose, natheless, neither upon the King's Highness' own instance towards the Warden, by the Ambassador of England afterwards and first, and next to the Queen of England from His Majesty's self. Wherefore, the Lord Buccleuch, being the King's officer, finding His Majesty's honour touched so apparently to the world, he did resolve himself to seek the relief of the prisoner by the means whereby it was performed, and that with such foresight and regard as could be, that through any rigorous circumstance of the action, in regard of the place wherein he was kept, that the same should breed no greater jar between the Princes than merely that which was to grow from the simple relief of a prisoner unlawfully taken.

And for such purpose the Lord of Buccleuch, upon intelligence taken that the Castle of Carlisle, where the prisoner was kept, was surprisable, and of the means, by sending some persons of trust to view a postern gate and to measure the height of the wall, he did immediately draw together very close a two hundred horse, assigned the place of meeting an hour before sunset at the tower of Morton, the which is ten miles from Carlisle, and upon the Water of Sark in the Debatable Land, where he had his preparations of ladders for scaling the castle wall, and other instruments of iron for breaking through the wall and forcing of gates, if the need had been.

The troop being assembled at the place, he marcheth forwards and entereth English ground within six miles of Carlisle, and passes the Water of Esk, where the Graemes did inhabit, at the falling of the night. From he entered English ground the order was this : there were sent some few horsemen before all the way to discover,[1] and they were seconded by a forty or fifty horse, in case of any rencounter ; there were next them

[1] Scout.

the ladders, carried two and two upon a horse, and horse carrying the other instruments mentioned before, and last of all himself with the rest of the troop. He marched on in this order, and passeth the Water of Eden about a two hours before day, at the Stanwix [1] Bank beneath Carlisle Brig, the water being at that time [in spate] through rains that had fallen well thick. He comes to the Sacery, a plain place, anunder the town and castle, and haps upon the side of a little water or burn that they call Cadaye. There he makes about a fourscore men to light from their horses, take the ladders and other instruments with them, and accompanies them himself to the foot of the wall, makes fast the ladders to be set on the wall and assayed, whilst the sentinels were on the top of the wall above them, looking over, crying and speaking one to another : but that it happened to fall to be very dark in that hindnight, and a little misty. The ladders proved too short through the error of them who had been sent to measure the wall, and then order was given for to make use of the other instruments that were carried, for opening the wall a little hard by the postern ; the which, being set in the way, the Lord of Buccleuch, seeing that the matter was likely to succeed well, and that no discovery was, did retire himself to about a six score of men, that he had reserved to stand on horseback with himself for the surety of them that he had sent upon the Castle, and against the sort of [2] the town, and so put himself and the horsemen betwixt the postern of the Castle and the next port of the town, upon the plain field, to assure the retiral of his own from the Castle again, who were sent also in such competent number as was known to be able to master them that were within the Castle, together with a trumpet to give a greater terror to them of the Castle upon occasion, and to give a signal to them that were without upon their entry, who did also correspond upon the first sound of the

[1] Stanwix village is on the Roman Wall, just due north of Carlisle across the Eden, nearly opposite its confluence with the Caldew Water—the writer's Cadaye.

[2] Sortie from.

trumpet with a cry and noise, the more to confirm his own that was gone upon the Castle, and to terrify both the Castle and the town by the imagination of a greater force.

They entered the Castle, the first of them single by the overture that was made, and there brake open the postern by such instruments as was fit, to give passage to the greater number. Then did occur[1] to their entry allanerlie the watchmen and sentinels, and some others after upon the alarm, and made some resistance with the weapons they had. But after they were put back and scattered, the rest that were within doors, hearing the noise of the trumpet and the Castle was entered, and the noise of the voices without, both the Lord Scroop himself and his Warden Depute Salkeld, being there with the garrison and their own retinue, did keep themselves close.

The prisoner was taken out of the house where he was kept, the which was known by the Lord of Buccleuch sending a woman upon a pretext to visit the prisoner a day before ; she reporting what place he was kept in, there lacked not persons enough that knew all the rooms, and so went directly after the rencounter with the watchmen, and some other with them that came to the alarm afterwards to the place, and brought him forth, and so by the postern got away.

Some other prisoners were brought out that were taken in the rencounter, the which were presently returned into the castle again by the Lord of Buccleuch, and any other spoil or booting hindered also ; yea, not so much as any other door that was open within the Castle entered, but that where the prisoner was, the which was broken up ; nor other door that was shut so much as knocked at, though they that entered might have taken prisoner the Warden and all the persons that were there, and made prey of the whole goods, seeing they were masters of the Castle. Such was the regard of the Lord of Buccleuch and the strict orders he gave, being present himself, that he would not have any circumstance to fall out in that

[1] Run up.

action, in so far as it could have been eschewed, that could have given the least cause of offence, either to the King his master or to the late Queen. By which time of bringing forth the prisoner, the town and Castle was in a great stir and alarm, and there was a putting themselves in arms. Drums were beating, bells ringing, and bales [1] put up on the top of the Castle to warn the country. The day was broken, and so the enterprise having so well succeeded, the Lord of Buccleuch, after that they that went upon the Castle and the prisoner were retired and horsed, marched close by the Sacery again, to the river, at the Stanwix bank, where, upon the alarm of the Castle and the town, some were assembled on the far side of the passage. And so unto that time, having retired himself close and without any noise from the Castle, he caused sound up his trumpet before he took the river, it being yet both misty and dank though the day was broken, to the end both to encourage his own and to let them that were abiding him upon the passage know that he looked for and was to receive any charge that they should offer him, whereupon they made choice to look to him and give him way, and not adventure upon so doubtful an event with him, who behoved to retire him homeward and not lodge there, if he could choose, after such an usage of his host. So having passed the river, within a little the day began to grow light, and he did retire himself in order, through the Graemes of Esk and Leven, and came back to Scots ground at about a two hours after the sun rising, and so homewards.

England raged furiously, and pelted King James with notes. James, well aware that Willie's arrest was a flat contravention of international law, met the protests by politely offering an international commission to investigate matters. Elizabeth, who knew this as well as he did, had to avoid the commission, or lose face badly, so she put up a smoke-screen of righteous indignation.

Fully to appreciate the very characteristic personal letter she

[1] Signal fires.

wrote to James on the 24th of June, one has to remember that, since its writer had attained her throne, every conspiracy against the Scots Crown had had a thriving tap-root in her court, while for centuries every Scottish rebel and traitor had been sure of help and refuge in her country.   One of the worst had even been given the Garter.

MY DEAR BROTHER,

I am to seek with what arguments my letter should be fraught, since such themes be given me that I am loath to send and slow to recite.   Yet, since I needs must treat of and unwillingly receive, I cannot omit to set before you a too rare example of a seduced king by evil information.   Was it ever seen that a prince from his cradle preserved from the slaughter, held up in royal dignity, conserved from many treasons, maintained in all sort of kindness, should remunerate with so hard measure such dear deserving with doubt to yield a just treater's response to a lawful friend's demand ?   Ought it to be put to a question whether a king should do another his alike right, or should a council be demanded for their good pleasure what he himself should do ?   Were it in the nonage of the prince it might have some colour, but in a father's age it seems strange, and I dare say without example.   I am sorry for the cause that constrains this speech, specially in so apert[1] a matter, whose root groweth far, and is of that nature that it, I fear me, will more harm the wronger nor the wronged : for how little regard soever be held of me, yet I should grieve too much to see you neglect yourself. . . .

After much more to the same effect, she continues :

Wherefore, for fine, let this suffice you, that I am as evil treated by my named friend as I could be by my known foe. Shall any castle or habitation of mine be assailed by a night larceny, and shall not my confederate send the offender to his

[1] Open, public.

due punishment ? . . . The law of kingly love would have said nay, and not, for persuasion of such as never can nor will stead you, but dishonour you to keep their own rule, lay behind you the due regard of me, and in it of yourself. . . .

For commissioners I will never grant, for an act that he cannot deny that made it. . . . For other doubtful and litigious causes upon our Borders, I will be ready to permit commissioners, if I shall find it needful, but for this matter of so villanous a usage, I answer you I will never be so answered as hearers shall need. . . . So praying God for your keeping.

Buccleuch was not handed over, but later, on his way to the Low Countries, where he had helped to found the famous Scots-Dutch, he cheerfully bearded the lioness in her den, and laughed her into regaining her sense of humour. Willie went about his more or less lawful occasions, and Scotland was richer by a great Riding Ballad.

155. A Riding Ballad

The Riding Ballads are still fairly well known even in their own country : but there are several scholarly and/or literary excuses for including one here as a specimen of the kind. " Kinmont Willie " is perhaps the finest of all, but its story has just been told at a certain length, and it is easily available. " Jamie Telfer," which is hardly inferior, is perhaps slightly less known, and it tells of a typical Border incident, such as might happen any night of the week. The version is the late eighteenth-century one, from Scott's "Border Minstrelsy." [1]

[1] The Border law of the Hot Trod illustrated in this ballad is summed up in Scott's *Black Dwarf*. " Hout, there's nae great skill needed ; just put a lighted peat on the end of a spear, or hayfork, or siclike, and blaw a horn and cry the gathering-word, and then it's lawful to follow gear into England, and recover it by the strong hand, or to take gear from some other Englishman, providing ye lift nae mair than's been lifted frae you. That's the auld Border Law, made at Dundrennan in the days of the Black Douglas. Deil ane need doubt it. It's as clear as the sun " . . . though under the moon some excess of enthusiasm might now and then forget the last limitation.

It fell about the Martinmas tyde,
 When our Border steeds get corn and hay,
The Captain of Bewcastle hath bound him to ryde,
 And he's ower to Tividale to drive a prey.

The first ae guide that they met wi',
 It was high up in Hardhaughswire ;
The second guide that we [they ?] met wi',
 It was laigh down in Borthwick Water.

" What tidings, what tidings, my trusty guide ? "
 " Nae tidings, nae tidings, I hae to thee ;
But gin ye'll gae to the fair Dodhead,
 Mony a cow's calf I'll let thee see."

And when they cam to the fair Dodhead,
 Right hasily they clam the peel ;
They loosed the kye out, ane an a',
 And ranshackled the house right weel.

Now Jamie Telfer's heart was sair,
 The tear aye rowing in his e'e ;
He pled wi' the Captain to hae his gear,
 Or else revenged he wad be.

The Captain turned him round and leugh ;
 Said, " Man, there's naething in thy house,
But ae auld sword without a sheath,
 That hardly now wad fell a mouse."

The sun was na up, but the moon was down,
 It was the gryming o' a new fa'n snaw,
Jamie Telfer has run ten myles afoot,
 Between the Dodhead and the Stob's Ha'.

And when he cam to the fair tower yate,
  He shouted loud and cried weel hie,
Till out bespak auld Gibby Elliot—
  " Whae's this that brings the fraye to me ? "

" It's I, Jamie Telfer o' the fair Dodhead,
  And a harried man I think I be !
There's naething left at the fair Dodhead
  But a waefu' wife and bairnies three."

" Gae seek your succour at Branksome Ha',
  For succour ye'se get nane frae me !
Gae seek your succour where ye paid black-mail,
  For, man ! ye ne'er paid money to me."

Jamie has turned him round about,
  I wat the tear blinded his e'e—
" I'll ne'er pay mail to Elliot again,
  And the fair Dodhead I'll never see.

" My hounds may a' rin masterless,
  My hawks may fly frae tree to tree,
My lord may grip my vassal lands,
  For there again maun I never be ! "

He has turned him to the Tiviot side,
  Even as fast as he could drie,
Till he cam to the Coultart Cleugh,
  And there he shouted baith loud and hie.

Then up bespak him auld Jock Grieve—
  " Wha's this that brings the fraye to me ? "
" It's I, Jamie Telfer o' the fair Dodhead,
  A harried man I trow I be.

" There's naething left in the fair Dodhead
  But a greeting wife and bairnies three,
And six poor ca's stand in the sta',
  A' routing loud for their minnie."

" Alack a wae ! " quo' auld Jock Grieve,
  " Alack, my heart is sore for thee,
For I was married on the elder sister,
  And you on the youngest of a' the three."

Then he has ta'en out a bonny black,
  Was right weel fed wi' corn and hay,
And he's set Jamie Telfer on his back
  To the Catslockhill to tak the fraye.

And when he cam to the Catslockhill,
  He shouted loud and cried full hie,
Till out and spak him William's Wat—
  " O wha's this brings the fraye to me ? "

" It's I, Jamie Telfer o' the fair Dodhead,
  A harried man I think I be !
The Captain o' Bewcastle has driven my gear ;
  For God's sake rise and succour me."

" Alas for wae ! " quo' William's Wat,
  " Alack, for thee my heart is sair !
I never cam by the fair Dodhead,
  That ever I fand thy basket bare."

He's set his twa sons on coal-black steeds,
  Himsel' upon a freckled grey,
And they are on wi' Jamie Telfer,
  To Branksome Ha' to tak the fraye.

And whan they cam' to Branksome Ha',
    They shouted a' baith loud and hie,
Till up and spak him auld Buccleuch,
    Said—" Whae's this brings the fraye to me ? "

" It's I, Jamie Telfer o' the fair Dodhead,
    And a harried man I think I be !
There's nought left in the fair Dodhead,
    But a greeting wife and bairnies three."

" Alack for wae ! " quoth the guid auld lord,
    " And ever my heart is wae for thee !
But fye gar cry on Willie my son,
    And see that he come to me speedilie !

" Gar warn the water, braid and wide,
    Gar warn it sune and hastilie !
They that winna ride for Telfer's kye,
    Let them never look in the face o' me !

" Warn Wat o' Harden and his sons,
    Wi' them will Borthwick Water ride ;
Warn Gaudilands, and Allanhaugh,
    And Gilmanscleugh, and Commonside.

" Ride by the gate at Priesthaughswire,
    And warn the Currors o' the Lea ;
As ye cum down the Hermitage Slack,
    Warn doughty Willie o' Gorrinberry."

The Scotts they rade, the Scotts they ran,
    Sae starkly and sae steadily !
And aye the ower-word o' the thrang
    Was—" Rise for Branksome readilie ! "

The gear was driven the Frostylee up,
   Frae the Frostylee unto the plain,
Whan Willie has looked his men before,
   And saw the kye right fast drivand.

" Whae drives thir kye ? " gan Willie say,
   " To mak an outspeckle o' me ? "
" It's I, the Captain o' Bewcastle, Willie ;
   I winna layne my name for thee."

" O will ye let Telfer's kye gae back,
   Or will ye do aught for regard o' me ?
Or by the faith o' my body," quo' Willie Scott,
   " I'se ware my dame's cauf's skin on thee ! "

" I winna let the kye gae back,
   Neither for thy love nor yet thy fear ;
But I will drive Jamie Telfer's kye,
   In spite of every Scott that's here."

" Set on them, lads ! " quo Willie then ;
   " Fye lads, set on them cruellie !
For ere they win to the Ritterford,
   Mony a toom saddle there sall be ! "

Then till't they gaed, wi' heart and hand ;
   The blows fell thick as bickering hail ;
And mony a horse ran masterless,
   And mony a comely cheek was pale !

But Willie was stricken ower the head,
   And through the knapscap the sword has gane ;
And Harden grat for very rage,
   When Willie on the grund lay slane.

But he's tane aff his guid steel cap,
    And thrice he's waved it in the air—
And Dinlay snaw was ne'er mair white,
    Nor the lyart locks of Harden's hair.

" Revenge ! revenge ! " auld Wat gan cry ;
    " Fye lads, lay on them cruellie !
We'll ne'er see Tiviotside again,
    Or Willie's death revenged shall be."

O mony a horse ran masterless,
    The splintered lances flew on hie ;
But or they wan to the Kershope ford,
    The Scotts had gotten the victory.

John o' Brigham there was slane,
    And John o' Barlow, as I hear say ;
And thirty mae o' the Captain's men,
    Lay bleeding on the grund that day.

The Captain was run through the thick of the thigh,
    And broken was his right leg bane ;
If he had lived this hundred year,
    He had never been loved by woman again.

" Hae back thy kye ! " the Captain said ;
    " Dear kye, I trow, to some they be !
For gin I suld live a hundred years,
    There will ne'er fair lady smile on me."

Then word is gone to the Captain's bride,
    Even in the bower where that she lay,
That her lord was prisoner in enemy's hand,
    Since into Tividale he had led the way.

" I wad lourd hae had a winding-sheet,
   And helped to put it ower his heid,
Ere he had been disgraced by the Border Scott,
   Whan he ower Liddel his men did lead."

There was a wild gallant amang us a',
   His name was Watty wi' the Wudspurs,
Cried, " On for his house in Stanegirthside,
   If ony man will ride wi' us ! "

When they cam to the Stanegirthside,
   They dang wi' trees, and burst the door ;
They loosed out a' the Captain's kye,
   And set them forth our lads before.

There was an auld wyfe ayont the fire,
   A wee bit o' the Captain's kin—
" Whae dar loose out the Captain's kye,
   Or answer to him and his men ? "

" It's I, Watty Wudspurs, loose the kye !
   I winna layne my name frae thee !
And I will loose out the Captain's kye,
   In scorn o' a' his men and he."

When they cam to the fair Dodhead,
   They were a wellcum sight to see !
For instead of his ain ten milk kye,
   Jamie Telfer has gotten thirty and three.

And he has paid the rescue shot,
   Baith wi' goud and white monie ;
And at the burial o' Willie Scott,
   I wat was mony a weeping e'e.

Hardhaughswire is the pass from Liddesdale to Upper Teviot-dale, and Borthwick Water runs into Teviot. Stobs Hall is on Slitrig Water : Jamie had paid protection-money to Elliot, who let him down. Branksome is Buccleuch's, the head of the name of Scott. The whole thing is of Scott country : Wat of Harden was the lineal ancestor of a more famous Sir Walter, and husband of the Flower of Yarrow : it is curious to think that in no more than a hundred and eighty years his descendant was a douce Edinburgh lawyer.

156. THE OTHER SIDE

There is another side to these things : and the Borders knew it. It comes out immemorially in one brief ballad whose source, according to the old tradition, is no more than a routine incident of justice. When at the end of his tumultuous minority, James V rode out in 1529 to enforce the King's Peace on the troubled Borders, he hanged Piers Cockburn of Henderland over his door, not far above St Mary's Loch of Yarrow. And tradition puts this in the mouth of Cockburn's wife :

> My love he built me a bonny bower,
> And clad it a' wi' lilye flour ;
> A brawer bower ye ne'er did see,
> Than my true love he built for me.
>
> There came a man, by middle day,
> He spied his sport, and went away ;
> And brought the King, that very night,
> Who brake my bower, and slew my knight.
>
> He slew my knight, to me sae dear,
> He slew my knight, and poin'd his gear ;
> My servants a' for life did flee,
> And left me in extremitie.

I sew'd his sheet, making my mane ;
I watched the corpse, myself alane ;
I watched his body, night and day,
No living creature came that way.

I took his body on my back,
And whiles I gaed, and whiles I sat ;
I digg'd a grave, and laid him in,
And happed him wi' the sod sae green.

But think na ye my heart was sair
When I laid the moul on his yellow hair ;
And think na ye my heart was wae,
When I turned about, away to gae ?

Nae living man I'll love again,
Since that my lovely knight is slain ;
Wi' ae lock of his yellow hair
I'll chain my heart for evermair.

And in our own time . . .

XII

THE AULD ALLIANCE

Deux patries, la sienne et la France.
Old saying

157. SHIELD AND ALLIANCE

In his " Rolment of Courtis " Habakkuk Bisset tells of the Auld Alliance, and its making between Achaius and Charlemagne in the year 809. As an Aberdeen man, he was probably an Episcopalian, and therefore Nationalist and pro-French.

And that the nobillis of Scotland suld be the mair mindfull of the foirsaid League, to the King of Scottis armes (quhilkis wes that tyme ane reid Lyoun rampand in ane feild of gold) wes eikit ane doubill tressour, with contrair lilleis, including about the Lyoun in all pointis : to signifie that the said Lyoun wes then armit, keipit, and defendit with the lilleis, richis, and freindschip of that nobill and maist puissant kingdom of France be the foirsaid League, and confederat with the samyn perpetuallie. And als to signifie that all the Kingis of Scottis sall fecht valiantlie for thair realm and libertie, fredome of religioun and innocence perpetuallie, and support Frenschemen for evir aganis all thair enemeis.

The history, of course, is mythical. Charlemagne and Eochaid of Scots may have made a treaty of some sort—there is a hint of an Irish one in Einhard : but armorial bearings do not arise till long after. Yet the myth expresses popular feeling.

158. FRIENDSHIP IS TESTED

In 1525, after the disastrous defeat of Francis I at the battle of Pavia, the Estates sent their condolences by one Patrick Houymes

*or Wymes.   Teulet renders this Hume, but from other indications
the name seems to have been Wemyss.   The original is in French.*

. . . First, the said Wemyss shall protest that the Lords of
the Council of the Kingdom of Scotland, having heard of the
troublesome misfortune which befell in the battle in which was
taken the first Christian King, they are as grieved and sorrowful
as if it had befallen themselves, and are not less disturbed and
unhappy than if the case had fallen upon themselves, and desire
above all things to hear some good change of fortune into relief
and prosperity.

*The message goes on to say that they have refused to make a
peace with England, unless France is included : but Henry VIII
will not make it unless they throw over France, which they will
not do.   As an English attack in force is being mounted, they
hope that France will send the promised help, including a couple
of hundred expert gunners.   The French were then supreme in
artillery.*

*The French Regent, Louise de Savoie, Duchesse d'Angoulême,
replied gracefully, though with some confusion of pronouns :*

. . . The ancient and inviolable love, alliance, federation,
and affinity which has been from the earliest times, and is now,
between the House of France and that of Scotland, the entire
faith and firm trust which the Kings of France have had in them,
so that they have given the guard of their persons to people of
their nation, and that the gentlemen of Scotland who have gone
to France have found there good welcome and great matches,
so that there are great houses in France sprung from the Scots
nobility, and such has been the love and confederation of French
and Scots that each has considered it indissoluble. . . .

And [the Lords of the Council, and the Estates] have shown
that the love they bear to the House of France is true and un-
feigned, insomuch as the friend reveals himself in adversity, and
that they, after having learned of the King's capture, have shown

themselves firm and constant in resolution to keep more than
ever the friendship and alliance they have with France, however
the English may try to force them to break it. . . .

159. KING FRANCIS IS ALARMED

*None the less, in 1531 Francis appears to have been much
afraid that Henry VIII would succeed in inducing his nephew
James V to break the Alliance. He therefore sent this letter to
King James. The body of it is a careful secretarial black-letter,
but the last commendation and the signature are in Francis's own
bold Italian hand. It is in French.*

Most High, most Excellent, and most Puissant Prince, our
very dear and beloved brother, cousin, and ancient ally, greeting,
love, and brotherly affection.   We have lately been informed by
way of Flanders that the Emperor had discussed sending you
shortly a gentleman of his, as much to bring you the collar of
his Order [1] as to speak to you and put forward certain projects
of his, in order to treat and draw up an agreement with you,
and in this way divide you from your good friends and old
allies—a thing which we could not and will not really believe
you would choose to do, considering the friendship and alliance
which has always and from old times subsisted between your
predecessors and our own, and the kind and courteous words
which have constantly been borne to us from you, indeed quite
lately by the Sieur de Beauvoye, gentleman of our Chamber,
whom we sent to you expressly to declare and make plain to
you our will and intentions, and the love and singular affection
which we bear to you and to your kingdom.[2]

[1] The Emperor was Charles V, who as both Emperor and King of Spain,
controlling Italy and the Low Countries, had France encircled, with the gap
closed by his ally England.   The Order is the Golden Fleece, which, in fact, was
sent: its insignia appear on James's great gate at Linlithgow with those of his own
Thistle, the French St Michel, and the English Garter.

[2] From its first trace in 1168 the Alliance had never been merely dynastic :
it is always definitely one of *peoples*.   This, in the Middle Ages and even later,
shows a quite exceptional attitude to such things.   One notices that in the

None the less, we have decided to let you know of the above by the bearer, whom we have sent expressly for this purpose, in order to inform you more certainly of this present.   Praying you that when it shall come to pass that they wish you to put forward the new proposals and try by this means to change and lessen the ancient friendship that is between us, you will in no wise agree, but on the contrary choose to persevere in and continue those things which your predecessors and ours have inviolably guarded and observed.   And on our side you will always see by our actions that we wish perpetually to remain your good brother and old friend.   And meanwhile, as we have discussed all the above-mentioned things more at length and in detail with our very dear and beloved cousin the Duke of Albany[1] who will write to you more fully on our behalf, we do not mean for the present to write you a longer letter, save that we pray you to believe him on this matter as you would ourselves, and you will do a thing which shall be most pleasing and agreeable to us.   And no less, most High, Excellent, and Puissant Prince, our very dear brother, cousin, and old ally, we pray the Creator to have you in His most holy and worthy keeping.

Written at Rouen, the 2nd day of February, the year 1531.

Your good brother, cousin, and ancient ally,

FRANÇOIS.

160. RENEWING ALLIANCE

As a matter of routine, the Auld Alliance was formally renewed on the accession of a new sovereign of either Scotland or France. In Mary's case, the situation had been complicated by the marriage treaty with England, which had caused the usual renewal to be delayed by the pro-English party.   Henry's bad faith in violating

preceding extract, Louise de Savoie, who was not a Frenchwoman, speaks of it merely as the usual dynastic alliance, but the Scots had not done so, nor does her son Francis.

[1] John, Duke of Albany, James's cousin and Regent in his minority.   He had returned to France, of which he was High Admiral, but frequently took a hand in Scots foreign negotiations.   Francis's son was shortly to marry Albany's niece by marriage, Catherine de Medici.

*the peace, which of course was a condition of the Treaty, had caused
the Estates to denounce it, and the formal ratification of French
relations was made as usual in the December of 1543, when the
little Queen was just a year old.*

The quhilk day in presens of ane richt nobill prince James
Erl of Arane, Lord Hamiltoun, etc. Tutour to our Soverain
Ladie and Governour of hir realm,[1] and [the] Thre Estaitis of
the samyn sittand in Parliament, compeirit Jacques de la Brosse,
knicht, and Maister James Ménage, Counsalour of Parlement of
Rouen, Ambassadouris to the Maist Cristen King of France,
and thair at lenth schew and declairit the caus of thair message
and cuming in this realm, quhilk wes principallie for the pairt
of the said King of France, and to desire for the pairt of Scotland
the Auld Ancient Ligis, Contractis, and Consideratiounis of
Amitie and Kyndnes passit at all tymis befoir betuix the Kingis
of Scottis and of France thair ambassadouris ; and eftir the sicht [2]
of all contractis passit betuix the Kingis of France and Scotland
sen King Robert the Bruce, hes thocht verie expedient and with
ane consent and assent hes declairit and ordainit the saidis contractis to be ratifeit, apprevit, and confermit and to be of new
contractit and renewit. And in special the contractis maid
betuix umquhile our Soverain Ladeis Fader, quham God
assoilzie, his guidsire and grantsire with the Kingis of France,
and of all uthir contractis sen the deceise of umquhile King
Robert the Bruce first King of Scottis of that name and Charlis
King of France and Navarre : And ordainit letteris to be direct
heirupoun in dew and ampill form in our Soverain Ladeis name
with consent of hir said Tutour and Governour of hir realm,
undir Hir Grace Greit Seil, the King of France doand in
semblabill maneir for his pairt.

[1] Second cousin of James V, the Queen's next of kin and heir presumptive,
and, as such, her guardian and Regent. He was up to the neck in intrigue with
England, and the clerk who wrote his name in this report may have allowed
himself a dry legal chuckle.
[2] Examination.

161. True Alliance

Jean de Beaugué tells how, after giving siege to the English,
Albanian, and other troops in Haddington, and making an attack
on the Spaniards holding Jedburgh,

we withdrew to Edinburgh, where, how short a time our
fighting men had stayed there, to see their intercourse with the
Scots, they might have been born and bred in Scotland.   For
beyond that these two peoples have always been good friends,
and that one could not in all the world find two nations so compatible, the singular prudence and justice of Monsieur d'Essé,
his gentle, humane, and intimate manner of command, were so
effective, that it seemed enough that it should be his will to
make every man do his duty.

162. Trouble

As we know in our own day, the position of foreign troops in an
allied country, however friendly, has its difficulties.   Beaugué goes
on to tell how this happy symbiosis was threatened by an unfortun-
ate incident.

So lived, good friends, the Frenchmen and the Scots, as
perfect friendship commonly subsists between good people who
are alike in virtue [*or* of like qualities] when a French soldier,
unknown and of small account, and three or four Scots of
Edinburgh insulted each other by outrageous words.   And after
some quarrelling they came to arms, several Scots running up
to take the Frenchman to prison, and some French soldiers to
help the mutineer : which was a mistake which almost became
a great scandal, though the officers, none the less, were not to
blame, for as soon as they heard the disturbance they ran up in
haste and with much difficulty quieted matters.   Later that same
day, in the Grande Place of Edinburgh where the trouble had
begun, they had the man who had led the disturbance hanged.
In so doing they applied such an effective remedy to this un-

seemly business that the accord held, and holds still today, without the intercourse between the two nations, although it has been most familiar and friendly, being able since to give fresh occasion for quarrel.

163. A Vote of Thanks

On the 1st February of 1551, the Estates decided on a testimonial to the retiring French Ambassador.

The quhilk day it wes put in rememberaunce to my Lord Governouris Grace, Thrie Estaitis being present in Parliament, how that Monsieure Dosel,[1] the Maist Christin Kingis Lieutenant and Ambassadour, wes hastilie to depairt of this realm to his Maister, and that his guid service done in thir pairtis, baith in tyme of peace and weir, suld be writtin to the said Maist Christin King, nocht allanerlie thankand His Grace of the samyn, but alswa suppleand to thank and rewaird the said Monsieure Dosel. And thairfoir it wes concludit be the Thrie Estaitis that my Lord Secretar suld maik letteris in our Soverain Ladeis name, my Lord Governouris, and thairis, to the said Maist Christin King, in ampill and effectuous maneir to the effect foirsaid.

164. International Rights

Louis XII gave to all Scottish subjects the full rights of French nationality without any formality being necessary, and without any loss of their national rights as Scots. The converse grant of Scottish rights to French subjects was postponed, however, by the death of James IV. On the marriage of the Dauphin to Queen Mary, the French grant was renewed by Henri II: and thereafter, as a routine formality on accession, it was renewed by every French sovereign up to and including Louis XIV (1643–1715). After 1603 a clause was added specially enacting that the grant held good even

[1] D'Oysel.

*when Scotland's associated kingdom of England was at war with
France. Owing, perhaps, to the gap between 1643 and 1715, no
renewal was made by Louis XV and his successors : but the grant
has never been formally rescinded.*

*This is the converse Scottish declaration, as passed by the Estates
in 1555 :*

Item, becaus the Maist Christin King of France hes grantit
ane lettir of naturalitie for him and his successouris to all and
sindrie Scottismen being in the realm of France, or sal happin
to be in the samyn in onie tyme to cum, makand thaim abil to
bruik landis, heritagis, officis, digniteis, and beneficeis, and to
dispone thairupoun, and thair airis to succeid to thair landis and
heritagis, lyke as the said lettir of naturalitie registrat in the
Parlement of Paris, in the Greit Counsall, and in the Chalmer of
Comptis in the self at mair lenth purportis, THAIRFOIR the
Quenis Grace Dowriare and Regent of this realm, and Thrie
Estaitis of the samyn thinkis it guid and agreabil that the lyke
letteris of naturalitie be gevin and grantit be the King and Quene
of Scottis, Dolphin and Dolphines of Viennoise,[1] to all and
sindrie the said Maist Christin King of France subjectis, being
or sal happin to go in the realm of Scotland in onie tyme to
cum, with siclyk privilegeis and faculteis as is gevin be the said
Maist Christin King of France to the subjectis of this realm.
And the said lettir of naturalitie to be registrat in the buikis of
Parlement, buikis of Counsall and Sessioun, and in the Chekker
Rollis. . . .

[1] The Dauphin's full title was Dauphin de Viennois, from the district round
Vienne in the Dauphiné. He held the Crown Matrimonial of Scotland, whose
lack was to be such a grievance to Darnley.

XIII

THE NEW ALLIANCE

Muckle on the north side of friendly.
SIR WALTER SCOTT, *Rob Roy*

165. FORESIGHT

In March 1603, Elizabeth was on that terrible death-bed—or rather, refusing to be placed in it, and sitting hunched on cushions on the floor, staring dumbly before her, her fingers in her mouth, or striking with a sword into the shadows. While she still crouched there, five English lords sent this letter to the King who would soon be their own. It is a breathless thing in one huge sentence, scrawled and blotted with haste, and signed with five cipher emblems instead of names—a wise precaution, for Elizabeth, had the matter come to her knowledge, would even then have had their heads for it.

May it please Your Majesty, we whose ciphers are here underwritten and three others of extraordinary quality and power to do Your Majesty service, whom for the purpose we have appointed unto us in this business, do most humbly and most instantly beseech Your Majesty to despatch away your minister in all possible haste, for that Her Majesty's great danger is now apparent and public, and for that discovery is lately made of a strong opposition intended against you by the Popish faction and their adherents, in which business the foreign ambassadors are not idle, they are resolute in the purpose and more diligent in their resolution than the better party can be, for want of correspondence and direction, to come furnished at least with credence and power for the nominating of such as you specially please to commit the managing of this important cause to, and for the authorising of them to address commissions into all parts and to all purposes necessary for Your Majesty's service, which may be by some brief and general commission, under Your Majesty's hand and seal, with a space for such names as Your Majesty's pleasure shall be to have used in that service, whose firmness will now be daily more and more discovered as their love to your person shall concur with their sufficiency and with their graciousness with the people, a matter greatly to be respected,[1] and although the minister cannot be so thoroughly furnished in this so urgent and necessary great haste, yet let his furniture[2] be despatched rather after him than that his presence here should be delayed, whereupon so much dependeth, and of this Your Majesty may be assured that your friends have made your party so strong that without some fatal disaster it cannot be overthrown, and those that stand for you are resolved not to have any being in this world except they may be yours as in right they ought to be, and this we most humbly beseech you that Your Majesty will not take any sudden alarm at this business until you be certainly advertised how God hath disposed of the Queen, but according to your accustomed wisdom to carry your business in such covert and peaceable manner as that no sudden terror be apprehended in our nation which might cause some evil effect, yet always wishing for Your Highness to be in perfect readiness but without any apparent show thereof till the time do call for it.

10 of March at 11 of the clock.

(There follow five cipher signs.)

To His Most Excellent Majesty, in haste.

166. SCOTLAND LEARNS OF THE UNION

A fortnight later, in the small hours of the 24th of March, Elizabeth died; and King James was proclaimed in London at ten that morning. The breath was hardly out of the Queen's body when Sir Robert Carey galloped north with the news, arriving

---

[1] Considered.　　　　　　[2] Equipment.

in Holyrood, much the worse for wear, after nightfall on Saturday the 26th. Scotland had been making quiet preparations for war if it should break out, and the ports were immediately closed. The official intimation of the Queen's death and England's acceptance of James as her lawful heir arrived, however, on Monday the 28th. The Privy Council was summoned, and next day sent out a proclamation announcing the news.

It meant that the Three Hundred Years' War was over, and instead of the King of England annexing Scotland, the King of Scots had become the King of England. We may say that the Scots could afford to be generous : the fact remains that they were generous, and that the King, Privy Council, and Estates worked hard from the outset to make of the Union a fair and acceptable federation of the countries.

This is how the news was to be proclaimed from the Market Crosses to

His Majesteis guid and loving subjectis within this realm, quhair through nane pretend ignorance of the same, and that His Majesteis undoubtit richt to the Imperiall Croun fallen to His Hienes, now unitit and incorporat with His Majesteis Croun of Scotland, and authorisit in maneir foirsaid, may nocht onlie be knawen to all His Hienes guid subjectis within this realm, bot lykewayis may kindil and stir up in the hairtis of all His Hienes Scottis subjectis to quhais knalege thir presentis sall cum, ane loving and kindlie dispositioun towardis all His Majesteis subjectis inhabitantis of England, of quhatsumevir qualiteis or degre thay be of : that thay represent and acknawlege thaim as thair deirest brethren and freindis, and the inhabitantis of baith his realmis to obliterat and remuve out of thair mindis all and quhatsumevir quarrellis, eleistis, or debaitis quhilk hes mainteinit discord or distractioun of affectioun amangis thaim in tyme passit, and with ane universall unanimitie of hairtis conjoin thaimselffis as ane natioun, undir His Majesties authoritie, for maintenaunce of His Majesteis royall estait and

persoun, defence of the haill Island aganis quhatsumevir
forrayneris wald disturb the quyetnes thairof, or seditius persounis within the samyn, quha aither be remembering of auld
querrellis or forging of new, wald minister matter of variance
betuix thaim quham God of His mercie hath thus happilie and
hairtilie unitit to His Majesteis obedience.

eleistis, discords.

167. England learns of the Union

*The English towns also were told of the fact by proclamation :
this is that made at Southampton. One observes that the tone
differs considerably : there is nothing here about giving up old
enmities. We have to remember that England had some excuse
for feeling sore. For centuries the English Kings and people had
poured out a constant stream of blood, gold, and treasure in a vain
attempt to wipe out a smaller kingdom, and more than once had
seemed to achieve success : yet Scotland had persisted in surviving,
and now her King took his place on the English throne.*

Whereas, upon the 24th day of this present month, it pleased
the Almighty God to call out of this mortal life our late Sovereign
and most noble queen, Elizabeth of happy memory, and we
doubt not to everlasting blessedness in Heaven ; whereupon
the noble persons and others that were of her Most Honourable
Privy Council and that were at her departure in her court at
Richmond eftsoons repaired to the city of London, and there,
on Thursday last past, upon deliberate consideration how necessary it was not only to make known to the world the death of the
said most Christian and godly Queen, but also to declare how
James the now King of Scotland, being royally and in right line
from both Houses of York and Lancaster descended, from the
Lady Margaret, the elder daughter of the famous King Henry the
Seventh, and sister to the late famous and noble King Henry
the Eighth, and there the said James King of Scotland, being

by the law of God, of Nature, and of this Realm of England the undoubted and lawful successor and inheritor to our late blessed Sovereign's kingdoms and dominions ; the said noble persons and others that had been of her Privy Council, publicly in the cities of Westminster and London, with the assent, assistance, and great joy of divers noble peers, bishops, and multitudes of the commonalty of this realm, proclaim him the said James, being the Sixth of Scotland of that name, to be the First James and lawful King and inheritor of the realms of England, France,[1] and Ireland, as he hath been likeways in other parts of this realm proclaimed.

Now we, the Mayor, Sheriffs, Bailiffs, Burgesses, and Commonalty of this town and county of Southampton, as our duty and allegiance bindeth us to do, do here declare and proclaim the said James King of Scotland to be by the grace of God King of England, France, and Ireland, whose life and reign over us the God Almighty, King of Heaven and all the Earth, grant may be long and most prosperous to the universal Church of God, and particularly to his realms and dominions.

And so, God save King James.

God save King James.   Amen.   Amen.

168. Seeking Peace

James really desired peace, and his first care was to end the occasions of strife between his kingdoms, and especially on the inflammable Borders. A few weeks after his accession, he had this proclamation read in all six Marches. This is an English copy, most probably drawn up by an English official on notes of the King's.

[1] Although the original claim of Edward III to France was, to his own knowledge, ineffective (since, by his own principles, two of his cousins had better), the Kings of England claimed to be Kings of France, and bore the French lilies, for two centuries and a half after losing the last of their various conquests in France. Elizabeth, who did this with the rest, strongly objected when Mary, whose claim to England was actually better than her own, was persuaded to use for a time the arms of England . . . and English historians still scold Mary for it.

The foul and insolent outrages lately committed upon the Border of our realms of England and Scotland by persons accustomed in former times to live by rapine and spoil, preying daily upon our good and loving subjects, without fear of God or man, hath given us just cause to use all means convenient, both for the relief of our subjects damnified, and for prevention of the like mischief hereafter.

Wherefore, as of late we gave commission to proceed against those persons that were guilty of these foul facts, we now again, because as yet such redress hath not followed as both our honour and our good subjects' love do require, we have thought good to renew that our commission to certain persons of quality and of good understanding in the affairs of those our Borders : and withal to publish by open proclamation to all men, but specially to such as are guilty or were partakers of the foul incursions made upon our first coming to the crown of this our realm of England, or any other before or since, that whereas some of them have of late submitted themselves, and some others seemed to be willing to submit themselves to our mercy : because they and all others shall know that as we are a Prince that, before all worldly respects whatsoever, affecteth the preservation of justice among our people, and the punishment of such as break the rules thereof, so that we are not indisposed to show mercy where there is cause to extend it, and where the same is sought at our hands in such dutiful manner as is meet :

We do therefore charge all persons whatsoever who know themselves to have been actors, partners, or of counsel to that incursion above mentioned, or to any other breach of our peace within the countries and limits heretofore called our Borders, both of the English side and of the Scottish, that they do, before the 20th day of June next coming, resort to such places where they shall understand our Commissioners to be, and there submit themselves to such mercy and favour as we shall think good to extend towards them : assuring them, in the word of

our royal and supreme power, that whosoever of them shall
not, before the said 20th day of June, have submitted himself,
according to the tenour of this our proclamation, shall hold
himself forever excluded from our mercy without hope at any
time to obtain grace or favour, but to abide the rigour of such
punishment as our power can lay upon him.

169. Reassurance

*In the time of her late Queen's father, and even since, England
had run up a long bill in Scotland : and one cannot be surprised
that Englishmen wondered if payment would now be exacted for it.
When James had been three months on his English throne, he had
to put out a reassuring proclamation. Incidentally, it suggests
that the subservience of the executive to the Crown which had been
so marked a feature of Tudor reigns was being continued, and that
James, in spite of his desire that the King should have a real power
in the state, found it too much for him.*

We have, since our entry into this realm of England, had
special care to make all our subjects know with how equal
affection we resolved to proceed in all things which should
concern the safety and honour of both kingdoms, for both
which we know we are to make one and the self-same account
to Almighty God, under Whom we hold all earthly things : in
which respect we were very curious [1] to prevent, at our first
coming, all manner of offences or affronts which naturally do
arise between several [2] nations at their first joining in society
and conversation, never ceasing to lay severe commandment
upon our greatest subjects that came in with us, to suppress any
injurious actions of any of their servants or train towards the
meanest subject of English birth : in whom, from the highest to
the lowest, we have observed so great a love and general obedience to us and our commandments, and whensoever it hath

---

[1] Careful.   [2] Separate.

come to our ears that any offence hath been done by any of them, we have made them know how much it hath displeasured us.

Notwithstanding, because we do hear of many insolences reported to be committed by our natives of Scotland to our English subjects, with this addition further, that the magistrates and justices are thought to be remiss towards such, in doubt lest the same should be offensively reported to us, we have thought it convenient, as well for the satisfaction of the one sort as for admonition of the other, to publish by open signification that seeing it hath pleased Almighty God to call us to the supreme power over both, we are purposed to be a universal and equal sovereign to them both, and to administer justice where there shall be occasion, without any worldly respect to either of them : and thereby do enjoin all Lieutenants, Deputy Lieutenants, Justices of Peace, and all other our officers and ministers of this kingdom, that whensoever complaint shall be made to any of them, that breach of peace is committed by those of our nation of Scotland upon the subjects of England, or by the subjects of England upon those of the nation of Scotland, in both which kinds we hear of many great abuses, though sometimes aggravated according to the humour [1] of the reporters, they shall carefully upon every complaint examine with indifferency the parties of every such action, and cause punishment to be inflicted upon the party offending, without respect of nation, according to the law of both realms.

Though the language is probably that of an English official, we can catch several echoes of James. To be a " universal " king —king holding an equal balance between all sections and parties of his subjects—had been his ambition since he grasped the reins as a boy of seventeen in mortal danger. It was that policy which had brought him in conflict with Melville and his party, and was now to rouse a good deal of grumbling in England : for what most

[1] Predisposition.

men understand by equal rule is apt to be freedom for them to be top dog.

The proclamation ends with the shrewd warning :

If any shall be slow to redress such grievances or punish the offenders, we shall have cause to think that they are willing to nourish some cause of such rumours, the rather to serve for colour or cause of further alienation. . . .

170. NATIONAL DIGNITIES

In the autumn of the next year, James told the English Parliament soothingly :

. . . What can be a more express testimony of God's authority of this work than that two mighty nations, having been ever from their first separation continually in blood against each other, should for so many years immediately before our succession be at peace together, as it were to that end that their memory being free from sense of the smart of former injuries, their minds might in the time of God's appointment more willingly come together, that it hath pleased Him so to dispose that this Union is not enforced by conquest and violence, nor contracted by doubtful and deceivable points of transaction, but naturally derived from the right and title of the precedent princes of both kingdoms, concurring in one person, alike lineally descended from the blood of both through the sacred conjunction of wedlock, an Union which is the work of God and nature, and whereat the works of force and policy cannot attain.

He leaves the details of the new federation to be worked out by the Parliaments of both kingdoms, but

seeing there is undoubtedly but one head to both peoples, which is ourself, and that unfeignedly we have but one heart and mind to communicate equally to both states, as lines issuing from one centre, our justice [and] our favours. . . we have thought it good to discontinue the divided names of England and Scotland out of our regal style, and do intend and resolve to take and assume unto us . . . the name and style of King of Great Britain.

The effects were less happy than the King had hoped. In pointing out that the Union was not by force, he had rather emphasised the spectacular failure of the constant English attempts to achieve just that : and the English had, and have, a strong dislike to the United Kingdom being regarded as anything whatever but simply England.

James showed the same care with regard to external signs of nationhood. In April of 1604 he issued an order concerning national flags.

Whereas some difference hath arisen between our subjects of South and North Britain, travelling by seas, about the bearing of their flags ; for the avoiding of all such contentions hereafter we have, with the advice of our Council, ordered that from henceforth all our subjects of this isle and kingdom of Great Britain and the members thereof, shall bear in their maintop the Red Cross commonly called St George's and the White Cross commonly called St Andrew's, joined together according to a form made by our heralds and sent by us to our Admiral to be published to our said subjects ; and in their foretop our subjects of South Britain shall wear the Red Cross only as they were wont, and our subjects of North Britain the White Cross only as they were accustomed.

The same principle was applied in such matters as coinage. Most of the coins bear the King's portrait and arms, but others have the thistle on one side and the rose on the other, and all are adorned with mottoes extolling union.

171. The Lost Opportunity

During the first four years of his reign in England, James worked hard to achieve a fair and friendly Union. In Scotland his efforts met with real success. By 1607 the Estates had drawn up and approved an excellent treaty, embodying terms for a friendly federation, trade with England being arranged on a "most favoured nation" basis, with an offer to negotiate with France for the admission of English merchants there to a share in Scottish commercial privileges. The language shows an exemplary courtesy and a willingness to lay aside old hatred and make the new alliance a real success.

England, unluckily, refused the Treaty, and furiously resented the offer it made. By hard work, with Bacon to help him, James brought about the abrogation of actual laws against Scots, in return for the equivalent abrogation of Scots laws against Englishmen. By still harder work, he secured that persons born after the Union of Crowns should have all privileges of nationality in both kingdoms. But the English Parliament furiously objected to the clause in the Treaty safeguarding Scotland as " a free monarchy," and complained that (a) the Scots did not want Union either ; and that (b) they were " so greedy of this Union, and apprehended that they should receive so much benefit from it, as they cared not for the strictness of any conditions." The Hon. Member for Buckinghamshire, Sir Christopher Pigott, objected to it on grounds of public morals, since " the Scots have not suffered above two Kings to die in their beds this two hundred years." [1]

Then they swung round, and demanded "perfect Union," making clear the sense of this attractive phrase in such speeches as that of Sir Herbert Crofts in the House of Commons in March 1606.

---

[1] If we take his period strictly by the letter, the Scots in that time had in fact murdered two kings and deposed a queen. But the corresponding English score is two murdered and one killed in battle with his subjects : and if we take Sir Christopher's round figure as meaning the Middle Ages generally, a Scottish sovereign's chance of being murdered was a good deal lower than that of an English one—as three to five, or even possibly six.

If we have not a perfect Union, they of Scotland will stand able to enjoy what they have taken, but not bound to yield either profit nor obedience further than themselves from time to time shall please.

The question of " perfect "—incorporating—Union, was hotly debated at Westminster month after month : and a year and four days after Crofts's enlightening remark, Laurence Hyde summed up :

We have spent a year and proceeded little.   For the Scottish Nation have reserved to themselves to continue a free Monarchy. They have saved their fundamental laws, their liberties, privileges, and rights, which being done, no perfect Union can be had.[1]

And the Estates at this point shrugged their shoulders, passed a vote of thanks to the King for his endeavours, and informed His Majesty, very politely, that it was not their wish that he should make further efforts.

[1] The speeches are taken from the Parliamentary diary of Robert Bowyer, member for Evesham and secretary to Lord Buckhurst.

XIV

THE STRANGER WITHIN THE GATES

At departing, courteously they will say, God thank you.
JEAN FROISSART, *Chronique* (Berners' version)

172. INTERNATIONAL AMITY

While their governments came to an unpleasing impasse, decent people of both countries contrived to be friends. Here are agreeable civic courtesies recorded by the Town Council of Aberdeen early in August 1622.

The samyn day, in presence of the Provost, Baileis, and Counsall, convenit in the Counsall Hous, compeirit Andro Meldrum, merchant burges of this burgh, and exhibit and presentit befoir thaim ane silver cup, with the cover, all doubil over-gilt with gold, havand the tounis armis with thair motto Bon Accord thairupoun, sent and propynit to the toun be Thomas Pendillburrie, merchand and citizen of London, in tokin of his luve and affectioun to this burgh, quhairof he is frie guild burges.

And here in the February of 1613, we find the Privy Council doing their best to keep out of trouble, with his own police, a poor Englishman, who has pluckily come to the help of a Scot in peril.

We the Lordis of His Majesteis Prevy Counsall in the Kingdom of Scotland, undersubscriband, greiting : Quhairas the berar heirof, James Hall, servitour to Benjamin Stout, oister-catchear in Ypchurch [1] being upoun the xiii day of Januar last bound to London in ane catche or oister boit, laidnit with oisteris, and as he wes upoun his dew cours upoun the revar of Thames about Halwodtrie, some ten miles above Gravisend,

---

[1] Possibly Ipswich in Essex. It sounds more like Upchurch, but although that is a common place-name in England, the Editor cannot find one on the coast.

having onlie ane auld man with him in the catche, thay wer persewit and bordit about ten of the clock at nicht be ane namit John Davidson, born at Ratleif besyde London, with fyve utheris in his cumpanie ; quha seisit upoun the catche and carryit the samyn, with the said James, to the sie, threitning the said James with present death gif he yeildit nocht to join with thaim and to assist thaim with thair piraceis. And eftir that thay had scourit the coast sum few dayis, at last cuming to Yarmouth, thay thair burdit a Scottis schip, quhairof Alexander Law in Kirkcaldy wes maister : tuik the schip and hir laidning, demittit and put away the catche, and caryit the schip with the said Alexander Law and ane uthir of his fellowis, to the sie, and resolving to haif thrawn thaim overburd, quhairby thay micht with the greitar securitie haif possessit the schip and gudis.

The said James Hall, heiring thair resolution, and acquenting ane William Normann, Dutcheman (the said William being lykewayis taen and deteinit in thair cumpanie, aganis his will) and the saidis James and William being movit with pitie and commiseratioun of the hard estait and conditioun of the said Alexander Law and his fellow, quha had nocht onlie lost thair schip and gudis, bot wer in present danger to haif lost thair lyvis, thay resolvit to withstand and resist the crueltie intendit aganis thaim, and to use thair endevouris alsweill to procure thair ain libertie and releif as to preserve the lyfe of the said Alexander and his fellow. And imparting thair resolutioun to the said Alexander, and thay all promising ane joint concurrence in this mateir, thay maid ane present onset upoun Davidson and his fellowis, and eftir a scharp conflict betuix thaim, quhairin twa of Davidsonis fellowis wer slain, thay tuik Davidson him-self, and ane of his fellowis callit John Low, and brocht thaim to the toun of Kirkcaldy in this kingdom ; and that being from thens brocht heir, and thay being all examinat, confrontit, and re-examinat, thay haif confessit the premisses to be of truth ; quhairupoun order and directioun is gevin for the tryall and punisching of Davidson and his fellow, according to the course

U

of law and justice : and we haif set frie the said James Hall and the Dutcheman, as honest men quha with the hasard and perrell of thair lyvis procurit thair ain libertie and releif and the saiftie and preservatioun of the lyvis of the said Alexander and his fellowis.

And now, since the said James is to return hame to his ain countrey, we haif thocht meit and expedient to accumpanie him with this our lettir of certificat and trew record that he wes violentlie taen be Davidson and his fellowis, aganis his will, and that he and the Dutcheman with the hasard of thair lyvis procurit thair ain relief and deliverie and the saiftie and preservatioun of the lyvis of the said Alexander Law and his fellow : quhilkis premissis, according to the tryall and examinatioun taen be us, we testifie to be of treuth.   Gevin at Edinburgh, the secund day of Februar in the yeir of God j^mvi^c and xiii yeiris.

Sic subscribitur

. . . *and there follow the signatures of the Lord Chancellor, the Lord President, the Lord Justice Clerk, and five Privy Councillors.*

catche, ketch.

173. Ducal Grand Tour

A dainty little Elzevir duodecimo published in Amsterdam in 1646 contains " Le Voyage du Duc de Rohan faict en l'an 1600 " . . . the account of a journey through Italy, Germany, the Netherlands, England, and Scotland.   The young Breton was head of one of the greatest houses in France, and, when the Edict of Nantes had ended his soldiering at twenty-one, had already been made Duc et Pair and betrothed by Henri IV to the daughter of the great minister Sully.   Rohan was something of a classical scholar, and wrote shrewdly on imperial politics . . . but his career covers no less than seven and a half pages of the curt Biographie Universelle. He seems to have been a young man of much charm.   Elizabeth of

England called him " her knight," but he obviously preferred the Scottish court, where he won such favour that he was invited to stand godfather to the King's younger son, the future Charles I.

His British journey was brief, and he did not see much of either kingdom beyond its court.

If the affection one naturally bears to a country, joined to the obligations one receives from it, not from an individual but from the people in general, should induce my pen to write well of it, Scotland surpasses not only all the other countries I have seen, but even compels me to equal it in this point with my own nation. If in all the rest of my journey, which has included almost all Christendom (I exclude France) I have lacked cause to speak of princes both truthfully and well at the same time (which is why I have been silent about them to this point) and if this isle of Britain—not the whole isle, but the smaller and more barren part of it—shows itself there more fertile than any other nation, and gives me here not one subject but two, not two subjects but two mirrors of virtue, from whom all people, according to sex, may take example, does it not deserve to be honoured ? I do not speak from a special passion, nor from the honours and courtesies, greater than I deserved, that I received there, but because the truth speaks of its own accord. For where will you find today princes, who for the most part wrest justice, the laws of their kingdom and of conscience, to their own utility, and who abound in vices above their subjects as much as they should abound above them in virtues—for the Prince is the example to his people. Truly, if we consider closely the private and public life of the King of Scotland, his character, his actions, the excellence of his intelligence, his learning and eloquence, we should judge him worthy to govern his kingdom and far more. . . .

To come then to the praise and the description of the second part of the isle of Britain or Albion. I will say that it is rather less than England, and much more barren and mountainous, but that it has this advantage over England, that since men first dwelt there it has never been conquered by any other nation.

He apologises for the shortness of his description, but says that he did not travel widely in Scotland : yet he must attempt a sketch, " not to show myself ungrateful to the places where I have had such good cheer, and to remind myself of the courtesy I have received from strangers." He speaks of Edinburgh as having most of its houses of wood, and remarks on the number of gentlemen's seats around it. Leith reminds him that " these two nations, the French and the Scots have given each other mutual help for 872 years." He did not see much more but the royal palaces : at Stirling he visited the future Queen of Hearts, Princess Elizabeth, already " Belle et bien jolie," at Dunfermline the Queen, at Linlithgow the boy Prince Henry.

That is all that I have seen in the kingdom of Scotland, which if I found it very barren of what is required to support human life, I found very fertile in *gens vertueux*.[1] For besides the gentry whom I knew, full of culture and courtesy, there are many very learned men ; and besides this, there is the great valour common to all that nation, and their fidelity, which is such that our own Kings of France have drawn from it their personal bodyguard.

174. Wise Men from the East

A good many other foreign visitors have already made their appearance in this book, under other headings—De Selve and that pleasant person Jean de Beaugué, Thomas Randolph, John Taylor, Fynes Morison, and others. Not all wrote their impressions : but

---

[1] *Virtù, vertu, virtue* at this time are almost untranslatable in modern speech. They have more than a merely moral connotation—indeed in Italian the word has almost none : the nearest sense one can give is a rich and accomplished fullness of personality.

one would like to have those of the two who asked the Privy Council
for passports in the January of the year 1611.

The quhilk day a pasport wes expeid to twa strangeris, ane a
Caldeane of the citie of Jerusalem, ane uthir a Persiane of the
citie of Tibris (*Tabriz*).

XV

WANDERING SCOTS

"I come to seek my fortune in France, or elsewhere, after
the custom of my countrymen."
SIR WALTER SCOTT, *Quentin Durward*

175. THE SOLDIER OF FORTUNE

*The stream of religious exiles of all faiths increased the thick
scatter of Scots already spread through the churches, armies,
colleges, and markets of all the countries of Europe, from Norway
to Spain. One could write a book—and good books have been
written—on the Scots in practically any country, and frequently
enough on a single one of these wanderers : Thomas Dempster, for
instance, duellist and scholar, Sub-Principal of the Paris Collége
de Beauvais and a member at various times of the universities of
Cambridge, Paris, Louvain, Rome, Douai, Tournay, Toulouse,
Montpelier, Pisa, and Bologna. Here there is only room for a
few glimpses of typical figures, famous and obscure. The temper
of most of them, soldiers, scholars, or merchants, shows in the
letter written from the Hague, in the September of the year 1608,
by one James Henderson, a younger son of Henderson of Fordell.*

I am a young man, and gif I haif litill, I haif als litill to fear.
I have my swerd undishonorit, and that is aneuch to me : yit
gif evir God send me a fortune, I hoip to use it weill.

176. ITALY

*The most dazzling of all, though he died at a few weeks short
of twenty-two, was that strange figure the Admirable Crichton.
Certain nineteenth-century historians, indeed, regarded him as the
old lady did the giraffe—looked at the creature and said, " I don't
believe it." But we have good contemporary evidence, from*

Italian scholars of very high repute, of his accomplishments, and he had many : " the soldier's, courtier's, scholar's, eye, tongue, sword." Born in 1560, a Lord Advocate's son, he sat under George Buchanan at St Andrews, and was one of the group of boys of gentle birth about the young King : but Catholic religion, or merely the ganging fit, took him abroad while he was in his teens. Handsome, a brilliant swordsman, a fine horseman, he had a quite uncanny erudition, being able to speak ten languages fluently, including among them Hebrew and Chaldaic, and to dispute in them on all branches of learning. His holding of the lists of dispute at Padua for three days against all comers was long talked of. The secret seems to have been a freak memory, of the kind that is occasionally found : he claimed to be able to repeat verbatim a Latin oration he had only heard once, and could make an epigram in Latin verse and then immediately recite it backward. That alarming body, the Council of Ten of Venice, was to celebrate his twentieth birthday thus :

There has arrived in this city a young Scot named James Crichton, who so far as is known with regard to his social position is of very good birth, and who has been, moreover, clearly proved to possess the most rare and singular attainments, by various tests carried out by most learned and knowledgeable men, and in special by a Latin oration delivered extempore this morning in our College, in such wise that he, though not past, or but little past, twenty,[1] astounded and bewildered all who heard him : a thing which as it is in all points extraordinary and unlike what Nature is wonted to produce, has moved this Council to make some courteous gesture in favour of this very remarkable person, who mainly through accidents which have befallen him, and the changes of fortune, is in serious straits.

Therefore be it resolved that out of the funds of this Council, there shall be handed to the aforesaid Crichton, gentleman of Scotland, a hundred crowns of gold.

[1] He was actually twenty that very day.

Of the twenty-eight Councillors who discussed the matter, twenty-two voted for it, and only two against, the other four reserving their opinion. The scholar-printer Aldus Manutius, the classicist Burchelati, and the famous old logician Speroni made Crichton welcome as their friend. In an evil day he took service with the Duke of Mantua, to help in building his Palace of the Teo : fortification, it seems, was one of his subjects. He was fitted to shine in an Italian court, and he shone too much. In six months, he had collided one night in the street with the Duke's heir, Don Vicenzo, and one of his gentlemen. The latter died on the spot : Crichton, next morning. Don Vicenzo declared that it was all a mistake, but told two different and conflicting stories. Mantua, shocked at the loss of its new treasure, put Don Vicenzo on trial and banished him : and his father confirmed the sentence. But Crichton was dead.

177. FRANCE

A more typical figure—though he also died comparatively young, in his early forties, in 1546—was Florentius Volusenus, Florence Wilson, an Elgin man, who graduated at Aberdeen in the reign of James V. Cardinal Sadoleto, Bishop of Carpentras, not far from Avignon, described in a Latin letter to his nephew how he met him in the year 1535.

I do not think there is any longer need to seek through your help a schoolmaster to instruct the youth of this place. For I will give you a little history, from which you shall immediately acknowledge how much more fortune may at times effect that human counsel.

Four days ago, when it was already night, I had by chance gone into my library, and was very eagerly turning over some books, when my chamberlain told me one wished to speak to me. I ask, Who is he ? A gownsman, was the answer. I order him to be brought in. He comes. I ask what he wants, that he comes at such an hour. (For I wanted to rid myself of him speedily, and return to my studies.)   Then he, introducing himself in most humble terms, spoke with such modesty, propriety, and correctness as to make me wish to question him in detail, and make his better acquaintance.   So, having closed my book and turned round to him, I began to ask of what country he might be, what was his profession, and what had brought him to this neighbourhood.   To which he answers, I am a Scot.   What, said I, do you come from the uttermost parts of the earth ?   Even so, said he.   Where have you studied the liberal sciences ?   (Which question I put because his discourse showed both high intelligence and elegant Latin.)   I studied philosophy, said he, first of all for several years in my own country, and later at Paris, where I taught a nephew of the Cardinal of York.[1]   Then, when the uncle's death caused the lad to be taken from me, I went to Monseigneur de Belley, [Arch]bishop of Paris, and was about to go with him to Rome, but a serious illness separated me from him on the journey.   I asked him, " What then do you look for here ? "   In the first place, said he, I had a great desire to see you.[2]   Then, since I had heard at Avignon that you needed someone to teach in the school of your city, I thought of offering myself, in case I might be fitted for that appointment, not indeed so much desiring the post itself as anxious to be admitted to your service, and realising that whatever appointment I might hold near your person, or by your selection, would be a good thing for my reputation.

What do you think ?   He pleased me so much that very early next morning I sent for the magistrate Glocerius, and for Helia.   I told them my expectations of the man, and described those things about him which had so pleased me, for certainly we should have had little chance of finding an Italian with the sense, the modesty, and the manners of this young man.

Not satisfied with this, however, I had Florence himself (for that is his name), our physician, of whom I have told you

[1] Cardinal Wolsey.
[2] Not necessarily flattery.   Sadoleto was a very distinguished scholar.

already, the Magistrate, and Helia, as my guests. Immediately after dinner, I launched a discussion, and while we talked of natural philosophy, our medical friend argued bitterly, grinning and panting. The other sat calm and modest, saying nothing irrelevant, nothing but what was both discreetly and accurately put, every word showing skill and understanding. Aye, and when I myself, facing the doctor in an argument, had stated an intricate and difficult case, which made him struggle, our stranger, asking pardon, suggested the best and most scientific solution. What more would you have ? All are ardent to keep such a character among us. The magistrates take him aside, the terms of the engagement are settled at 100 gold pieces, and with so much approval from the citizens that I hear they all consider his application as a piece of rare good fortune for the town. There are tales of talks of his with the magistrates, so learned and wise that nothing can surpass them. So I hope that we have done as well as can be with regard to the appointment and its concerns. The man has also—what specially pleases me —enough even of Greek to teach our boys. On this business, therefore, you need have no more trouble.

For one Florence Wilson or Arthur Johnstone, Andrew Melville or George Buchanan, famous through Europe, there were, of course, a score of lesser men, filling decent unspectacular positions. There is a glimpse of one in this letter of commendation from Bochetel, the French Secretary of State, to Marie de Guise.

MADAME,

Having found Master Henry Scrimgeour, the bearer of these presents, a man of good character and respectable life, and of great learning, as well in Greek as in Latin, I have given him charge of my children these three or four years, in which position he has so borne himself, that I have reason, Madame, to congratulate myself and be greatly pleased. And because, Madame, he is of the Scottish nation, and has begged me to let him go over there for some time to set some family affairs in order, I am bold, Madame, to accompany him with this letter, and most humbly entreat that it shall please you to have him and his house in your good protection and recommendation. Which doing, Madame, with so much of other gracious kindness that it has pleased you to grant me, I shall remain more and more obliged, and entirely and humbly at your service.

Madame, recommending myself most humbly to your good grace, I will pray Our Lord to give you in perfect health long and good life.

Written at La Muette, this 16th day of February,

Your most humble and most obedient servant,

BOCHETEL.

178. SWEDEN

Soldiers have always been a main Scottish export, and with Sweden, newly broken loose from Denmark, beginning on the lively course of wars that was to make her mistress of the Baltic and a Great Power, there were naturally Scottish soldiers in Sweden. John III, then fighting Russia as ally of Poland, writes in 1573 to Sir Archibald Ruthven : the letter is in Latin.

To our sincerely beloved and faithful, the noble and well-born Sir Archibald Ruthven, our singular good will and favour. That you have proved to us your faith and constancy in levying and leading thither a Scottish force is very acceptable to us, and therefore of our royal good will we are about to acknowledge it heartily. Further, we have given commission to the bearer of these presents, our trusty and beloved the noble Andrew Keith, our butler [*pincerna*], that in our name he may let you know our will in certain affairs. We therefore kindly desire you to give him as certain and undoubting credence in these things as if we ourselves were present : thus both of you shall do us acceptable favour. Farewell.

Given from our castle of Stockholm, v of the Ides of July, in the year of Christ 1500 73.

JOHN, R.S.

But the great age of the Scots in Swedish service came later. During the first two-thirds of the Thirty Years' War, Scotland was in a state of unwonted peace, and her stirring youth went abroad to seek fame and fortune. They found the fame more often than the fortune, but the fame they did find, on both sides of the conflict. Gustav Adolf of Sweden, the chief of the leaders on the Protestant side and one of the greatest soldiers of his age, is reputed to have had thirty-four Scots colonels in his service, with Scots commands. He made over sixty Scots governors of captured towns, and, like the Kings of France, had a Scots bodyguard. At the taking of Frankfurt Lumsden's Regiment captured nine stands of colours from the enemy, and at Leipzig the Scots Brigade led the advance.

Knowing his Scots as he did, he had a strong and natural objection to finding them against him in the field, and in 1623 he sent this protest to the Scots Estates. The original is in Latin, ending with the King's huge bold signature with its elaborate paraph.

Gustav Adolf, by the grace of God King of the Swedes, Goths, and Vandals, Grand Prince of Finland, Duke of Esthonia and Karelia, Lord of Ingria,

Greeting and our especial favour. Illustrious, mighty, and noble lords, by us sincerely beloved, we have learned that this last summer there has been in Poland a countryman of yours, one Robert Stewart, who had sometime served us ; and that there he received money for a promise of 8000 Scots foot for the King of Poland, to employ them against us and to invade our province of Vastergottland. Stewart has now, we hear, gone to England, and so far as he can, is diligently setting about the fulfilment of his promise. It has seemed to us that this is a thing which should hardly be permitted, and we would both advise our dearest brother the King of the affair, and inform you more clearly of what is done against us, praying that you will petition your King to turn aside and inhibit such plans and movements, hostile towards us, and that you yourselves, so far as you may, will also avert the same.

You know how greatly the Roman Catholics, puffed up by the success of their good fortune, are taking heart, and with what hope and enterprise they begin to set going their long-planned schemes against Evangelicals, lest this, or any, chance of crushing us should slip untried from their hands. They have never rested from such plots, and never yet have greater hopes of carrying them through been presented to them in this dangerous time, when the minds and counsels of those who should oppose them are divided. All other things you will do as seems to you fitting : only we wish to warn you of this thing, that the Roman Catholics are now, with all their power, attempting to break a way through this our kingdom, the sole Northern bulwark of the Evangelicals, which by its own danger and at its own expense has hitherto kept safe the kingdom of Denmark, great part of Saxony, and if all things are properly considered, Scotland itself and many more states and nations : and if this bulwark were in Papist hands, with these excellent harbours and other advantages, it will not be hard for a sensible man to guess in what dangerous case will be Protestant affairs, throughout the world and in special among our neighbours. This indeed the Papists scarcely hope to achieve, unless with the help of the Evangelicals themselves and their internal quarrels : and so that they may sever your nation from ours, and abandon the urgings of hatred, they have judged that the first thing which should be done was to stir against us a man of your nation, under pretext of a quarrel of Sweden and Poland. Yet we sincerely trust in both your King, our most friendly brother, and in you yourselves, that the memory of that friendship and goodwill which between our predecessors, ourselves, and our two nations has been of perpetual exercise, shall be much stronger : nor shall we permit it to be in any way weakened by such hostile motions, professing to be in your name. There are men of your nation (of whom many have fixed their business and home among us) held in the highest honour in these kingdoms, and many are in command in our army, all enjoying, as much as if they had really been born here, the rights and privileges of nobility.   It would indeed be unjust behaviour to us, and not less to them, if anything should be done to lessen our friendliness, and the Scots should be led to hate a nation which has so favoured them.

All these things which concern the Evangelical cause in general, or our nation and yours, we trust you will consider according to your piety and prudence, and endeavour, both by your King and by your own action, to forbid the levy of any Scottish force either by Stewart or by his accomplices, or that they should do anything to the prejudice and detriment of us and our kingdoms, either in the kingdom of Scotland or in its harbours and islands.   Your constant regard for the conservation of the Purer Church, and the material friendship of the kingdoms of Sweden and Scotland, assure us of this.   And when occasion shall be offered us, we will endeavour with the same goodwill to fulfil our obligations towards your state, and show favour to your people dwelling among us.   Of these things, more fully shall speak the magnificent and well-born Sir James Spence of Wermston, Knight [*eques auratus*], to us truly faithful. And by these we commend you to God

Given at Gripsholm, the 23rd day of September, in the year 1623.

GUSTAV ADOLF.

To the Illustrious, Magnificent, and High-born, our Well-beloved the Senators of the Kingdom of Scotland.

179. HOLLAND

One of the most famous fighting units of the time was the Scots Brigade in Dutch service.   Like their French equivalent, they were the Right of the Line, and in the two centuries and more of their existence they never lost a stand of colours in action.

The Dutch War of Independence began in 1572, and the Scots Brigade was founded that same year, the Buccleuch who lifted

Kinmont Willie being one of their original officers : they were allowed their own forms of discipline, on the grounds that " Scotsmen would not easily be brought to bear German punishments." Very soon they were in the great defence of Haarlem, and among those who cut a way across the frozen Meer to relieve the city. Its guns were commanded by a Scot, and others captured four Spanish standards in a night attack. They took part, too, in the great siege and relief of Leyden—Holland's Bannockburn—and fought at Reymenant and Aerschot, though the Spanish systematically drowned Scots prisoners, on the grounds that being neutrals they ought not to be there. We hear a great deal of Elizabeth's help to Holland : but in 1579, when the Union of Utrecht laid the foundation of the United Netherlands, there were eight English companies in Dutch service, and eighteen Scots. They helped to defend Antwerp against Parma, and preceded later compatriots at Eindhoven and Hertogenbosch, Zutphen, Nimeguen, Turnhout, Ostend, and Nieuport.

Their long service, which often became hereditary, was not without its troubles, naturally. In 1589 there was an international incident over their pay, which was so far in arrears that the Scots Government gave their Colonel Letters of Marque to collect it. This letter of 1607 shows another difficulty.

To the Council of State,
My Lords,

Your communication of the 24th April last was handed to me on the last of the following month, and from it I understand that Your Honours' decision and intentions, conform to the note of His Excellency appended to the request of Ensign William Stewart, is to the effect that I should receive him in my company, and permit him to benefit fully by the said note, unless I could offer strong reasons against so doing.

Will it please Your Honours therefore to accept these considerations and take them into account : that the deceased, killed by the said remonstrant, is my cousin-german, and a near blood relation ? Clearly, therefore, it would not be possible for me to endure to have the remonstrant going about before my eyes, and more difficult still to have him serving in my company without loss of respect : and his being in it would cause grave inconveniences, which owing to natural affection for a kinsman, might be the cause of more and greater grievances to the other than those which already have been put forward.

Therefore I hope that your lordships, duly weighing what has been said, will be pleased to take action as may be most requisite for securing quiet, peace, and tranquillity to both parties. Moreover, may it please you to order the said Ensign to keep himself anywhere else out of my sight.

Herewith I pray the Almighty to have Your Lordships under the shield and protection of His grace, to whom also I very humbly commend myself.

Your Honours' most obedient servant,

DAVID RAMSAY.

From Bergen op Zoom, the 1st May, anno 1607.

The Brigade was part of the Dutch forces till towards the end of the eighteenth century, when—though only the officers by that time were Scots—the men threatened to mutiny when the Scots words of command were changed to Dutch. When Britain and Holland went to war in 1781, the officers were repatriated, and re-formed in a Brigade which not long after was to assist in taking the Cape from the Dutch. But the War Office was not interested. By 1871 the unit had been linked with an Irish regiment, and in 1881 it became the Second Battalion of the Connaught Rangers, with Galway assigned as its recruiting district.

180. POLAND

There had always been a good deal of coming and going between the Scots ports and those of the Baltic, Danzig in special. It was on the Long Bridge of Danzig that Douglas of Liddesdale, the Flower of Knighthood, was murdered by men in the pay of his

*enemy Clifford : and the Höhe Thor of the town, accordingly, was
known for centuries as the Douglas Gate.*[1]

*Here are the Scots in Danzig in 1577, a contingent on loan
to the town from the Scots-Dutch.   And a much worried captain
writes in stately German to the civic authorities :*

Dread, noble, worthiest, ? high-born, ? namely, and most
gracious gentlemen,[2]

Having offered you my most willing and humble services,
I beg to call your attention to the fact that a few weeks ago, at
my own charges, I have brought all the men under my colours
from the Low Countries, to serve this good town of Danzig
against its enemies.   To this end I have laid out, at my own
cost, over 600 thalers, in commissariat and carriage and other
expenses, to pay which I had to pawn my best clothes at Elsinore
in Denmark.   And although I have already applied for reim-
bursement, I was told only that I must set down clearly in
writing all sums paid by me for the men in my command, and
forward the list to the magistrates, when I should duly be paid
what was owing me.   By this time, however, it is quite impossible to put down every item of the said expenses, as I have kept
no written accounts.   I therefore leave it to you to decide the
matter, and trust that I shall receive what is owing me, with
which I shall be well satisfied.

In the hope of a favourable answer,

Your humble servant,

WILHELM MONKREIFF, Captain.

*In the late war, the apparent natural affinity of Scots and Poles
was often remarked on by their English comrades.   There would
seem to be some historical reason for it, as Poland was almost as
full of Scots as France.   In the sixteenth and seventeenth centuries,*

[1] The English editor who translated John Major for the Scottish History
Society makes *Dansken in Sprusa* Dunglass on the Pease ! But as Mr Fischer
points out, the Danzig story—a European scandal in its day—is reported in a
French chronicle, two German ones, and six Scots.

[2] Gestrenge, edle, ehrveste, erbare, nahmhaffte, gross gunstige Herren.

Scotland's chief commercial connections were largely Polish. In the time of James VI, when King Stephen Bathany gave the Scots merchants their own quarter in Cracow, no less than eight were "aulic"—Royal Purveyors. And, after Warsaw became the capital, a Scot called Chalmers was three times its Provost.

William Lithgow, who travelled Poland in 1616, received much kindness from his countrymen.

Being arrived in Crocko or Crocavia, the capital city of Poland, I met with divers Scottish merchants, who were wonderful glad of mine arrival there, especially the two brothers Dickson, men of singular note of honesty and wealth. . . .

Poland is a large and mighty kingdom, puissant in horsemen and populous of strangers, being charged with a proud nobility, a familiar and manly gentry, and a ruvidous vulgarity.[1] They are all for the most part of square and thick bodies, having bull necks, great thighs and legs, grim and broad faces, and commonly their shaven heads are finely covered with overthwarting strokes of crooked shables : for they and the Armenians of Asia are of stature the biggest and grossest[2] people the world affords.

The soil is wonderful fruitful of corns, so that this country is become the girnel of Western Europe for all sorts of grain, besides honey, wax, flax, iron, and other commodities : and for auspiciousness I may rather term it to be a mother and nurse for the youth and younglings of Scotland, who are yearly sent thither in great numbers, than a proper dame for her own birth, in clothing, feeding, and enriching them with the fatness of her best things, besides 30,000 Scots families that live incorporate in her bowels. And certainly Poland may be termed in this kind to be the mother of our commons, and the first commencement of all our best merchants' wealth, or at the least most part of them. . . .

[At Lublin] I found abundance of gallant rich merchants my countrymen, who were all very kind to me, and so were they

---

[1] Common people.   [2] Heaviest.

by the way in every place where I came, the conclusion being ever sealed with deep draughts and God be with you. . . .

And now ceasing to peramble through any more particulars of this familiar nation to us, I was kindly transported from Warsaw to Danzig, being fifty leagues distant, with a generous young merchant William Baillie my Clydesdale countryman, to whose courtesies I still rest thankful.

Here in Danzig I fell deadly sick for three weeks space, insomuch that my grave and tomb was prepared by my countrymen there. . . .

But the Scots in Poland were by no means all merchants. Many soldiers went also, for Poland, though a strongly Catholic country, was not a persecuting one, and gave an opening to Protestant exiles as well as to Catholics. In the seventeenth century George Guthrie, with his own regiment of hussars, helped King Jan Sobieski to save Vienna—and incidentally Europe. King Jan made him a Polish noble, and so late as 1914 there were Barons de Guttry near Posen. We have already seen the Swedish reaction to the efforts of Mary's nephew, Robert Stewart, to raise 8000 Scots for the Polish King. And the connection outlasted the mercantile. In the Prior's room at the fortress monastery of Częstochowa there used to hang the portrait of one Cajetan Stuart, a Polish-born Scot who defended the place against the Russians in 1806.

The scholars came and went, too. In the middle of the seventeenth century, one Dr William Davidson was Physician to King Jan Casimir, while in 1693 Edinburgh University established a bursary for Polish students.

181. UNITED NATIONS IN CRETE

Scholars, soldiers, merchants . . . but there were others who went " for to admire and for to see, for to be'old this world so wide," as a later Scoto-Englishman was to put it. Among them was the William Lithgow who wrote the passage which precedes this. He was born at Lanark in 1582, and by 1609 he had begun some nineteen years of wandering which took him, mainly on foot, through Germany, Bohemia, the Low Countries, France, Spain, Italy, Istria, Croatia, Dalmatia, Slavonia, Epirus, Corfù, Cephalonia, Zante, Greece, Crete, Palestine, the Greek islands, Macedonia, Troy, Constantinople, Thrace, Rhodes, Cyprus, Syria, Idumea, " the sabulous conspicuosities of stony deserts," Cairo, Egypt, Algiers, Fez, Libya, Malta, Sicily, Rome, Poland, England, and Ireland.

His " Totall Discourse of the Rare Adventures and Painfull Peregrinations of long nineteene Years Travayles from Scotland to the most famous Kingdomes in Europe, Asia, and Africa " was published in London in 1632, with gorgeous woodcuts—Lithgow in the Libyan Desert, Lithgow tied to a tree by thieves in Moldavia, Lithgow in the ruins of Troy wearing Turkish dress with a turban the size of a millstone, and Lithgow on the rack in a Spanish prison when his too frank tongue had got him into trouble.

His language, so late as this, is Scoto-English rather than Scots, and his London printer, of course, Englished the spelling. The extract here tells of his adventures in Crete, then Venetian territory, in 1609–10.

In my first abode at Canea, being a fortnight, there came six galleys from Venice, upon one of which there was a young French gentleman, a Protestant, born near Montpelier in Languedoc, who being by chance in company with other four of his countrymen in Venice, one of them killed a young noble Venetian about the quarrel of a courtesan. Whereupon they flying to the French Ambassador's house, the rest escaped, and he only, apprehended by a fall in his flight, was afterwards condemned by the Senators to the galleys during life. Now the galleys lying here six days, he got leave of the Captain to come ashore with a keeper, when he would, carrying an iron bolt on his leg : in which time we falling in acquaintance, he complained heavily of his hard fortune, and how because he was a Protestant (besides his slavery) he was severely abused in the galley, sighing forth these words with tears, Lord have mercy upon me, and grant me patience, for neither friends nor money can redeem me.

At which expression I was both glad and sorrowful, the one moving my soul to exult in joy for his religion, the other for his misfortune working a Christian condolement for intolerable affliction. For I was in Venice at that time when the accident fell out, yet would not tell him so much. But pondering seriously his lamentable distress, I secretly advised him the manner how he might escape, and how far I would hazard the liberty of my life for his deliverance, desiring him to come ashore early next morning. Meanwhile I went to an old Greekish woman, with whom I was friendly inward, for she was my laundress, and reciting to her the business, she willingly condescended to lend me an old gown and a black veil for his disguisement. The time came, and we met. The matter was difficult to shake off the keeper : but such was my plot, I did invite him to the wine, where after tractal discourse and deep draughts of Leatick, reason failing, sleep overcame his sense. Whereupon conducting my friend to the appointed place, I disburdened him of his irons, clothed him in a female habit, and set him out before me, conducted by the Greekish woman : and when securely past both guards and gate, I followed, carrying with me his clothes, where, when accosting him in a field of olives, and the other turned back, we speedily crossed the vale of Suda, and interchanging his apparel, I directed him the way over the mountains, to a Greekish convent on the south side of the land, a place of safeguard, called commonly the Monastery of Refuge, where he would kindly be entertained till either the galleys or men of war of Malta arrived. It being a custom at their going or coming from the Levant to touch here, to relieve or carry away distressed men. . . .[1] And now many joyful

[1] It is pleasant to know that when, a long time after, Lithgow called on the young man's father in Montpellier, he learned that his protégé had reached home safely.

thanks from him redounded. I returned keeping the high
way, where incontinent I encountered two English soldiers,
John Smith and Thomas Hargrave, coming of purpose to
inform me of an eminent danger, showing me that all the officers
of the galley, with a number of soldiers, were in searching the
city and hunting all over the fields for me. After which relation, consulting with them what way I could come to the
Italian monastery Saint Salvator, for there I lay (the vulgar
town affording neither lodging nor beds) they answered me
that they would venture their lives for my liberty, and I should
enter at the Eastern (the least frequented) gate of the city,
where three other Englishmen were that day on guard, for so
there were five of them here in garrison : where when we came,
the other Englishmen, accompanied with eight French soldiers,
their familiars, came along with me also, and having passed
the market-place and near my lodging, four officers and six
galley soldiers ran to lay hands on me, whereat the English and
French, unsheathing their swords, valiantly resisted their fury
and deadly wounded two of the officers. Meanwhile fresh
supply coming from the galleys, John Smith ran along with me
to the monastery, leaving the rest at pell mell to intercept their
following.

At last the captain of the garrison approaching the tumult,
relieved their own soldiers and drove back the others to the
galleys. A little thereafter the General of the Galleys came to
the monastery, and examined me concerning the fugitive, but
I clearing myself so, and quenching the least suspicion he might
conceive (notwithstanding of mine accusers) he could lay
nothing to my charge. Howsoever it was, he seemed somewhat
more favourable, partly because I had the Duke of Venice his
passport, partly because of mine intended voyage to Jerusalem,
partly because he was a great favourer of the French nation,
and partly because he could not mend himself, in regard to my
shelter and the Governor's favour. Yet nevertheless, I detained
myself under shelter of the cloister until the galleys were gone.

He then left Canea, passed Suda Bay, " the only key of the island," and describes the rich Suda Valley, with sixty-seven villages, " the garden of the whole universe." He found the Candiotes the bravest of all Greeks, and great singers. Having explored the antiquities and seen, though he did not enter, the Labyrinth, he had a " sassinous and marine passage," back to Canea, where he was able to repay his debt to his English friend.

I was forced to return to Canea the same way I went ; when come I was exceeding merry with my old friends the Englishmen. Meanwhile there arrived from Tunis in Barbary an English runagate named Wilson, bound for the Rhodes, where after short acquaintance with his natives,[1] and understanding what I was, he imparted these words. " I have had my elder brother," said he, " the master or captain of a ship, slain at Burntisland in Scotland by one called Kerr, and notwithstanding he was beheaded, I have long since sworn to be revenged of my brother's death on the first Scotsman I ever saw or met, and my design is to stob him [*sic*] with a knife this night as he goeth late home to his lodgings," desiring their assistance. But Smith, Hargrave, and Horsfield refused, yet Cook and Rollands yielded. Meanwhile, Smith knowing where I used sometimes to dine, found me at supper at a sutler's, a soldiers' house, where acquainting me with this plot, the host, he, and three Italian soldiers conveyed me to my bed, passing by the arch-villain and his confederates, where he was prepared for the mischief : which when he saw his treachery was discovered, he fled away and was seen no more there.

Remarking the fidelity and kindness that Smith had twice shown me, first in freeing me from the danger of gallery slavery, and now in saving my life, I advised to do him a good deed in some part of acquittance, and thus it was. At his first coming to Venice, he was taken up as a soldier for Candy,[2] where when transported, within a short time he found the Captain's promise

[1] Countrymen.　　　　　　　　　　[2] Crete.

and performance different, which enforced him at the beginning to borrow a little money of his Lieutenant. The five years of their abode expired, and fresh companies come from Venice to exhibit the charge, Smith, not being able to discharge his debt, was turned over to the new Captain for five years more, who paid the old Captain his money. And his time also worn out, the third Captain came, when likewise he was put in his hands, serving him five years longer.

Then having served three Captains fifteen years, and never likely able (for a small trifle) to attain his liberty, I went to the Captain and paid his debt, obtaining also of the Rector his license to depart and the allowance of the State for his passage, which was wine and biscuit-bread. Thereafter I embarked him for Venice in a Flemish ship, the Master being a Scotsman, John Allen, born in Glasgow and dwelt at Middelburgh in Zeeland. His debt was only forty-eight shillings sterling.

XVI

SALT WATER

Utheris hes sailit als weill as ye.
QUINTIN SCHAW, *The Vyage of Court*

182. SHIPS

*A string of ships' names has always something about it that
haunts like a song.   Here are some Scots ones of round about
1600.*

Pruss Mayden.   Ly by the Fyr.   Falcon.   Unicorn.   Hund.
Little Pink.   Grace of God.   Swan.   Mary Gallant.   Klink-
bellis.   Expeditioun.   Dragon.   Engell.   Dow.   Gift of God.
Good Fortun.   Elspet.   Margaret and James.   Jonas.   Swift.
Robuck.   Hope of Grace.

183. SEA SYMPHONY

*Here, from the " Compleynt of Scotland," is a ship putting out
and engaging an enemy.   Like the author's other pictures, it is
done almost wholly in terms of sound.*

I sat doun to sie the flowing of the faem, quhen that I luikit
far forth on the salt fluid.   Thair I beheld ane galliasse gaily
graithit for the weir, lyand fast at ane anker, and hir sailis in
hou.   I herd monie wordis amang the marinalis, bot I wist
nocht quhat thay meinit ;   yit I sal rehers and report thair
crying and thair call.

In the first, the master of the galliasse gart the botisman pas
up to the top, to luik far furth gif he culd sie onie schippis.
Then the botisman luikit sa lang quhill that he saw ane quhyte
sail.   Than he cryit with ane skirl, quod he, " I sie ane greit
schip."

Then the maister quhissilit, and bad the marinalis lay the
cabil to the cabil-stok, to wind and wey. Than the marinalis
began to wind the cabil with monie loud cry, and as ane cryit,
al the laif cryit in that samyn tune, as it had bein Echo in ane
hou heuch : and as it appeirit to me, thay cryit thir wordis as
eftir followis.

> Ware a', ware a',
> Gentil gallandis, gentil gallandis,
> Wynd I sie him, wynd I sie him,
> Pour bossa, pour bossa,
> Haul al and ane, haul al and ane,
> Haul him up til us, haul him up til us.

Then quhen the anker wes haulit up abuve the watir, ane marinal
cryit and al the laif followit in that samyn tune :

> Caupon caupona, caupon caupona,
> Caupon hola, caupon hola,
> Caupon holt, caupon holt.
> Sarabossa, sarabossa.

Than thay maid fast the schank of the anker.

And the maister quhissilit, and cryit, " Twa men abuve to
the foir ra. Cut the raibandis and lat the foir sail fall. Haul
doun the steirbord luff hard aburd. Haul eftir the foir sail
scheit. Haul out the bollein." Then the maister quhissilit,
and cryit, " Twa men abuve to the main ra. Cut the raibandis
and lat the main sail and top sail fall. Haul doun the luff close
aburd. Haul eftir the main scheit. Haul out the main-sail
bollein." Than ane of the marinalis began to haul and to cry,
and al the marinalis answeirit of that samyn sound.

> Hou hou, hou hou,
> Pull weill a', pull weill a',
> Bollein a', bollein a'.
> Dart a', dart a',
> Hard out steif, hard out steif,

Afoir the wind, afoir the wind,
God send, God send
Fair wethir, fair wethir,
Monie prisis, monie prisis,
Guid foirland, guid foirland,
Stow, stow, stow, stow,
Maik fast and belay.

Than the maister cryit and bad reze ane bonet. " Vire the trossis. Hou heise." Than the marinalis began to heise up the sail, cryand

Heisum heisum
Worsa, worsa,
Wou wou, wou wou,
Ane lang draucht, ane lang draucht,
Mair maucht, mair maucht,
Yong bluid, yong bluid,
Mair muid, mair muid,
Fals flesche, fals flesche,
Ly abak, ly abak,
Lang swak, lang swak,
That that, that that,
Thair thair, thair thair,
Yallou hair, yallou hair,
Hippis bair, hippis bair,
Til him a', til him a',
Widdefullis a', widdefullis a',
Greit and sma', greit and sma',
Ane and a', ane and a',
Heise a', heise a'.

" Nou maik fast the teiris."

Than the maister cryit, " Top your topinels. Haul on your topsail scheitis. Vire your liftaris and your topsail trossis, and heise the topsail hyar. Haul out the topsail bollein. Heise the missen and change it ower to leuart. Haul the linche and the scheitis. Haul the tross to the ra."

Than the maister cryit on the rudirman, " Mait, keip ful and by. A-luif. Cum na hyar. Holabar. Arrya. Steir clein. Up the helm. Thus and so."

Than quhen the schip wes taiklit, the maister cryit, " Boy to the top. Schaik out ane flag on the top mast. Marinalis, stand to your geir in takling of your sailis. Everie quarter-maister til his ain quarter. Botis-man, beir stanis and lyme pottis ful of lyme in the craklin pokis to the top, and paveis weil the top with paveisis and mantillis. Gunnaris, cum heir and stand by your artailzie, everie gunnar til his ain quarter. Maik reddy your cannonis, culvereinis moyennis, culvereinis bastardis, falconis, sakiris, half sakiris and half falconis, slangis and half slangis, quarter slangis, heid stikkis, murderaris, pesvolans, bersis, doggis, doubil doggis, doubil bersis, hagbuttis of croche, half haggis, culveraris, and hail schot. And ye sol-dartis and companziounis of weir, maik reddy your crossbowis, hand bowis, fyr speiris, hail schot, lancis, pykis, halbardis, rondellis, twa handit swerdis and targis."

Than the gay galliasse, beand in guid order, sche followit fast the samyn schip that the botisman had sein, and for mair speid the galliasse put forth her stoyten sailis and ane hundred aris on everie syde. The maister gart al his marinalis and men of weir hald thaim quyet at rest, be resoun that the muving of the pepil within ane schip stoppis hir of hir faird. Of this sort the said galliasse in schort tyme cam on windwart of the tothir schip. Than eftir that thay had hailit utheris, thay maid thaim reddie for batail. Than quhair I sat I herd the cannonis and gunnis maik monie hideous crak, duf duf duf duf duf duf. The bersis and falconnis cryit tirdif, tirdif, tirdif, tirdif, tirdif, tirdif. Then the small artaillzie cryit tik tak, tik tak, tik tak, tik tak. The reik, smuik, and the stink of the gun puldir fylit all the air, almaist lyke as Plutois paleis had bein birnand in ane bauld fyre, quhilk generit sic mirknes and mist that I culd nocht sie my lenth about me. Quhairfoir I rais and returnit to the fresche feildis that I cam fra.

The chanties are evidently written down by ear. I have guessed at a meaning in places, though these things need not have much. "Pull weill a'" is actually "pulpela." "Pour bossa" may be "Pu' oor best a'." Messrs. R. & R. Clark's reader makes the interesting suggestion that "Caupona" may be "Caup on a'," "Cop (catch) on, all," and "Sarabossa", "Ser' oor best a'."

galliasse, sailing warship provided with sweeps. *in hou*, ? hollow, ? filling ? or housed—which seems to fit the later orders better. *cabil-stok*, capstan. *hou*, hollow. *ra*, yard. *raibandis*, gaskets. *eftir*, aft. *bonet*, jib. *vire the trossis*, let go the braces. *heise*, hoist. *muid*, pith. *topinels*, topsails. *leuart*, leeward. *linche* ? *arrya*, ? as you are. *thus and so*, keep her as you go. *craklin pokis*, ? canvas bags. *paveisis and mantillis*, big wooden screens to defend the tops. *stoyten sailis*, stunsails. *stoppis hir of hir faird*, checks her way. *foirland*, landfall.

In his artillery, as in his helm orders, his delight in technicalities has rather run away with him. *Culverines* (from *couleuvre*, serpent) were long-barrelled. *Sakers* were short. *Bers* is a mortar. A *murderer* seems to be a big gun: Mons Meg is so described. *Slangs* may be slings for stones, *heid stikkis* possibly staff-slings. A *hagbut* is the characteristic musket of the time, with a much bent stock, a hagbut *à croche*, fired from a stand. *Rondellis* are small round shields or bucklers, smaller than the target. *Doggis* are pistols. *Pesvolans* and *culveraris* are guns of sorts, but this editor cannot define them.

184. PASSENGERS

This plaintive epistle was written to Marie de Guise, apparently between her marriage in 1538 and her widowhood in 1542. The writer has apparently set out from Leith and had to put back for stress of weather.

TO THE QUEEN,

Madame, to obey the King's order and yours, which Monsieur de Fonpertuis [1] and I would not disobey for the world, we are back again in this place of Little Leith, with all the company, waiting for a fair wind and God's mercy, assuring you, Madame, that if it had pleased you to let me go by land, you would have done much for me and for my health, for never was woman so ill as I, so little as I have been there, and I have taken such a stomach-ache as I fear will do me much harm, and think I will have much more of it before I am in France.

[1] The writer's husband.

For the rest, Madame, if you please to command further to
Monsieur de Fonpertuis and myself, we beg you most humbly,
Madame, to let us hear in order to obey you, and in this place
we beg the Creator, Madame, to give you good and long life.

From Little Leith, this 17th of the month.

Your more than most humble and most obedient servant,

A. DE BARBANÇOIS.

*Here is William Lithgow again, in 1609, sailing from Corfù to
Zante in a Greek ship, whose company of forty-eight souls included
Greeks, Slavonians, Italians, Armenians, Jews, and himself.*

[Off Leucadia] the Captain of the vessel spied a sail coming
from sea, he being presently moved therewith sent a mariner
to the top, who certified that she was a Turkish galley of
Bizerta, prosecuting a straight course to invade our bark.
Which sudden affrighting news overwhelmed us almost in
despair. Resolution being by the amazed master demanded of
every man what was best to do, some replied one way, and some
another ; insomuch that the most part of the passengers gave
counsel rather to render than to fight, being confident their
friends would pay their ransoms and relieve them. But I the
wandering pilgrim, pondering in my pensive breast my solitary
estate, the distance of my country and my friends, could conceive no light of deliverance. Upon which troublesome and
fearful appearance of slavery, I absolutely arose, and spoke to
the master, saying, " The half of the carmosado [1] is your own,
and the most part also of the loading," (all which he had told me
before) " wherefore my counsel is that you prepare yourself to
fight, and go encourage your passengers, promising to your
mariners double wages. Make ready your two pieces of
ordnance, your muskets, powder, lead, and half pikes, for who
knoweth but the Lord may deliver us from the thraldom of
these Infidels." My exhortation ended, he was greatly animated

---

[1] Ship of a distinctive Mediterranean rig.

therewith, and gave me thanks; whereupon, assembling the passengers and mariners, he gave good comfort and large promises to them all, so that their affrighted hopes were converted to a courageous resolution, meaning rather to give the first assault than to receive the second wrong.

To perform the plot [1] of our defence, every man was busy in the work, some below in the gunner-room, others cleansing their muskets, some preparing the powder and balls, some their swords and short weapons, some dressing the half-pikes, and other making fast the doors above : for so the master resolved to make combat below, both to save us from small shot and besides for boarding us on a sudden. The dextrous courage of all men was so forward to defend their lives and liberty, that truly in mine opinion we seemed thrice as many as we were. All things below and above being cunningly perfected, and every one ranked in order with his arquebus and pike, we recommended ourselves into the hands of the Almighty, and in the meantime attended their fiery salutation.

In a furious spleen, the first hola of their courtesy was the progress of a martial conflict, thundering forth a terrible noise of galley-roaring pieces. And we in a sad reply sent such a back-sounding echo of fiery flying shots, which made an aequivox to the clouds, rebounding backwards in our perturbed breasts the ambiguous sounds of fear and hope. After a long and doubtful fight, both with great and small shot (night parting us) the Turks retired till morning, and then were mindful to give us the new rencounter of a second alarum. But as it pleased Him Who never faileth His, to send down an irresistible tempest, about the break of day we escaped their furious designs, and were enforced to seek into the Bay of Largostolo in Cephalonia, both because of the violent weather, and because a great lake was stricken into the ship.

In this fight there were of us killed three Italians, two Greeks, and two Jews, with eleven others deadly wounded, and I also

[1] Plan.

hurt in the right arm with a small shot. But what harm was done by us among the Turks, we were not assured thereof, save only this, we shot away their middle mast and the hinder part of the poop, for the Greeks are not expert gunners, neither could our arquebusades much annoy them, in respect they never boarded. But however it was, being all disbarked on shore, we gave thanks to the Lord for our unexpected safety, and buried the dead Christians in a Greekish cemetery, and the Jews were interred by the seaside.

185. THE FREEDOM OF THE SEAS

With a good deal of gusto for a man of peace, James Melville tells how Anstruther coped with a pirate. The affair took place in 1587, when he was minister of the neighbouring charge of Kil-renny.

Ane of our crearis, returning from England, was umbesett be ane Englis pirat, pillit, and a verie guid honest man of Anstruther slain thairin. The quhilk lown, cuming pertlie to the verie road of Pittenweem, spulzit a schip lying thairin, and misusit the men thairof.

This wrang culd nocht be sufferit be our men, lest thay suld be maid a comoun prey to sic limmaris. Thairfoir, purchasing a commissioun, thay riggit to a propir flie-boat, and everie man incouraging uthir, maid almaist the haill honest and best men in all the toun to go in hir.

James, though deeply concerned for their probable fate, would not interfere, but was very anxious

till aucht or ten dayis wes endit, and thay in sicht returning, with all guid tokinnis of joy, flaggis, stremaris, and enseinzie displayit, quhom with greit joy we resavit, and went togidder to the kirk and praisit God.

The Captain for the tyme, a godlie, wyse, and stout man,

recompted to me trewlie the haill proceiding : That thay meiting
with thair Admirall, a greit schip of Sanct Androis, weill riggit
out be the Burrowis, being fyne of sail, went before hir all the
way, and maid everie schip thay foirgatherit with, of quhatsumevir natioun, to stryk and do homage to the King of Scotland,
schawing thaim for quhat caus thay were riggit furth, and in-
quyring of knavis and piratis. At last they met with a proud
stiff Englishman, quha refusis to do reverens : thairfoir the
Captain, thinking it wes a lown, commandis to gif thaim his
nose-peice, the quhilk delashit lichtis on the tye of the English-
manis main sail, and doun it cumis ; then he yeildis, being bot a
merchant. Bot thair wes the mercifull providence of God in
staying a greit peice of the Englishman, lying out his starn in
redines to be schot, quhilk if it had lichtit amang our folkis,
being monie in litill roum, without fence, wald haif cruellie
demeinit thaim all. Bot God directing, that first schot preservit
thaim.

For thaim, thay approchit to the schore at Suffolk, and finding
be Providence the lown, quha had newlingis taikin a crear of
our awin toun and wes spulzeing hir. Howsoun thay spie ane
cuming weirlyk, the lownis levis thair prize, and rinnis thair schip
on land, our flie-boat eftir, and almaist wes on land with thaim ;
yit staying hard by, thay delaish thair ordnance at the lownis,
and a numbir going aland persewis and takis a half a dizzoun of
thaim, and puttis thaim abord in thair boat. The gentilmen of
the countrey and tounis besyde, heiring the nois of schotting,
gatheris with haste, suppoising the Spanyardis had landit, and
apprehending a numbir of the lownis in our mennis handis,
desyrit to knaw the mateir. The quhilk, quhen the Justiceis of
Peace understude, and saw the King of Scotlandis armis, with
twa gallant schippis in warlyke maneir, yeildit and gaif reverence
thair to, suffering our folkis to taik with thaim thair prisonaris
and piratis schip, quhilk thay brocht haim with thaim, with half a
dizzoun of the lownis ; quhairof two wer hangit at our Pier-end,
the rest in Sanct Androis, with na hurt at all to onie of our

folkis, quha evir sinsyne hes bein frie from Englis piratis. All prais to God forevir. Amen.

crear, light coasting vessel.   *umbesett*, set about.   *commissioun*, letters of marque, permission to take reprisals, with the temporary status of a King's ship.   *flie-boat*, small fast vessel.   *Burrowis*, Convention of Royal Burghs. *stryk*, strike topsails, the naval salute of the day, due from a merchantman to a royal ship.   *nose-peice*, bow gun.   *delashit*, délâché, let off.   *fence*, protection.   *howsoun*, as soon as.

SUPPLEMENTARY GLOSSARY

For nouns and one or two adjectival words, chiefly *quhilk*, *uthir*, *said*, and *foirsaid*, the regular plural is *-is*. The possessive is also regularly in *-is*. The preterite and past participle of verbs are commonly in *-it*. The vowel in both terminations is almost elided, merely serving to give room for the sharp emphasis on the final consonant that is still characteristic of modern Scots and Scoto-English. In the present participle, *-ing* by this time is more usual than *-and*, which by the later sixteenth century is almost confined to very formal or official writing.

Many of the words glossed below have several senses besides those given here, and several can only approximately be rendered in English.

Air, heir
Allanerlie, alone, solely
Als, as
Alsweill, as well, also
An, if
Assoilzie, clear of a charge
Attour, as well

Be, by
Bigg, build
Birl, to send (glass, etc.) about
Black-mail, protection money
Brodit, prodded
Boundis, district
But, without
By, excepting
Byd, abide, endure

Caller, *frais*, agreeably cool and fresh
Chalmer, chamber
Choppin, a liquid measure
Cleiding, clothing
Clengeing, cleansing, acquittal
Collatioun, light refreshments
Craftie, skilful, workmanlike
Cuschat, wood-dove

Dag, pistol
Decern, give for judgment
Decreit, ordinance
Ding, smite
Disjune, breakfast

Dispone, leave by will, assign
Dou, dow, dove
Douk, dive
Dowriare, dowager
Drie, endure, *also* drive
Dwine, dwindle, pine away

Effeir, n., readiness
Effeir, vb., become, be suitable
Eik, increase, add to
Ein, eyes
Exerceisis, (has sense of) devotions

Feid, feud
Festuall, festival
Fewar, feuar, renter of land
Foirhammer, smith's heavy hammer
Fornent, facing
Forsamekil, forasmuch
Fraye, alert, alarm
Furth, outside. *Fill furth*, fulfil

Gait, street
Gar, cause to
Gavel, gable
Gif, *gif that*, if
Gled, kite
Gowk, cuckoo
Graith, equip, put in readiness. *Worst graithit*, made most useless

Hain, save, economise
Heirintil, heretofore

Hollin, holly

Horn, put to, formally declare contumacious to the law

Ilk, adj., each ; pron., same, *only used in phrase as* Orrok of that Ilk, Orrok of Orrok

Intromit, take to do with, generally used in bad sense

Kaim, comb
Kais, daws
Kirn, churn
Knapscap, steel cap
Know-heid, top of hillock

Landwart, landward, country, rural
Laverok, lark
Layne, conceal
Liefull, lawful
Limmar, person of dubious character
Linn, waterfall
Loan, lane
Lourd, liever
Lowe, blaze
Lown, low fellow
Lyart, grizzled

Maik, mate
Mairattour, moreover
Manrent, acceptance of another as one's chief
Mavis, thrush
May, maid
Mekil, large
Merle, blackbird
Minnie, mammy
Mou, mouth
Moul, loose earth

Nevoy, nephew
Newlingis, newly
Nolt, cattle

Or, before
Ousen, oxen

Paiks, spanking
Pairtrick, partridge
Paroche, parish
Pasch, Easter
Pertlie, cheekily
Pillit, pillaged
Poind, confiscate
Pratik, practice. *Preve pratticks,* test, practise
Propone, propose
Propyne, to present, gift presented

Quha, who
Quhair, where
Quhairthrouch, whereby
Quhais, whose
Quham, whom
Quhat, what
Quhilk, which
Quhill, while, until
Quhissilit, whistled

Redd, disentangle
Relict, widow
Resett, to shelter and aid (a criminal)
Rigg, ridge
Rigging stanis, roofing stones
Rok, distaff
Rout, lowe

Samyn, same
Sark, shirt
Seawair, sea-weed
Set, suit, become
Sevensum, strictly seven at once : here merely seven-more-or-less
Shable, cutlass
Simples, herbs
Sinsyne, since
Skail, disperse
Skaith, harm
Sowning to, suggesting
Speir, ask
Spulzie, sack, loot
Steik, to close, *also* stitch
Suppone, suppose
Syne, then, afterward

Tail, train
Tent, *taik*, pay attention
Thir, these
Tint, lost
Toom, empty
Tutour, legal guardian of a minor
Twasum, two by two
Tymeous, in good time
Tyne, lose

Ugsome, revolting
Umquhill, sometime, the late

Upbraids, rises

Waill, choose, pick out
Want, lack
Wappit, folded round
Ware, to use, employ
Whinger, dagger
Wudspurs, Wildspurs
Wyte, blame

Yett, gate, especially iron grille
Yow, ewe

INDEX OF BOOKS AND AUTHORS

The numbers are those of extracts, not of pages